STUDY GUIDE

Larry Elowitz

Georgia College and State University

TEXAS EDITION

POLITICS IN AMERICA

FOURTH EDITION

Thomas R. Dye

Florida State University

Prentice Hall, Upper Saddle River, New Jersey 07458

© 2001 by PRENTICE-HALL, INC.
PEARSON EDUCATION
Upper Saddle River, New Jersey 07458

ISBN 0-13-027179-9

Printed in the United States of America

TABLE OF CONTENTS

CHAPTER ONE
POLITICS: WHO GETS WHAT, WHEN, AND HOW

I. **POLITICS AND POLITICAL SCIENCE:** Politics is the process of deciding who gets what, when, and how. Political Science is the study of politics, or who governs, for what ends and by what means.

II. **POLITICS AND GOVERNMENT:** Two factors distinguish governmental politics from other organizations. First, governmental decisions extend to the whole of society, as opposed to only small parts of it. Secondly, governments can use force legitimately. Explain why democratic governments enjoy a special claim to legitimacy.

III. **THE PURPOSES OF GOVERNMENT:** Why do people come together and form governments? In the United States, the answer to that is found in the Preamble to the U.S. Constitution. It lists the purposes of government as:

   A. To Establish Justice and Domestic Tranquility: Government manages conflict and protects its citizens from each other. Accordingly, it is to the citizens' advantage to agree to be governed. **DEFINE SOCIAL CONTRACT**.

   B. To Provide for the Common Defense: One of the main tasks of government is protect its citizenry from outside forces. Some scholars believe this to be the origins of government. Today in the U.S., however, national defense accounts for only a small proportion of the federal government's activities.

   C. To Promote the General Welfare: This is done in numerous ways. Governments provide public goods, they regulate society, and they also use income transfers to help provide for the general welfare of the citizenry. **DEFINE PUBLIC GOOD. DEFINE INCOME TRANSFER.**

   D. To Secure the Blessings of Liberty: Democratic governments have the responsibility to protect the liberty of the individual citizens by ensuring that all people are equal under the law. This means that all people, including governmental leaders, are subject to the laws of the land.

IV. **THE MEANING OF DEMOCRACY:** There is no single definition of democracy, even though the idea of democracy originated with the early Greek philosophers. The best way to understand democracy is to think about it as a set of traditions and ideas.

   A. Individual Dignity: The basis of the democracy is the idea that individual human beings are entitled to a certain amount of dignity. This dignity requires that people be given freedom from their government as well as its protection. The political philosopher John Locke argued that this dignity was not given to people by governments, but rather came from a higher "natural law." This is where we get the idea, as stated in the Constitution, that people are endowed with certain "inalienable rights."

B.   Equality: True democracy requires equal protection of the law for all citizens, regardless of race, ethnicity, wealth, gender, or any other personal characteristic.

C.   Participation in the Decision Making: One of the key ideas in democracy is that the people should be involved in the decision making. This means that the citizens should be involved in the process for determining laws and policy. There is no guarantee that the people will always make the proper decisions, but being involved in the process at least provides the opportunity for fairness and freedom.

D.   Majority Rule: One Person One Vote: The decision-making process in a democracy should be governed by majority rule with each person having equal input.

V.   THE PARADOX OF DEMOCRACY: Any democracy entails a paradox. That is the potential for conflict between individual freedom and majority rule.

A.   Limiting the Power of Majorities: The framers of the U.S. Constitution feared that simple majority rule might intrude on the freedoms of some individuals. To protect the individuals, they established the concept of limited government and put some personal liberties beyond the reach of majority action. Explain the concept of limited government.

B.   Totalitarianism: Unlimited Government Power: **DEFINE TOTALITARIANISM.**

C.   Constitutional Government: Governmental powers are limited by constitutions. Constitutions set forth the structure, powers, and limitations of governments, They also set forth the personal liberties of the citizens and restrain the government from limiting such freedoms.

VI.   DIRECT VERSUS REPRESENTATIVE DEMOCRACY: **DEFINE DIRECT AND REPRESENTATIVE DEMOCRACY.**

VII.   WHO REALLY GOVERNS: Democracy is a great idea, but there are few who would argue that all people are willing and able to participate equally. So who then is really governing?

A.   The Elitist Perspective: The basic idea of elitism is that society is divided into two groups: those who have power and influence (and often money) and those who do not. The group that has the power is referred to as the elites. In a society as large as ours, this division into groups is inevitable according to the theory. Elitism does not mean that the leaders will neglect or exploit the masses, it simply refers to the political decision, making power.

B.   The Pluralist Perspective: **DEFINE PLURALISM**.

VIII.   DEMOCRACY IN AMERICA: Is democracy alive and well in America?

CHAPTER ONE SAMPLE QUESTIONS

TRUE-FALSE:

1. Politics arises out of conflict.

2. American trust in government is at an all-time low since 1964.

3. One of the main purposes of government is to protect citizens from each other.

4. The first political philosopher to conceptualize the social contract was John Locke.

5. "Civil disobedience" implies a willingness to accept a penalty for breaking the law.

6. National defense would be an example of a public good.

7. Second-hand smoke could be considered an externality.

8. All governments have the responsibility to provide for individual liberties.

9. The paradox of democracy is the tension between majority rule and individual freedom.

10. The United States is a direct democracy.

MULTIPLE-CHOICE:

11. The purposes of government include all of the following EXCEPT:
    a. Provide for the common defense
    b. Promote the general welfare
    c. Establish justice
    d. All of the above are purposes of government

12. A good which could not be withheld from those who do not pay for it is called:
    a. A public good
    b. A private good
    c. A national good
    d. An externality

13. Governments regulate society in order to:
    a. Prevent fraud
    b. Prevent unfair competition
    c. Limit the effects of externalities
    d. All of the above

14. Which of the following is/are protected by democratic governments?
    a. Freedom of speech
    b. Freedom of religion
    c. Freedom to petition
    d. All of the above

15. All but one of the following are essential elements of democracy:
    a. Communal dignity
    b. Equal protection of the law
    c. Equal opportunity to participate in public decisions
    d. Majority rule decision making

16. All but one of the following were used by the framers of the U.S. Constitution to limit the power of the political majority:
    a. Republican government
    b. Separation of powers
    c. Checks and balances
    d. Judicial review

17. Which of the following is the principal means used to limit government?
    a. Laws
    b. Regulations
    c. Constitutions
    d. Statutes

18. A representative democracy has all but one of the following attributes:
    a. Representatives selected by a vote of all the people
    b. Closed elections
    c. Freedom of expression for both candidates and voters
    d. Periodic elections

19. The small group of people who maintain the power of governing are called the:
    a. masses
    b. insiders
    c. elite
    d. power brokers

20. The theory that states that Democracy can be achieved through the competition of groups is called:
    a. Elitism
    b. Interest group politics
    c. Pluralism
    d. None of the above

CHAPTER ONE SAMPLE QUESTION ANSWERS

TRUE-FALSE

1. **TRUE.** Politics arises out of conflict and involves all the activities by which conflict is carried on. See page 2.

2. **TRUE.** See graph on page 4.

3. **TRUE.** The U.S. Constitution states that government is to establish justice and ensure domestic tranquility. See page 7.

4. **FALSE.** Thomas Hobbes was the first. See page 7.

5. **TRUE.** See Conflicting View on page 8, second column.

6. **TRUE.** No private investor has the capital to invest in national defense. See page 7.

7. **TRUE.** Second-hand smoke affects nonparticipants and may be an appropriate area for the government to regulate. See page 9.

8. **FALSE.** Providing for personal liberties is a special responsibility of democracies. See page 11.

9. **TRUE.** See page 13.

10. **FALSE.** The United States is a representative democracy. See page 17.

MULTIPLE CHOICE

11. **D.** The purposes of government include all of those listed. See pages 7-9.

12. **A.** A public good is one which could not be withheld from those who do not pay for it. See page 7.

13. **D**. Governments regulate society in order to prevent fraud, prevent unfair competition, and limit the effects of externalities. See page 9.

14. **E**. Democratic governments protects freedom of speech, freedom of religion, freedom to petition, and the freedom to form groups. See pages 10-11.

15. **A** Individual dignity, not communal dignity. See pages 12-13.

16. **D**. Judicial review was not part of the Constitution but pronounced by the U.S. Supreme Court as a judicial power. See page 16.

17. **C**. Only a constitution can restrain government; all the others can be changed at will by the government. See page 16.

18. **B**. Open elections are essential; closed elections would be more typical of a totalitarian regime when only the regime's candidates would be on the ballot. See page 17.

19. **C**. The small group of people who maintain the power of governing are called the elite. See page 18.

20. **C**. The theory that states that Democracy can be achieved through the competition of groups is called pluralism. See page 20.

CHAPTER TWO: POLITICAL CULTURE:
IDEAS IN CONFLICT

I. POLITICAL CULTURE: Political culture refers to the widely shared ideas based on values and beliefs in a society that help to determine who should govern, how, and for what end. Values are more deeply rooted and deal with ideas about what is good or desirable. A belief on the other hand is a shared idea of truth and is more subject to change. Variations in values and beliefs are sometimes referred to as subcultures and develop from diverse religious, racial, and/or ethnic identities.

   A. Contradictions between Values and Conditions: Political culture can often have contradictions, e.g. equality versus slavery and segregation. Still, the value of equality can often be a catalyst for change.

   B. Inconsistent Applications: Political culture of shared ideas does not mean that the principles will be consistently applied in all cases. A classic example is the support in the U.S. for the idea of freedom of speech and the willingness of the U.S. public to limit such freedoms for unpopular groups of people.

   C. Conflict: The idea of Political Culture and shared common beliefs does not mean that there will be an absence of conflict over ideas or beliefs.

II. INDIVIDUAL LIBERTY: No political value has been given as much emphasis in our nation as individual liberty. This value is based in the political philosophy of classical liberalism, which asserts the worth and dignity of the individual.

   A. Political Liberty: Classical liberalism began in the 18th century as an attack on the feudal hierarchy in place in Europe. Noted political philosophers who promoted liberalism included Voltaire, Locke, Rousseau, Smith, and Jefferson. It is this belief in liberalism that caused the American founders to declare independence from England, write the U.S. Constitution, and form this nation.

   B. Economic Freedom: Classical liberalism is a political idea which is very similar to capitalism as a economic idea. **DEFINE CAPITALISM**.

III. DILEMMAS OF EQUALITY: Equality is an honored value in the American political culture. Yet the struggle for equality and the determination of the meaning of equality is ongoing.

   A. Political Equality: The founders believed in legal equality, meaning that the laws should apply equally to all. This was not the same as political equality.

DEFINE POLITICAL EQUALITY AND GIVE AN EXAMPLE.

B. Equality of Opportunity: Equality of opportunity refers to the removal of artificial barriers to success in life. Most Americans support the idea that everyone should be given the opportunity to make the most of their own abilities. Differences arise over the policies used to remove the artificial barriers.

C. Equality of Results: Equality of results refers to the equal sharing of income and material rewards. Proponents of this idea argue that if people are truly equal they should all enjoy basically the same standard of living. Under this concept inequalities in income are intolerable. This concept is not a widely shared value. See Figure 2-1.

D. Fairness: Most Americans believe in fairness, but disagree on what is fair. Most support the concept of a public safety net which should provide a basic income level below which people should not be forced to live, but there is disagreement over how low the floor should be. Most do not support any cap or limitation on earnings although there is some concern about the growing gap between CEO and worker incomes.

E. Equality in Politics Versus Economics: **FILL IN.**

IV. INEQUALITY OF INCOME AND WEALTH: Political conflict is most often caused by inequalities within a society.

A. Inequality of Income: Dividing the U.S. population into fifths (quintiles), we see that since 1929, the lower fifth of our population receives a small share of U.S. wealth, while the upper fifth receives almost half of U.S. income. This group has lost some relative ground since 1929. However, since 1970, the income gap of the poorest and richest quintiles has increased.

B. Explaining Recent Increases in Income Inequality: The increase in the income inequality in the U.S. has been caused by four major factors. **FILL IN.**

C. Inequality of Wealth: Wealth is the total family assets, not limited to income. There is greater inequality of wealth than income in the U.S.

V. SOCIAL MOBILITY: The possibility of social mobility (better job, more income, etc.) reduces class conflict and diminishes class consciousness.

A. How Much Mobility?: Social mobility seems to be slowing in recent years.

B. Mobility, Class Conflict, and Class Consciousness: Conflict over wealth and power, otherwise known as class conflict, is not as common in the U.S. as in other nations. The belief in social mobility may partially explain this. **DEFINE CLASS CONSCIOUSNESS.**

VI.   RACE, ETHNICITY, AND IMMIGRATION: America has always been an ethnically and racially pluralist society.

    A.   African Americans: Historically, the nation's largest minority. Today 35 million comprise 12.1 percent of U.S. population.

    B.   Hispanic Americans: "Hispanic" refers to Spanish-speaking ancestry and culture, including Mexican Americans, Cuban Americans, and Puerto Ricans. There are an estimated 31 million, comprising 11.4 percent of the total population.

    C.   A Nation of Immigrants: Immigrants have come to America for a better life. Immigration policy is a responsibility of the national government. Quotas and restrictions on immigrants have been used in the past. In 1986, the Simpson-Mazzoli Act tried to reform immigration, but the Act failed to reduce the flow of either legal or illegal immigrants.

    D.   Illegal Immigration: Estimates range from 400,000 to 3 million per year. INS estimates that 4 million illegal immigrants currently reside in the U.S. Aliens are entitled to due process.

    E.   Citizenship: Persons born in the U.S. are citizens. People can go through the naturalization process provided they meet certain legal and intellectual requirements.

VII.   IDEOLOGIES: LIBERALISM AND CONSERVATISM: An ideology is a consistent and integrated system of ideas, values, and beliefs. Political ideology tells us who should get what, when, and how. When we use the terms liberal or conservative, we are implying a set of values or beliefs, an ideology. Many Americans avoid labeling themselves based on ideology. Nevertheless, ideology plays a key role in politics.

    A.   Modern Conservatism: Individualism plus Traditional Values: Modern conservatism combines a belief in free markets, limited government, and individual self-reliance in economic affairs with a belief in tradition, law, and morality in social affairs. These ideas are consistent with classic liberalism (discussed earlier). At the same time, modern conservatives recognize frail human nature and consequently emphasize the role of traditional values.

        Conservatives: Conservatives generally prefer a limited role for government in economic affairs and would increase the ability of government to regulate social conduct. Both the liberals and conservatives can be said to be inconsistent in their views toward government, wanting government intervention in one area of policy, but not in another.

B.   Modern Liberalism: Governmental Power to "Do Good": Modern liberals see government as necessary to provide economic security and protect civil rights. Government power is seen as a positive force. Modern liberalism retains the idea of individual dignity put forth in classical liberalism and combines that with an emphasis on social and economic security for the whole population.

C.   Populists: Populists are individuals who are liberal in economic affairs, but conservative on social issues. These people are very consistent on their view of government. They want an active strong government in both economic and social affairs.

D.   Libertarians: Libertarians prefer minimal government, both in regards to the economy and society.

VIII.   DISSENT IN THE UNITED STATES: Dissent from American political culture has developed on both the right and left sides of the political spectrum. Extreme radicals on both sides reject the democratic model.

A.   Antidemocratic Ideologies: Those at the far right of the political spectrum are fascists who believe in the supremacy of the state (under their control) and the white race. On the far left are Marxists who wrote about the exploitation of the working class. Marxism-Leninism became the philosophical basis of Communism which included government ownership of all the means of production and distribution. The concept of private property was abolished. All property belonged to the state. The Party controlled the government.

B.   Socialism: Socialism is on the left spectrum, but not as far as communism. Socialists believe in government ownership of main industries, but not all private property. They also support the democratic political process.

C.   The End of History? Much of the history of the twentieth century has been The conflict between capitalism and communism. The collapse of of communism increased the movement to free markets and political democracy. This process has been labeled the "End of History."

D.   Academic Radicalism: Academic radicalism is found in the "politically correct" movements on academic campuses. The problems of capitalism are attacked as well as Western civilization--institutions, language, and culture which are labeled as racist, sexist, etc.

CHAPTER TWO SAMPLE QUESTIONS

TRUE-FALSE:

1.   Subcultures arise from diverse religions, races, and ethnic identities.

2.   Capitalism motivated the American founders to declare independence from England.

3.   Political equality is synonymous with legal equality.

4.   Most Americans support the idea of equality of results.

5.   Income inequality increased in the United States because of reduced federal social welfare payments in the 1980s.

6.   Inequality of wealth is even greater than inequality of incomes in the United States.

7.   The United States accepts more immigrants than all the other nations of the world combined.

8.   State governments accurately track the immigration status of welfare recipients.

9.   Modern liberalism emphasizes the importance of economic and social security for the whole population.

10.   Conservatism is a belief in the value of free markets and limited government.

MULTIPLE-CHOICE.

11.   Class conflict is rare in the U.S. because:
      a. There is a belief in social mobility
      b. There is a diminished sense of class consciousness
      c. All of the above
      d. None of the above

12.   The idea of the founders that the laws should apply equally to all people is called:
      a. Legal equality   b. Political equality
      c. Equality of results   d. None of the above

13. Americans believe strongly in equality of _____ but not in equality of _____.
    a. Opportunity, results   b. Results, outcome
    c. Opportunity, politics   d. All of the above

14. Recent increases in income inequalities have been caused by:
    a. A decline in manufacturing
    b. An increase in the number of elderly people
    c. Global competition
    d. All of the above

15. Social mobility in the U.S. has _____ in recent years.
    a. Increased   b. Decreased
    c. Remained constant   d. Changed radically

16. Both modern conservatism and modern liberalism share elements of:
    a. Classical conservatism   b. Neo-liberalism
    c. Classical liberalism   d. None of the above

17. Senator Barbara Boxer is mainly a defender of:
    a. Liberalism   b. Conservatism
    c Populism   d. Libertarianism

18. Which of the following would not be favored by liberals?
    a. Government regulation of business
    b. Protection of civil rights
    c. More prisons
    d. Decriminalize marijuana

19. Which of the following would be associated with minimal government interference in both the economic and social spheres?
    a. Liberals   b. Conservatives
    c. Populists   d. Libertarians

20. Academic radicalism is most associated with:
    a. Affirmative action   b. Conservatism
    c. Political correctness   d. Populism

TRUE-FALSE:

1. **TRUE**. Subcultures arise from diverse religions, races, and ethnic identities. See page 26.

2. **FALSE**. Classical liberalism motivated the founders to declare independence from England. See page 26.

3. **FALSE.** The Constitution speaks of equality under the law. This is quite different than political equality such as voting or citizenship which was not made part of the Constitution until after the Civil War (Fifteenth Amendment). See page 29.

4. **FALSE.** Most Americans do not support the idea of equality of results. See page 27.

5. **FALSE.** Government spending for welfare did not decline per se, but only the rate of growth in welfare spending. See page 31.

6. **TRUE.** The top 1 percent of U.S. citizens own 40 percent of the nation's wealth. For example, Bill Gates of Microsoft is considered to be the richest private individual in the world at this time. See page 33.

7. **TRUE.** Surprising, but true. America is still the beacon as the land of opportunity that attracts people from all over the world. See page 33.

8. **FALSE.** The federal and state governments do not accurately track the immigration status of welfare recipients. See page 39.

9. **TRUE.** Modern liberalism emphasizes the importance of economic and social security for the whole population. See page 42.

10. **TRUE.** See page 42.

MULTIPLE CHOICE:

11. **C**. Class conflict is rare in the U.S. because there is a belief in social mobility and there is a diminished sense of class consciousness. See page 35.

12. **B**. The idea of the founders that the laws should apply equally to all people is called political equality. See page 28.

13. **A**. Americans believe strongly in equality of opportunity but not in equality of results. See page 29.

14. **D**. Recent increases in income inequalities have been caused by a decline in manufacturing, an increase in the number of elderly people, and global competition. See page 29.

15. **B**. Social mobility in the U.S. has decreased in recent years. See page 33.

16. **C**. Both modern conservatism and modern liberalism share elements of classical liberalism. See page 39.

17. **A**. Barbara Boxer is a liberal. See pages 45, 48.

18. **C**. Liberals prefer rehabilitation. See page 45.

19. **D**. See page 48.

20. **C**. The agenda of academic radicalism is labeled "political correctness." It has an Orwellian toleration of dissent. See page 50.

CHAPTER THREE: THE CONSTITUTION:
LIMITING GOVERNMENTAL POWER

I. CONSTITUTIONAL GOVERNMENT: A written constitution establishes governmental authority and limits the actions of those who hold power. Personal freedoms are protected and beyond the reach of governments or popular majorities. Constitutions usually provide a policy decision mechanism. Constitutions are the supreme law of the land. They are superior to ordinary laws passed by a legislative body. The sanctity of a constitution is based on respect--that of the government and people.

II. THE CONSTITUTIONAL TRADITION: There are several important precedents to the U.S. Constitution.

   A. Magna Carta (1215): This was the first written document which forced the king of England to recognize feudal rights and set a precedence of limiting monarchial power.

   B. Mayflower Compact (1620): The Mayflower Compact was in essence, the first written "social contract." The governed established a government by popular consent.

   C. Colonial Charters (1630-1732): The colonies were established by royal decrees which officially created governments either as proprietary colonies (Maryland, Pennsylvania, and Delaware), or royal colonies. Two colonies were granted self-rule (Connecticut and Rhode Island).

   D. The Declaration of Independence (1776): The First Continental Congress met in 1774 to prepare a petition of grievances to send to the king. In response, the British sent in troops. The Second Continental Congress met in 1775 and designated George Washington to take command of the colonial troops. Although there was still some hope for reconciliation, this hope died by the summer of 1776, and on July 2nd, the Congress decided to declare independence from Great Britain. Thomas Jefferson was selected to write the Declaration, which was formally approved on July 4, 1776. Jefferson used several of Locke's ideas regarding the rights of individuals and consensual government.

   E. The Articles of Confederation (1781-1789): During the period 1776-1781, the emerging nation was governed by the Second Continental Congress. This Congress proposed the Articles of Confederation which provided for a single legislative house with each state having one vote. Congress appointed judges and military officers. It did not have the power to collect taxes, but could borrow and print money. This was a confederation government of independent states. It was not a national government of the people.

III. TROUBLES CONFRONTING A NEW NATION: The new U.S. government had made several notable advancements but the difficulties facing a new nation remained.

A. Financial Difficulties: With no power to tax under the Articles of Confederation, the new government had no way to pay back the money it had borrowed to finance the war. U.S. bonds lost 90 percent of their face value.

B. Commercial Obstacles: Each state could erect their own tariffs for imported goods from either outside the country or a neighboring state. The national government had no power to regulate interstate commerce. Under this situation, it was impossible even to develop a national market. High tariffs led to a thriving industry of smuggling. This situation has a modern sequel. High cigarette taxes in New York City led some entrepreneurs to purchase cheap cigarettes in North Carolina and smuggle them into New York.

C. Currency Problems: Both the national government and state governments printed currency. States had "legal tender" laws which required creditors to accept the state currency for payment of debts in the state. Some states printed too much money, which lost value. If the creditor refused this devalued money, the debt was canceled. Naturally, banks and creditors felt threatened by this "cheap money."

D. Civil Disorder: Debtors resisted efforts of creditors to collect debts and resisted efforts of tax collectors and sheriffs. The most serious incident occurred in western Massachusetts with Shays' Rebellion. While relatively a minor incident, it did arouse anxiety of the nation's leaders and commercial interests who began to call for a strong central government to "ensure domestic tranquility."

E. The Road to the Constitution: Both Virginia and Maryland claimed the Potomac River and the Chesapeake Bay. In the Spring of 1785, a conference was held to try to resolve this problem. One result of the meeting was a call for another general economic conference to convene in Annapolis, Maryland, in 1786. Instead of concentrating on commerce and navigation, this conference called for a general constitutional convention to remedy the defects in the Articles of Confederation. In 1787, the Congress called for a convention to meet in Philadelphia for the sole and express purpose of revising these Articles.

F. The Nation's Founders: The 55 delegates to the Philadelphia convention quickly discarded the idea of revising the Articles. The Virginia delegation led by James Madison drafted a new constitutional document which became the basis of further discussion.

IV.   CONSENSUS IN PHILADELPHIA: Consensus was achieved on most issues.

    A.   Liberty and Property: The framers strongly believed in Locke's writings about natural law and each person having the inalienable rights of life, liberty, and property. They held these beliefs even though they conflicted with the institution of slavery.

    B.   Social Contract: The framers agreed that government originates from the contract among the people. People establish a government and agree to obey its laws and pay taxes for the protection of their natural rights. This is what gives a government legitimacy. If a government violates individual liberties, they break the social contract, lose legitimacy, and can be overthrown by the people.

    C.   Representative Government: Although most of the world's governments at the time were monarchies, the founders decided to form a republican government. **DEFINE REPUBLICANISM.**

        Still, the Constitution provided for only one part of the government to be directly elected by the people-the House of Representatives. It is for this reason that the House still calls itself "The People's House."

    D.   Limited Government: The founders believed that unlimited power was dangerous and that the Constitution should limit the power of the government. A system of checks and balances was established to divide power among the branches of government.

    E.   Nationalism: Most founders believed in the necessity of a strong, national government. **DEFINE NATIONALISM.**

V.   CONFLICT IN PHILADELPHIA: While there was consensus on the basic principles of government at the convention, conflict arose over the implementation of these principles.

    A.   Representation: This was the most controversial issue at the convention. Several plans were presented including the Virginia and New Jersey plans, as well as the Connecticut compromise.
        1.   The Virginia plan called for a two chamber legislature--a lower house elected by the people of each state and an upper house chosen by the lower house. The Congress would have the power to nullify any state law thought to violate the Constitution thus assuring national supremacy. The legislature would choose the executive and judicial

officers of the government (somewhat like a parliamentary system). A "council of revision" could veto congressional acts. This plan was greatly debated, but not adopted.

2. The New Jersey plan favored state supremacy. As under the Articles of Confederation, each state would have just one vote. It proposed separate executive and judicial branches and provided for powers of taxation and regulation of commerce for the new Congress. It also included the now famous National Supremacy clause--the Constitution and federal laws would be supreme over state constitutions and laws.

3. Connecticut Compromise. **FILL IN.**

B. Slavery: Another contentious issue at the convention was slavery, even though slavery was legal in 12 of the 13 states. The South believed that slaves should be included in the population count of their states for representation purposes in the lower House. Nonslave holders argued that only free men should be counted. The infamous Three-fifths Compromise emerged wherein a slave would count as three-fifths of a person for population and direct tax purposes. No direct taxes were ever enacted until the demise of slavery, so the South won more than they lost. The South was also successful in writing a clause in the Constitution that supported the return of runaway slaves. Another compromise involved the prohibition of the importation of more slaves--under the Constitution, Congress was forbidden to halt further importations until the year 1808.

C. Voter Qualifications: There was much discussion whether voters and officeholders should be men of property (note the discussion concerned only men). After much discussion on the meaning of property ownership, the Constitution left voter qualification to the states. (This was later changed by amendments to the Constitution.)

VI. RESOLVING THE ECONOMIC ISSUES: This was one of the main concerns of the Constitutional Convention.

A. Levying Taxes : The national government was given its own taxing authority. Article VI of the Constitution obligated the new national government to pay the debts of the old "national" government. The government collected most of its revenue from tariffs. **DEFINE TARIFF.**

Direct taxes on individuals was prohibited. The power to tax and spend was given exclusively to the legislature.

B. Regulating Commerce: This gives the national government power to regulate foreign commerce among the states. The Constitution specifically forbid the states to levy tariffs on goods shipped across state lines. In effect, these provisions created the world's first common market.

C.   Protecting Money: Only the Congress was given the power to coin money and regulate its value. States no longer could print money.

VII.   PROTECTING NATIONAL SECURITY: During the Revolutionary War, there was no regular army. Troops came from state militias.

A.   War and Military Forces: Under the new Constitution, Congress was given the authorization to declare war and support a regular army and navy, and call the state militias into service.

B.   Commander in Chief: The new office of president was made the commander in chief of the armed forces. Over the next 200 years, questions would arise over the overlap between Congress's ability to declare war and the president's power as commander in chief.

C.   Foreign Affairs: The national government assumed this responsibility. This power is shared by the executive and legislature. The president can appoint ambassadors, but these must be confirmed by the Senate. The president can negotiate treaties, but these must be ratified by the Senate. The power of the purse also gives Congress a hand in foreign affairs.

VIII.   THE STRUCTURE OF THE GOVERNMENT: The new government's structure was designed to implement the founders' belief in nationalism, limited government, republicanism, the social contract, and the protection of liberty and property.

A.   National Supremacy: The Constitution, laws, and treaties take precedence and are the supreme law of the land which judges are to uphold and state laws shall not supersede.

B.   Federalism: Federalism was a novel concept where power is divided between two distinct, autonomous authorities--the national government and state governments. Each have their sphere of independence and authority.

C.   Republicanism: Delegated or representational power from the people to gifted individuals to govern. Of the four decision-making bodies of the federal government (the House, Senate, Presidency, and Supreme Court) only one (the House) was directly chosen by the people.

D.   Democracy: The people do not make decisions at the national level, but rather these decisions are made by representatives of the people. At the state level, there are certain decisions which are made by the people themselves. While this national arrangement may appear to be "undemocratic" in modern terms, even a representative government was radical when the Constitution was enacted in 1787. **DEFINE REFERENDA.**

IX.   SEPARATION OF POWERS AND CHECKS AND BALANCES: The framers believed that unlimited power was dangerous, so they limited the power of any one individual within government through a system of checks and balances. The separation of power is accomplished by the creation of three branches of the government--legislative, executive, and judicial. Each has distinct powers which can act as a check on the others.

Legislation originates in the Congress. Once approved, it must be signed or vetoed by the president. However, Congress can override a presidential veto if both the House and Senate pass the bill again by a two-thirds margin. Presidents may suggest legislation in State of the Union addresses, and executive departments may even draft proposed legislation. But the actual bill must be proposed by a member of the legislature.

The president appoints ambassadors, federal judges, and other high officials, but the Senate must concur in the appointments. The president and State Department can negotiate treaties, but the Senate must ratify these treaties. The president must execute the laws, but Congress provides the funds. Congress must authorize the creation of executive departments and agencies. And Congress has the power of impeachment of executive officers, including the president.
DEFINE JUDICIAL REVIEW

X.   CONFLICT OVER RATIFICATION: The founding fathers were clever in devising a ratification procedure that gave the new Constitution a fighting chance. Two devices were used: the ratification vote and the ratification procedure. The ratification vote called for the approval of only nine states to ratify the document, instead of a unanimous approval of the states. The ratification procedure specified that special ratifying conventions would be used, instead of state legislatures.

The founding fathers urged speedy approval and waged a very professional (for those days) media campaign to convince the people to support the new Constitution. Three supporters, James Madison, Alexander Hamilton, and John Jay wrote a series of articles under the pen name *Publicus* that were published in major newspapers. In these articles, they provided a detailed defense of the new document. These articles were later collected and published as a complete set simply called *The Federalist Papers*. Even today, they serve as a source of understanding of the thinking and rationale that guided the drafters of the Constitution. Two of these articles are included in the textbook appendix. The supporters of the Constitution called themselves Federalists--their opponents were known as Anti-Federalists. The latter opposed the Constitution because it would create an "aristocratic tyranny," would trample state governments, and lacked a Bill of Rights.

XI.   A BILL OF RIGHTS: There were a few liberties specified in the original Constitution. The Federalists did not think any further definition was required because the people's liberties were protected by state constitutions and the new national government was one of specified or enumerated powers. They could not interfere in liberty, because this was not an enumerated power. However, this did not satisfy the skeptics, and to secure ratification in such states as New York, Massachusetts, and Virginia, the Federalists promised to support the addition of a Bill of Rights to the Constitution.

XII.   CONSTITUTIONAL CHANGE: In order to limit governmental power, the federal government is prohibited from altering the Constitution. Yet the U.S. Constitution had changed over time.

     A.   Amendments: Amendments are used to formally change the Constitution. There is a two-step process:

         1.   Proposal. An amendment may be proposed by a two-thirds vote in each branch of Congress. An amendment may also be proposed by a constitutional convention called by Congress at the request of two-thirds of the states.

         2.   Ratification. A proposed amendment needs a three-quarter approval of state legislatures or ratifying conventions. Congress specifies which method will be used.

All successful amendments except one were passed by Congress and ratified by state legislatures. The 21st Amendment repealing prohibition was handled by ratifying conventions. Congress who was Congress was fearful the legislatures dominated by prohibitionists would defeat the proposed amendment.

     B.   Judicial Interpretations: Using the doctrine of judicial review, the Supreme Court has given meaning to the "necessary and proper" clause, "equal protection of the law," which was used in segregation and voting cases, and found the right to privacy in the Constitution which was used to establish the right to an abortion.

     C.   Presidential and Congressional Action: Presidents have expanded presidential power by acting. President Jefferson purchased the Louisiana Territory from France in 1803, but the Constitution is silent on this presidential action. Congress on the other hand has tried to restrict presidential power, even when the Constitution is silent.

D. Custom and Practice: Finally, the Constitution has changed over time as a result of generally accepted custom and practice. For example, the Constitution is silent on political parties, yet these can play a key role in the checks and balance of the government.

CHAPTER THREE SAMPLE QUESTIONS

TRUE-FALSE:

1. Constitutionalism is a government of laws based on the principle that government power should be limited.

2. Under the Articles of Confederation, the Continental Congress had the power to tax the states, but not the people.

3. Under the Articles of Confederation, each state printed its own money.

4. The framers of the U.S. Constitution had been selected by their state legislatures.

5. Under the original Constitution, the people elected Representatives and Senators to the Congress.

6. The founders believed in a strong independent national government.

7. Most of the delegates to the Constitutional Convention favored extending voting rights to all people.

8. A central purpose of the Constitution was to give the national government the power to tax.

9. The power of judicial review is contained in the original Constitution.

10. The Bill of Rights was originally intended to limit the power of state governments.

MULTIPLE-CHOICE

11. Which of the following is considered as the first written "social contract"?
    a. Magna Carta   b. Mayflower Compact
    c. Colonial charters   d. Declaration of Independence

12. Under the Articles of Confederation, the Congress had all but one of the following powers:
    a. Taxation   b. Print money   c. Make war and peace   d. Borrow money

13. The founders shared a consensus on all but one of the following ideas early in the Constitutional Convention:
   a. Liberty and property
   b. Representation in the Congress
   c. Social Contract
   d. Limited government

14. During the Constitutional Convention, there was conflict over all but one of the following:
   a. Representation b. Slavery c. Voter qualifications d. Nationalism

15. The first ten amendments to the U.S. Constitution are called:
   a. Bill of Rights   b. Informal changes
   c. judicial review   d. Custom and Tradition

16. Informal changes to the Constitution include all but one of the following:
   a. Presidential interpretation   b. Congressional interpretation
   c. Judicial interpretation   d. Amendments

17. Primary responsibility for economic policy was given to _____ in the Constitution.
   a. The President   b. The congress
   c. The federal reserve   d. The council of economic advisors

18. In order to create a strong national government while at the same time protecting liberty and property, the Constitution includes:
   a. A republican form of government
   b. National supremacy
   c. A federal form of government
   d. All of the above

19. In order to increase the chance that the Constitution would be ratified, the Founders:
   a. Required that the constitution only be ratified by nine states
   b. Permitted Constitutional conventions to be used to ratify
   c. Waged a media campaign to convince the states to ratify
   d. All of the above

20. The group of people who opposed ratification of the Constitution were:
   a. Federalists
   b. Anti-federalists
   c. Constitutionalists
   d. Anti-constitutionalists

CHAPTER THREE SAMPLE QUESTION ANSWERS

TRUE-FALSE

1. **TRUE**. This is the essence of Constitutionalism. See page 56.

2. **FALSE**. The Continental Congress did not have the power of taxation; they could only make requests. See page 57.

3. **TRUE**. See page 58.

4. **TRUE**. See page 60.

5. **FALSE**. Only one part of the government was directly elected by the people--the House of Representatives. See page 64.

6. **TRUE**. The founders believed in a strong independent national government. See page 61.

7. **FALSE**. Most of the delegates to the Constitutional Convention favored extending voting rights only to men of property. See page 66.

8. **TRUE**. A central purpose of the Constitution was to give the national government the power to tax. See page 66.

9. **FALSE**. It was a self-announced power of the Supreme Court in the case of *Marbury v. Madison*. See page 72.

10. **FALSE**. The Bill of Rights was originally intended to limit the power of the national government. See page 78.

MULTIPLE-CHOICE

11. **B**. See page 56.

12. **A**. The Congress had to petition the states for money. They only provided an estimated 10 percent of the money so requested. Congress did not have the power to levy any taxes on the states or individuals. See page 58.

13. **B** Representation in the legislature proved to be one of the main obstacles to consensus. See page 63.

14. **D**. Nationalism was one of the points of consensus. See pages 61-62.

15. **A**. The first ten amendments are called the Bill of Rights. See page 77.

16. **D**. Amendments are formal changes to the constitution. See pages 79-82.

17. **B**. Primary responsibility for economic policy was given to Congress in the Constitution. See pages 66-68.

18. **D**. In order to create a strong national government while at the same time protecting liberty and property, the Constitution includes a republican form of government, national supremacy, and a federal form of government. See page 70.

19. **D**. In order to increase the chance that the Constitution would be ratified, the founders required that the Constitution only be ratified by nine states, permitted constitutional conventions to be used, and waged a media campaign to convince the states to ratify. See page 74.

20. **B**. The group of people who opposed ratification of the Constitution were anti-federalists. See page 75.

CHAPTER FOUR: FEDERALISM:
DIVIDING GOVERNMENTAL POWER

I. INDESTRUCTIBLE UNION, INDESTRUCTIBLE STATES: The Civil War tested the proposition whether the nation was a voluntary association of states, or a permanent, indissolvable union. The answer was delivered in the nation's bloodiest carnage where over 500,000 lost their lives. After the Civil War, in *Texas v. White*, the Supreme Court noted that the Constitution looked at an indestructible union formed by indestructible states.

One of the checks and balances envisioned by the founding fathers was the division of power between the national government and state governments. Both are autonomous--that is, have a separate existence and powers. This division is called federalism.

A Unitary system of government is one where the national government is supreme and any powers exercised by lower governments are granted by the national government. State governments are really unitary models: i.e., local governments receive their power from their state government. Some of these powers are specified in state constitutions and others are transferred in a more blanket "Home Rule" which allows the local government to pass any law provided it does not conflict with national or state laws. **DEFINE CONFEDERATION. DEFINE INTERGOVERNMENTAL RELATIONS.**

II. WHY FEDERALISM? THE ARGUMENT FOR A "COMPOUND REPUBLIC": The founding fathers sought to protect minorities from the "tyranny of the majority" and saw federalism as one way this could be accomplished. There are several arguments used to support federalism.

   A. Protecting of Liberty: The founding fathers saw federalism as part of a double security system: the division of power between national and state governments (federalism) and the separation of powers between the three branches of the national government. Competition among these entities was seen as a means of protecting liberty.

   B. Dispersing Power: The founders believed that the dispersing of power among different sets of leaders (national, state, and local) would offer more protection from tyranny. It also helps party competition.

   C. Increasing Participation: In creating numerous governments on many levels, federalism increases the ability of the masses to participate by voting and holding office.

D. Improving Efficiency: Local and state governments can provide many services more efficiently than the national government-police, given their proximity to the people.

E. Ensuring Policy Responsiveness: The mobility of business and people make the numerous and competing governments strive to be sensitive to the policy preferences of the people.

F. Encouraging Policy Innovation: The founders hoped that numerous governments would provide for greater experimentation and innovation in problem solving.

G. Managing Conflict: Federalism permits people of different states and/or regions to pursue their own policies without having to make decisions exclusively on the national level. This greatly reduces conflict over policy preferences.

H. Some Important Reservations: The decentralization of power which can be seen as a strong point of federalism, can also lead to slighting of important but controversial issues, the unequal distribution of policy costs, and the frustration of national policy by local leaders.

III. THE ORIGINAL DESIGN OF FEDERALISM: The original scheme of government envisioned the national government as one with limited, specified powers, national and state governments exercising some concurrent powers, all other powers reserved to the states, with some powers being specifically denied within the Constitution, and the states playing some role in the composition of the national government.

A. Delegated Powers: Article I, Section 8 lists 17 specific powers granted to the national government. These collectively are referred to as delegated or enumerated powers. The last clause in this section enables Congress to make laws which are necessary and proper to carry out the delegated powers. This clause is known as the "Necessary and Proper Clause," which has been the major source of all the implied powers of Congress. This is also called the "elastic" clause since it is so flexible.

B. National Supremacy: The supremacy clause clearly provides for the supremacy of federal law over state or local laws.

C. Concurrent and Reserved Powers: **DEFINE CONCURRENT AND RESERVED POWERS.**

D. Powers Denied to the States: In order to protect national unity, some powers are prohibited to the states. These include coining money and making treaties with other nations.

E. Powers denied to the Nation and the States: The Bill of Rights clearly limits both the national and state governments from abridging individual liberties.

F. State Role in National Government: States are the basic units of the national government. They are used as the units for representation within Congress,and the Constitution cannot be altered without their participation.

IV. THE EVOLUTION OF AMERICAN FEDERALISM: Although not much has changed in the formal documentation of power over the 200 years of our country, it is unarguable that power has flowed up, that is, from the state and local government level to the national level. There have been various periods in the development of federalism:

A. State-Centered Federalism, 1787-1868: The states reigned supreme in this period. The national government was just beginning to define itself. The Civil War played a key role in this development.

B. Dual Federalism, 1868-1913. The national government limited its role to its delegated powers and the states handled domestic issues. This relationship is often compared to a "layer cake." **DEFINE DUAL FEDERALISM**.

C. Cooperative Federalism, 1913-1964: The distinction between national and state responsibilities began to erode and was caused by many factors: the Industrial Revolution and nationalization of the U.S. economy; the shifting of financial resources to the federal government as a result of the imposition of the federal income tax; two world wars; and the Great Depression. FDR's New Deal funded massive public works projects which were welcomed by state leaders. During this period, the federal government intervened in labor, agriculture, business practices, public assistance, employment services, child welfare, public housing, urban renewal, highway construction, and vocational education. Most of these programs were carried out at the local or state level but funded with federal money. This period featured cooperation between the national and state/local governments and is often described as "marble cake."

D. Centralized Federalism, 1964-1980: With the introduction of LBJ's Great Society, national goals became predominant. Congress went way beyond its enumerated powers relying on the "elastic clause" to legislate on almost any program. The U.S. Supreme Court did not consider the reserved states' powers of the Tenth Amendment to be any barrier to this increased federal activity. Sometimes this period is referred to as "pineapple upside-down cake" where the frosting is on top.

E.   New Federalism 1980-1985: **DEFINE NEW FEDERALISM**.

While there was some shift of responsibilities, federal money did not always go with the flow resulting in the states having to assume responsibilities and pay with their own resources. This situation is described as "unfunded mandates."

F.   Representational Federalism, 1985-1995: The 1985 Supreme Court *Garcia* decision virtually eliminated the concept of state powers conflicting with the national government. The Supreme Court essentially told the states that they elect political representatives and it is their job to protect state's rights. Thus, the concept of "representational federalism." This decision essentially eliminated the constitutional division of powers between the federal and state governments.

V.   KEY DEVELOPMENTS IN AMERICAN FEDERALISM. (From Up Close Insert, pages 102-103)

A.   *McCulloch v. Maryland* and the Necessary and Proper Clause: The crux of this issue was creation of a national bank. There is no discussion in the enumerated powers of a national bank, but some argued that the enumerated powers included the printing of money and that a bank was a depository of money and the creation of the bank could be implied by the necessary and proper clause. The issue came to a head when the state of Maryland attempted to impose a tax on the operations of the national bank in that state. In reaching a decision in the *McCulloch v. Maryland* case, the Supreme Court first had to consider: Was creation of the bank constitutional? Chief Justice Marshall gave a broad interpretation to the clause: If the end is legitimate and within the scope of the Constitution and the appropriate means are adopted toward that end and which are consistent with the letter or spirit of the Constitution, then it is constitutional. Thus, the Court found the national bank to be constitutional. The second issue was whether a state could tax the operations of the national government, not if the national supremacy clause had any meaning-state governments cannot interfere with federal laws.

B.   Secession and the Civil War: The Civil War was the greatest challenge of the federal system. At the heart of the debate was the question of how far a state could go in its opposition to the national government. **DEFINE SECESSION AND NULLIFICATION.**

This debate was settled by the North's victory in the Civil War. In addition, three amendments were added to the Constitution as a further limitation on states: the Thirteenth Amendment which abolished slavery, the Fourteenth Amendment which established due process for the deprivation of life, liberty and property; and equal protection of the law, and finally the Fifteenth Amendment which prohibited the states from denying the vote to black males.

C. National Guarantees of Civil Rights: Starting in 1925, the Supreme Court began to require states to protect civil liberties in the Bill of Rights by a process called "selective incorporation." That is, the Court on a case by case basis found the civil liberties of the Bill of Rights applicable to the national government also applicable to state/local governments. The *Brown v. Board of Education* was a watershed in that the Supreme Court for the first time used the Fourteenth Amendment to call for a full assertion of national authority in the field of civil rights. Mainly southern states resisted the efforts of the federal government to integrate schools. In extreme cases, state authorities tried to interpose themselves by ordering state military forces to block integration. These efforts were rejected by the Supreme Court and national government, which ordered regular army units or federal marshals to enforce the Court's decision.

D. Expansion of Interstate Commerce: Prior to the New Deal, the Supreme Court had interpreted the regulation of interstate commerce clause very narrowly; however in the 1930s interpreted it to mean any activity which substantially affects the national economy. This shift greatly increased the ability of the national government to regulate state behavior.

E. Federal Grants and Income Tax: With the funds provided by a federal income tax, the federal government began a program of establishing programs subject to federal direction that provided money grants to states for highway construction, vocational education, etc. In accepting the money, the states had to comply with the federal requirements.

VI. FEDERALISM REVISED? In recent years, the U.S. Supreme Court has become more respectful of the powers of the states.

A. *U.S. v. Lopez* (1995): The Court found that the Federal Gun Free School Zones Act was unconstitutional because it exceeded Congress's powers under the Interstate commerce clause.

B. *Seminole Tribe v. Florida* (1996): The Eleventh Amendment shields states from lawsuits by private parties that seek to force states to comply with federal laws enacted under the commerce power.

C. *Alden v. Maine* (1999): States were also shielded in their own courts from lawsuits in which private parties seek to enforce federal mandates.

D. *Printz v.U.S.* (1997): Provision of Brady law invalidated. Law's mandate to local police to conduct background checks on gun purchases violated "the very principle of separate state sovereignty."

VII. MONEY AND POWER FLOW TO WASHINGTON: Through its power to spend for the general welfare, there is almost no activity or program beyond the reach of the federal government--education, welfare, transportation, police protection, housing, hospitals, libraries, urban development, etc.

The single most important source of federal influence over state and local activities are the grants-in-aid. This is defined as a transfer for funds from one higher level of government to a lower level on some type of matching basis for some specific purpose and subject to prescribed conditions of the grantor. Participation in the grant-in-aid program is voluntary. More than 25 percent of state funds come from federal grants. There are three principal types of federal grants:

1. Categorical Grant: **FILL IN**.

2. Block Grant: This is a grant for a general governmental function such as health, education, or law enforcement in which the state and local governments have fairly broad discretion on deciding how to spend the money and are distributed on a formula basis.

3. General Revenue Sharing (GRS): Originally given to states and local governments with minimum strings. Money could be used where needed. The amount of money given to any state or local government is determined by a complex formula based on population, tax effort, and population income level. The program died in the 1986 budget crunch of national government and due to opposition to the program by states.

4. State and local government dependence on federal aid increased during the Clinton administration.

VIII. COERCIVE FEDERALISM: PREEMPTIONS AND MANDATES: In place of offering money with strings attached, Congress has undertaken to intervene in areas traditionally reserved to the states and forced states to comply with its programs and regulations.

A. Federal Preemptions: The national supremacy clause allows the federal government to preempt a state law. This preemption can be total or only partial. In total preemption the federal government assumes all responsibility for regulation. Examples include the areas of copyrights, bankruptcy, railroads, and airlines. **DEFINE PARTIAL PREEMPTION.**

In standard partial preemption the state standards are permitted to supersede federal standards, if the state standard is more stringent. This has been most applicable in environmental regulation area.

B. Federal Mandates: These are direct orders to a state or local government to perform a service or comply with a federal law. These mandates can cover a wide spectrum of policy areas.

C. "Unfunded Mandates." Federal mandates often cause state and local government to spend money to comply with the mandate. If the federal mandate does not include money for the states/local governments, this is, in effect, an "unfunded mandate."

IX. A DEVOLUTION REVOLUTION? The 1994 election of a Republican House to join the Republican Senate and a majority of states' governors who are Republicans brought a renewed call of decentralization from Washington back to the states. This is called "devolution."

A. Reliance on Block Grants: Devolution may take the form of consolidating and changing categorical grants to block grants, thus giving states more discretion on spending.

B. Welfare Reform and Federalism: This has been the key area of devolution. Significant changes in the welfare programs have given the states greater freedom and flexibility.

C. The Beginning of the End to Federal Entitlement? The major changes in welfare policy may be the model for shedding of all federal entitlement programs.

D. Federalism Impact Assessments: Reagan's 1987 order for reports on how new rules and regulations would impact upon state powers, laws, or programs was largely ignored.

E. Political Obstacles to Devolution and Federalism: Politicians gain little if they tell constituents that a particular problem is not a federal responsibility. Also, neither presidents nor members of Congress are inclined to restrain their powers.

CHAPTER FOUR SAMPLE QUESTIONS

TRUE-FALSE:

1. Federalist-type governments are the most common in the world today.

2. An example of a confederation would be the United States during the period 1781-1787.

3. The elastic clause refers to the necessary and proper clause in Article I, Section 8 of the Constitution.

4. One of the key advantages of federalism is that is disperses power among numerous governments.

5. A key feature of new federalism was the centralization of power in the national government.

6. Representational federalism in effect obliterates the historic meaning of federalism.

7. John C. Calhoun was an ardent nationalist prior to the Civil War.

8. A block grant is in one in which money is given for a narrow, specific purpose and must be approved by a federal agency.

9. Partial preemption stipulates that state laws are valid so long as they do not conflict with national laws.

10. Unfunded mandates are illegal.

MULTIPLE-CHOICE:

11. A system which places all the power in the hands of the national government and subnational governments have only those powers given to them by the national is called:
    a. Federal
    b. Confederate
    c. Unitary
    d. None of the above

12. The interaction between different levels of government is called:
    a. Home Rule
    b. Confederation
    c. Unitary
    d. Intergovernmental relations

13. The power of local government to pass laws affecting local affairs as long as they do not conflict with state or federal laws is:
   a. Home rule
   b. Local rule
   c. City rule
   d. None of the above

14. All but one of the following are favorable arguments for federalism:
   a. Protects liberty
   b. Concentrates power
   c. Increases participation
   d. Encourages policy innovation

15. All but one of the following are disadvantages of federalism:
   a. Improve efficiency
   b. Can obstruct action on national policies.
   c. Obstructs uniformity
   d. Local issues can override national priorities.

16. Which of the following was not part of the original Constitution?
   a. Enumerated powers
   b. National supremacy
   c. Concurrent powers
   d. Implied powers

17. Those powers listed in the Constitution which are to be shared by both the national and state governments are the:
   a. Reserved powers.
   b. Delegated powers
   c. Shared powers
   d. Concurrent powers

18. The period of U.S. federalism in which the national government narrowly interpreted the delegated powers and states handled most domestic policy was:
   a. State-centered federalism
   b. Centralized federalism
   c. New federalism
   d. Dual federalism

19. Which of the following was important to the development of U.S. federalism?
   a. The Civil War
   b. The federal income tax
   c. The broad interpretation of the Necessary and Proper clause
   d. All of the above.

20. Direct orders to state and local governments to perform a certain function are:
   a. Federal mandates
   b. Total preemptions
   c. Categorical mandates
   d. All of the above.

CHAPTER FOUR SAMPLE QUESTION ANSWERS

TRUE-FALSE:

1. **FALSE**. Unitary system of government is the most common. See page 89.

2.   **TRUE**. Today there are few examples of confederation. Switzerland is one of the few. See page 92.

3.   **TRUE**. Because the courts have used the clause to extend the power of the government in almost every area. See page 96.

4.   **TRUE**. One of the key advantages of federalism is that is disperses power among numerous governments. See page 93.

5.   **FALSE**. An effort was made to shift power from Washington back to the states. See page 99.

6.   **TRUE**. See discussion page 105.

7.   **FALSE**. The idea of states' rights' was promoted by Calhoun and others prior to the Civil War. See page 97.

8.   **FALSE.** A categorical grant is one in which money is given for a narrow, specific purpose and must be approved by a federal agency. See page 108.

9.   **TRUE**. Partial preemption stipulates that state laws are valid so long as they do not conflict with national laws. See page 111.

10.   **FALSE**. Although unpopular, unfunded mandates are not illegal. See page 112.

MULTIPLE-CHOICE:

11. **C**. A unitary system places all the power in the hands of the national government and subnational governments have only those powers given to them by the national. See page 90.

12. **D**. The interaction between different levels of government is called intergovernmental relations. See Page 90.

13. **A**. The power of local government to pass laws affecting local affairs as long as they do not conflict with state or federal laws is home rule. See page 90.

14. **B**. Rather than concentrate power, federalism diffuses power. See page 93.

15 **A**. Promoting efficiency is an advantage of federalism. See page 93.

16. **D**. Implied powers were a result of the *McCulloch v. Maryland* case. See page 102.

17. **D.** Those powers listed in the Constitution which are to be shared by both the national and state governments are the concurrent powers. See page 96.

18. **D.** The period of U.S. federalism in which the national government narrowly interpreted the delegated powers and states handled most domestic policy was dual federalism. See page 99.

19. **D.** See pages 102-103.

20. **A**. Direct orders to state and local governments to perform a certain function are federal mandates. See page 111.

CHAPTER FIVE: OPINION AND PARTICIPATION

I. POLITICS AND PUBLIC OPINION: Public opinion is important in a democracy because the government depends on the consent of the governed. The public's opinion is often weak, unstable, ill-informed or non-existent on specific policy issues. The absence of well-formed public opinion provides greater leeway to politicians and also increases the influence of special interest groups who are well informed on issues. Still, politicians ignore public opinion polls at their peril. The determination of public opinion is a thriving industry called survey research.

   A. Knowledge Levels: Most Americans do not follow politics closely and have little knowledge of government, thus making it difficult to form opinions on specific issues or policy proposals. Polls often "create" opinion by asking respondents about topics that respondents will not admit they know nothing about.

   B. The "Halo"Effect: **DEFINE HALO EFFECT**.

   C. Inconsistencies: Inconsistent survey results are often caused by asking uniformed respondents questions in a leading manner. Thus the same question asked in two different ways may yield conflicting results.

   D. Instability: Many people answer questions spontaneously with little thought, but do hold fairly fixed attitudes. Therefore it is possible to get inconsistent answers to the same question when asked at different times.

   E. Salience: **DEFINE SALIENT ISSUES**.

II. SOCIALIZATION: THE ORIGINS OF POLITICAL OPINIONS: Socialization is the learning of political values, beliefs, and opinions. It begins at an early age with acquiring of images and impressions of public authority figures such as policy officers and presidents. The sources of political socialization are numerous.

   A. Family: This is the first agent of political socialization. Early political identification mirrors that of family. When family has split party loyalty, child most often mirrors mother's political leanings or becomes independent. Policy identification is less certain--usually not discussed in families.

   B. School: There is no strong evidence that what is taught in schools determines the political attitudes of the students. There is an effort to inspire support for the political system in most schools, but the success of this fades in older students.

C.   Church: Religious beliefs and the importance of religion in one's life have a significant impact on political views. Religion plays an important role in opinion determination on issues such as drugs, abortion, and the death penalty.

D.   Generational and Life-Cycle Effects: Opinion differences are evident in people of various ages. This can be due to both generational (referring to the historical time-frame a person was born in--e.g., baby boomers) and life-cycle effects (what stage in life--e.g., middle or old age).

E.   Media Influence: Most Americans get their news via and trust TV as their source. The effect is not really to persuade people to one side or another of an issue but rather it alerts people to issues and thus "sets the agenda." There is little evidence that the media can change existing opinions, but it can create new ones and reinforce existing ones.

III.   IDEOLOGY AND OPINION: Ideology is a fairly consistent and integrated set of principles, often set in liberal-conservative framework. Most people do not have a consistent application of their ideology on policy issues, e.g., they claim to be liberals but are in favor of the death penalty. Therefore, the simple liberal-conservative dimension of ideology may be too simplistic to explain public opinion.

IV.   GENDER AND OPINION: Men and women do not differ greatly on most policy issues, even on so-called women's issues. There are two areas of difference: use of force (men are more supportive of the death penalty and less in favor of gun control than are women) and political party affiliation. More women identify themselves as Democrats.

V.   RACE AND OPINION: There are major differences of opinion here. Most whites believe there is little discrimination against blacks in jobs, housing, or education and that societal differences are caused by lack of motivation. Most blacks believe the opposite. Blacks are more likely to identify themselves as liberals and generally favor a more activist government role.

VI.   POLICY AND OPINION: Democracy assumes that political leaders will be guided by public opinion. But this is difficult if the public is apathetic and uninformed. In this situation political leaders are more inclined to be persuaded by special interest groups. Therefore, the influence of elites (those who participate in the political process) is strengthened by the weak or nonexistent public opinion on most issues. Political participation is the essential link between opinion and policy.

VII.   INDIVIDUAL PARTICIPATION IN POLITICS: There are numerous avenues of participation open in a democracy, from voting to wearing a political pin, to joining an interest group, to running for office.

VII. SECURING THE RIGHT TO VOTE: There were many steps necessary in securing the right to vote for all Americans.

  A. Elimination of Property Qualifications, 1800-1840: The Constitution left the qualification of voters up to the states. Most states had some kind of property qualification for voting up until 1840.

  B. The Fifteenth Amendment, 1870: **FILL IN**.

  C. Continued Denial of Voting Rights, 1870-1964: Southern states used the white primaries, literacy tests and other "legal" means to prevent blacks from participating. Social and economic threats were also used to intimidate and discourage black voting.

  D. The Civil Rights Act, 1964, the Twenty-Fourth Amendment, and Voting Rights Act, 1964-5: The Civil Rights Act of 1964 made it illegal to use unequal standards in registration of voters (i.e., the literacy tests). The Twenty-Fourth Amendment made poll taxes unconstitutional, and the Civil Rights Act of 1965 permitted the attorney general to replace local registrars of voters with federal officials if needed to prevent discrimination.

  E. The Nineteenth Amendment, 1920: **FILL IN**.

  F. The Twenty-Sixth Amendment, 1971: **FILL IN**.

  G. National Voter Registration Act, 1993: This has often been called the Motor-Voter Act because it mandates that people be allowed to register to vote when they apply for a driver's license or welfare services.

VIII. WHY VOTE?: About half of the voting age population in the U.S. typically does not vote, even in Presidential elections. Turnout in local elections is even lower and has been declining for the last several decades. **DEFINE VOTER TURNOUT.**

  A. The Rational Voter: Some would argue that to be completely rational, one should only vote if the cost of voting--(registration, information gathering, voting) is less than the expected benefit voting (your candidate wins), taking into consideration the chance that your vote will be the decisive vote. Clearly, according to this model it is rarely "rational" to vote. This model can only explain voting when it incorporates the intrinsic rewards of voting. These are the rewards one gets from participating in the voting process, regardless of the outcome.

  B. The Burden of Registration: **FILL IN: WHAT ARE THE BURDENS AND**

WHY IS REGISTRATION USED?

IX. THE POLITICS OF VOTER TURNOUT: The debate over easing registration requirements is clearly political. Democrats generally favor fewer requirements, Republicans more (currently most nonvoters fall into groups that typically support the Democrats). The Motor-Voter bill is an example of politics at work; it was passed by a Democratic Congress and signed by a Democratic president.

A. Stimulus of Competition: The more exciting the race, the greater the voter turnout. People are more likely to perceive that their vote counts in a tight race.

B. Political Alienation: Those who do not feel politics affect their life or that they cannot influence government are less likely to vote.

C. Voter Intensity: People who feel strongly about politics and who hold strong opinions are more likely to vote.

D. Explaining Turnout: The decline in voter turnout may by explained by increased political alienation, increased percentage of the voting population being young people (who tend to have lower turnout rates), and the declining role of party organizations in the political system.

X. VOTERS AND NONVOTERS: There are several factors that distinguish those voting and not voting. Education appears to be the most important determination in voting. The more educated one is, the more likely he/she is likely to vote. Education heightens political awareness and interest in politics.

Age also influences turnout. Young people (18-21) have the highest levels of nonvoting. Wealth also stimulates turnout in that high-income individuals turn out more than low-income people. With income and education held constant, there is no difference between white and black voter turnout. The greatest racial disparity in turnout is between Hispanics and other groups. Hispanics have a much lower turnout.

XI. NONVOTING: WHAT DIFFERENCE DOES IT MAKE? The lack of participation may call into question the legitimacy of democracy. It is important to remember, however, that nonvoting is not the same as being denied the right to vote. Perhaps more importantly is the class bias of nonvoters. Poor and less educated individuals are less likely to vote, and this may be a cause for concern.

XII. PROTEST AS POLITICAL PARTICIPATION: The First Amendment guarantees the right to peaceful assembly and redress of grievances. However, some forms of protest are less acceptable than others.

A.   Protests: Protests are designed to call attention to an issue. Publicity is sought. Media coverage of protest is important. Goal is to arouse public support.

B.   Civil Disobedience: This involves peacefully breaking "unjust laws." People using this strategy are willing to accept punishment in an effort to call public's attention to unjust laws. The Civil Rights Movement is a good case example of this type of protest.

C.   Violence: Political violence is a form of protest, but it is not protected by the Constitution. This extreme form of protest can include riots, assassinations, etc.

D.   Effectiveness: Protests are more effective when aimed at specific problems or laws, when targeting officials who have power to make change, and when goals are limited--getting a hearing. They are not too effective in changing laws or improving conditions that caused protest.

CHAPTER FIVE SAMPLE QUESTIONS

TRUE-FALSE:

1.   Public opinion is generally weak and ill-informed.

2.   The halo effect refers to the propensity of survey respondents to give what they believe to be the socially acceptable answer.

3.   The most powerful agent of political socialization is religion.

4.   There is strong evidence between the teaching in our public schools and the political attitudes of students.

5.   College seniors are generally more liberal than college freshmen.

6.   The media often cause people to change their opinions.

7.   Opinion socialization due to age is called life-cycle effects.

8.   The print media have the most influence in shaping our political opinions.

9.   There is a large gender gap between men and women on most issues.

10.   Women are more likely to be Democratic than men.

MULTIPLE-CHOICE:

11.   All of the following may cause survey results to be inaccurate EXCEPT:
      a. Inconsistency   b. Halo effect
      c. Unreliability   d. Instability

12.   Political socialization comes from all of the following EXCEPT:
      a. Church   b. Family   c. School
      d. Media   e. All of the above ARE sources of socialization

13.   Gender differences are most likely to arise on _____ issues.
      a. Use of force   b. Women's
      c. Economic   d. All of the above

14. Comparing blacks and white, all but one of the statements is more descriptive of blacks:
    a. Support for a positive, active role of government
    b. Are more liberal
    c. Belief that education is the key to black success
    d. Differences in living standards is due to discrimination

15. All of the following were used by southern states to limit black voting, EXCEPT:
    a. Poll taxes   b. White primaries
    c. Registration fences   d. Literacy tests

16. Which of the following forms of political participation enjoys the most support?
    a. Running for office
    b. Writing or calling officials
    c. Discussing politics
    d. Voting

17. Which of the following amendments gave the right to vote to women?
    a. Fifteenth   b. Nineteenth   c. Twenty-fourth   d. Twenty-sixth

18. The poll tax was outlawed by the:
    a. National Voter Registration Act
    b. Civil Rights Acts of 1964-65
    c. The Twenty-sixth Amendment
    d. None of the above

19. Voter turnout is affected by:
    a. Competitive races
    b. Political alienation
    c. Intensity of opinion
    d. All of the above

20. Which of the following factors is most predictive regarding voters?
    a. Education level   b. Age   c. Race   d. High income

CHAPTER FIVE SAMPLE QUESTION ANSWERS

TRUE-FALSE:

1.   **TRUE**. Public opinion is very fickle. See page 119.

2.   **TRUE**. The halo effect refers to the propensity of survey respondents to give what they believe to be the socially acceptable answer. See page 121.

3.   **FALSE**. The most powerful agent of political socialization is the family. See page 123.

4.   **FALSE**. Students seem to be more influenced in college than in K-12 schooling. See page 126.

5.   **FALSE.** The influence of liberal professors and more general acquisition of learning tend to make seniors more liberal. See page 126.

6.   **FALSE**. The media may stimulate interest and new opinion but rarely causes people to change existing opinions. See page 132.

7.   **FALSE**. Opinion socialization due to age is called generational effects. See page 129.

8.   **FALSE.** This is the age of TV, and it gets the prize for being most influential. See page 132.

9.   **FALSE.** Most men and women see alike even on "women's issues." See page 134.

10.   **TRUE.** This difference started in 1980. See page 133.

MULTIPLE-CHOICE:

11. **C**. Inconsistency, halo effect, and instability may cause survey results to be inaccurate. See page 121-122.

12. **E**. Political socialization comes from church, family, school, and the media. See pages 122-132.

13. **A**. Gender differences are most likely to arise on use of force issues. See page 133.

14. **C**. Majorities of both blacks and whites agree that education is the key. See pages

135-136.

15. **C**. Registration fences were never used by southern states to limit black voting. See pages 139-140.

16. **D**. Voting is by far the most practiced political participation. See Figure 5-6. See page 138.

17. **B**. In 1920 all women finally received the right to vote by ratification of the nineteenth amendment. See page 141.

18. **B**. The poll tax was outlawed by the Civil Rights Acts of 1964-65. See page 140.

19. **D**. Voter turnout is affected by competitive races, political alienation, and intensity of opinion. See pages 144-145.

20. **A**. The more education, the more likely to vote. See page 146.

CHAPTER SIX: MASS MEDIA:
SETTING THE POLITICAL AGENDA

I.   THE POWER OF THE MEDIA: Our knowledge of politics and political leaders comes to us largely through the mass media. Few of us have the firsthand opportunity to work in the inner circles of government nor are we usually intimate friends of political leaders. The media have often been called the "fourth branch of government."

A.   National News Media: Media power is concentrated in the hands of a very few reporters, editors, anchors, and producers of the national networks and papers.

B.   The Power of Television: Of all the media, television is the most powerful. It is multi-dimensional. We see and we hear. There is virtually at least one TV set in every American home, and studies show it is turned on for at least seven hours per day. For this reason, TV is the first true <u>mass</u> media. Television is watched and believed as accurate by more people than any other medium.

C.   The Myth of the Mirror: Media people claim they merely "mirror" reality and what they see in society. However, they decide what will be reported, how much time will be allotted, what footage will be used, etc. This gives them the power to shape the news, not merely report it.

II.   SOURCES OF MEDIA POWER: The media are protected by the First Amendment. The media is not neutral, but are active participants in challenging government officials, debating public issues, and defining society's problems.

A.   Newsmaking: **DEFINE NEWSMAKING**.

Politicians have a love/hate relationship with the media. While they resent the media's power to make news, they also seek the attention of the media. The need of politicians and interest groups to gain media attention in order to further their causes has lead to the growth of "media events" and "sound bites."

B.   Agenda Setting: This is the power to decide what will be decided. It is the power to frame issues, present alternatives, and create political issues. By having absolute power to screen the news, the media have the power to set the public agenda. Starvation in Africa is nothing new and when ignored by the media, most are unaware. But let the media feature a few minutes of vivid footage of starving children and suddenly it becomes an issue.

C. Interpreting: Media not only frame the news, but they also provide interpretation of the event. News is reported in "stories." The selection of visual footage is very important. People remember better what they see than hear. Some common themes are present in most news stories--good guys versus bad guys, little guys versus big guys and appearance versus reality. Media also selects expert sources to help explain the meaning and significance of events.

D. Socializing. **DEFINE SOCIALIZATION**.

E. Persuading: In paid advertisements, news, and entertainment the media often attempts to persuade the public. Governments and political leaders rely on persuasion of the media to carry out their programs. Political leaders attempt direct persuasion through press conferences, etc., and indirectly by giving information to reporters.

III. THE POLITICS OF THE MEDIA: Media politics are shaped by economic interests, professional environment, and ideological leanings.

A. Sensationalism: The economic interests of the media (the need to capture audiences) causes news to be selected for its emotional impact. There is a bias toward violence, conflict, scandal, corruption, sex, personal lives of politicians and celebrities. These stories attract and keep an audience's attention.

B. Negativism: **DEFINE NEGATIVSM**.

C. Muckraking: **DEFINE MUCKRAKING**.

D. Liberalism: Most of the media elite have liberal leanings. Talk radio is the one medium where conservatism is dominant.

IV. MEDIATED ELECTIONS: Political campaigning is a media activity, and the media play an important role in shaping American politics.

A. The Media and Candidate-Voter Linkage: The media are the link between voters and candidates. In the past, strong party organizations in local communities could get out the vote. Today, this has been replaced largely by TV. Candidates, therefore, must have great communication skills, i.e., appearance, personality, warmth, friendliness, humor, etc. Image is more important than substance. TV is tougher than the print media. People see as well as hear the candidate. In the print media, people can only read words of the candidate.

B. The Media and Candidate Selection: The media can have a tremendous influence on the early selection of candidates by helping to create name recognition. Discussion of potential candidates and the tone of the discussion can help create an awareness of the candidate as well as give that candidate credibility. Awareness and credibility can translate into campaign contributions.

C. The Media and the Horse Race: **DEFINE HORSERACE COVERAGE**.

D. The Media as Campaign Watchdogs: The media generally see their function in political campaigns as reporting on the weaknesses of the candidates. Media focus their attention on every aspect of a candidate's life: personal, financial, past history, etc. Personal scandal captures more audience attention than policy issues.

E. The Media and Political Bias: The media try to balance their coverage of both the Republican and Democratic candidates. They are usually more critical of front-runners than the underdog.

V. FREEDOM VERSUS FAIRNESS: Early press was very partisan. Not until the beginning of this century did the media try to become independent. The Constitution protects freedom of the press; it does not guarantee fairness.

A. Prior Restraint: Prior restraint refers to the limitation of press before publication. This was originally designed to prohibit the government from closing down or seizing newspapers. The U.S. Supreme Court ruled in the *Pentagon Papers* case that the government may not prohibit even the publishing of stolen, top secret government documents. While the government may not censure, they may be able to muzzle the press, especially in combat areas.

B. Press versus Electronic Media: The Federal Communications Commission was created in order to allocate broadcast frequencies. In doing so, broadcasters, unlike newspapers and magazines, are licensed by the government and thus come under regulation.

C. Equal-Time Requirement: The Federal Communications Commission requires broadcast media to offer equal time and rates to political candidates wishing to use the media for advertisements. But this requirement does not apply to news programs, news specials or talk shows. Nor does it apply to presidential addresses or press conferences. Sometimes the media offer,free time for the opposition party to respond, although it is much more truncated in terms of time.

VI.   LIBEL AND SLANDER: False, harmful written communication is called <u>libel.</u> The same type of communication if spoken is called <u>slander.</u> These types of communication are not protected by the First Amendment.

    A.   Public Officials: As a result of the *New York Times v. Sullivan* case (1964) it is more difficult for public officials to prove slander or libel. They must not only prove the communication to be false and that it was known to be false, but that it was made with "malicious intent" which has been interpreted as reckless regard for the truth. This is very difficult to prove in court,, and as a consequence the media can say virtually anything about a public official. In fact, they have tried to broaden public officials to include public figures.

    B.   "Absence of Malice": The Constitution protects the right of the media to be biased.

    C.   Shielding Sources: Reporters often give a promise of confidentiality (Shield) to sources. The media feel their ability to gather information would be seriously compromised if they had to reveal the identity of sources to the police or in court proceedings. The U.S. Supreme Court has not given blanket protection to the media, but several states have passed shield laws that would apply in their states.

VII.   POLITICS AND THE INTERNET: The Internet has a unique impact on public affairs by providing for "interactive mass participation" in politics.

    A.   Chaotic by Design: The Internet was designed (Note: Rand Corporation) "to operate without any central authority or organization. In 1999, there were 92 million users.

    B.   Political Websites Abound: Websites exist for federal agencies, cabinet departments, members of Congress, political parties, political campaigns, and all major interest groups.

    C.   Internet Uncensored: Internet allows unrestricted freedom of expression. Legislation tried to control "indecent material," but the Supreme Court gave the Internet First Amendment protection in *Reno versus. American Civil Liberties Union* (1997).

    D.   The Privacy Problem: Internet information can be easily accessed.

Websites can track visitors and even send out "cookies."

VIII. **MEDIA EFFECTS: SHAPING POLITICAL LIFE**: The media affect public opinion and political behavior in three categories, (1) information and agenda setting, (2) values and opinions, (3) behavior.

A. Information and Agenda-Setting Effects: Media does not tell us what to think, but does tell us what to think about. However, information overload (too much information) may diminish effectiveness of the media. This is especially true for political news.

B. Effects on Values and Opinions: The media can reinforce existing values and opinions, but seldom change preexisting opinions. **DEFINE SELECTIVE PERCEPTION.**

C. Direct Effects on Public Opinion: Studies show that opinion changes were heavily influenced by media messages. Anchors, reporters, and commentators had greatest impact. Independent experts had less impact. A popular president can change some public opinion. An unpopular one cannot. Interest groups have a slightly negative impact on public opinion.

D. Effects on Behavior: TV is likely to reinforce behavior rather than change it. Political ads are more useful in getting supporters to the polls than in changing opponents into supporters. TV political advertising is more influential with marginal voters.

CHAPTER SIX SAMPLE QUESTIONS

TRUE-FALSE:

1. Media power is widely distributed among numerous cable channels.

2. The power of television derives not only from the number of viewers, but also its ability to relate emotion as well as information.

3. Television is the most powerful medium in communication.

4. Newsmaking is the power to decide what and who is newsworthy.

5. Media professionals are neutral observers of American politics.

6. The real power of the media is the power to set the political agenda.

7. Politicians have a love-love relationship with the media.

8. The media is biased towards bad news.

9. Most direct persuasion comes to us through paid advertising.

10. Image is crucial to modern political campaigning on the TV medium.

11. All major interest groups maintain websites.

12. Surfing the Internet is protected for one's privacy.

MULTIPLE-CHOICE:

11. Which of the following is NOT one of the sources of media power?
    a. Newsmaking
    b. Agenda setting
    c. Interpreting
    d. Determining

12. The politics of the media is shaped by:
    a. Professional environment
    b. Economic interests
    c. Ideological leanings
    d. All of the above

13. Political reporting which focuses on which candidate is in the lead is called:
    a. Muckraking coverage
    b. Horserace coverage
    c. Watchdog coverage
    d. None of the above

14. Which media do people believe the most?
    a. TV   b. Radio   c. Newspapers   d. Magazines

15. Written communication which wrongly damages an individual is called:
    a. Libel   b. Slander   c. Defamation   d. All of the above

16. The media bias toward bad news is called:
    a. Agenda setting   b. Sensationalism
    c. Liberalism   d. Negativism

17. The watchdog activity of the press is also called:
    a. Agenda setting   b. Sensationalism
    c. Muckraking   d. Negativism

18. The rule which requires the demonstration that comments against public officials were made with "reckless disregard" for the truth is the:
    a. Equal time rule   b. Westmoreland rule
    c. Sullivan rule   d. None of the above

19. A newspaper is about to publish an article which tells how to make a pipe bomb. Because of terrorist activities, the U.S. government thinks the publication could be injurious to national security. They ask a court to issue an injunction to stop publication of the article. This would be called:
    a. Prior restraint   b. Slander
    c. Libel   d. Equal time requirement

20. The general distrust of political leaders and cynicism toward government caused by media coverage is called:
    a. Selective perceptions   b. Information overload
    c. Television malaise   d. None of the above

21. As of 1999, how many Internet users were there?
    a. 22 million   b. 58 million
    c. 79 million   d. 92 million

22. In the 1999 case of *Reno* versus. *American Civil Liberties Union*, the U. S. Supreme Court ruled that material on the Internet could be
    a. Censored   b. Protected by the Constitution
    c. Controlled by the government   d. None of the above

CHAPTER SIX SAMPLE QUESTION ANSWERS

TRUE-FALSE:

1. **FALSE**. Media power is concentrated in the leading networks and newspapers. See page 157.

2. **TRUE**. See page 158.

3. **TRUE.** We live in the TV age. See page 158.

4. **TRUE** See page 162.

5. **FALSE.** They are active participants, not neutral observers. See page 159.

6. **TRUE**. See page 164.

7. **FALSE.** It is a love-hate relationship. See page 162.

8. **TRUE**. See page 166.

9. **TRUE.** Whether persuading us to buy a product (commercial advertising) or vote for a candidate (Political advertising). See page 165.

10. **TRUE.** Because the viewer can see as well as hear the candidate, image is very important. See page 172.

11. **TRUE.** See page 179.

12. **FALSE.** See page 180.

MULTIPLE-CHOICE:

11. **D**. Media power is derived from newsmaking, agenda setting, persuading, and socializing. See pages 159-165.

12. **D**. The politics of the media is shaped by professional environment, economic interests, and ideological leanings. See page 166.

13. **B**. Political reporting which focuses on which candidate is in the lead is called horserace coverage. See page 173.

14. **A.** TV by far. See page 158.

15. **A**. Written communication which wrongly damage an individual is called libel. See page 185.

16. **D**. Bad news is a focus on negativism. Reporting good news would be a positive approach to the news. See page 166.

17. **C**. In the old days, it was called "muckraking." Today the modern term is the "watchdog" function of the press. See page 168.

18. **C**. The rule which requires the demonstration that comments against public officials were made with "reckless disregard" for the truth is the Sullivan rule. See page 176.

19. **A**. Prior restraint is the government's attempt to censor news. See pages 184-185.

20. **C**. The general distrust of political leaders and cynicism toward government caused by media coverage is called television malaise. See page 181.

21. **D**. See Figure 6.5 on page 179.

22. **B**. First Amendment freedom was the issue here. See page 179.

CHAPTER SEVEN: POLITICAL PARTIES: ORGANIZING POLITICS

I.   THE POWER OF ORGANIZATION: Politics depends on organization--organizing people to run for office and influencing public policy. Political organizations serve as intermediaries between individuals and the government. Political parties are concerned with winning public office, whereas interest groups are concerned more with public policies.

II.   AMERICAN PARTIES: A HISTORICAL PERSPECTIVE: Although parties were not mentioned in the Constitution and the framers viewed them as divisive factions, the rise of political parties was inevitable.

   A.   The Emergence of Parties: Federalists and Democratic-Republicans: Hamilton, John Adams, and others formed the <u>Federalist</u> Party. This party was centered in New York and New England and tended to represent merchants, manufacturers, and shippers.

   Jefferson and his followers formed the <u>Democratic-Republican Party</u>. This party represented agricultural interests, from the small farmer to the plantation owner.

   In the election of 1796, Adams narrowly defeated Jefferson. The election of 1800 featured the same candidates. The Democrat-Republicans appealed to the populace by printing campaign literature and grass-roots organization. The Federalists, who were more elitist, did not. The result was the victory of the Democrat-Republicans. But a major problem came out of this election. Under the original Constitution, electors had two votes. The person receiving the most votes would be President and the second highest number of votes would be the vice-president. If no one received a majority, the House of Representatives would elect the President. Aaron Burr was Jefferson's running mate. The Democrat-Republican electors dutifully cast their ballots for Jefferson and Burr, resulting in a tie with neither receiving a majority of the electoral votes. The election passed to the House of Representatives which the Democratic-Republicans controlled. Some of the Federalist representatives thought of trying to cast their vote for Burr (which he encouraged), but in the end Jefferson was elected as the third President of the United States. This 1800 election was remarkable because it was the first time in history the control of a government passed peacefully from one party to another as a result of an election outcome. It is still rare in the world today.

   B.   Jacksonian Democrats and the Whigs: In the elections of 1824, Andrew Jackson won more popular votes and more votes in the electoral college than any other candidate, but did not receive a majority of votes in either.

The election of the president passed to the House of Representatives where the Democratic-Republican Party was fractionalized, and they elected John Quincy Adams as president. In 1825. In essence, Jackson and his supporters formed a new party: the Democratic Party. Jacksonian ideas democratized and nationalized the party. **EXPLAIN DEMOCRATIZATION AND NATIONALIZATION.**

Jackson's opponents formed the <u>Whig Party</u> which included the remnants of the Federalist Party. They also adopted the Democrats' tactics of a national campaign and popular organizing. By 1840, they were able to capture the White House with William Henry Harrison as their candidate.

C. Post-Civil War Republican Dominance: The Whigs and Democrats shared power until the conflict over slavery caused the creation of the Republican Party in 1854. In 1860, the issue of slavery had split the Democratic Party into northern and southern wings. The Whig Party disintegrated and most supporters joined the new Republican Party. The election of 1860 saw four main candidates. None won a majority of the popular vote, but Lincoln was elected president by the electoral college.

The aftermath of the Civil War found the Republican Party representing the industrial North and the Democratic Party the agricultural South. The Republican Party was dominant during the period 1860-1912, winning every presidential election except two won by the Democratic candidate Grover Cleveland.

The 1896 election was notable because of William Jennings Bryant. A Populist, he was nominated by the Democrats. He sought to have the Democratic Party represent the "have-nots," particularly the debt-ridden farmers of the South and West. He proposed changing from the gold standard to a silver standard, which probably would have led to inflation, lowering the value of the dollar. This would have enabled the indebted farmers to pay their debts with "cheaper" dollars. The Republican Party appealed to the industrial North, calling for high tariffs, protection for manufacturers, and a solid monetary (gold) standard that would lead to prosperity for industrial workers. Thus, the Republican Party cast its lot with industrial workers, small business owners, bankers, and large manufacturers. Black Americans also supported the party of Lincoln. The wealthy class, worried about a possible victory of a Populist raised a huge amount of money. Republican William McKinley won in a landslide.

The Republican Party dominated the presidential scene until 1912 when the party was split by Teddy Roosevelt, who wanted to run again as president but was not chosen by the Republican Party. He formed the Bull Moose Party and as a third party candidate split the Republican vote enabling the

Democratic candidate, former Princeton political science professor Woodrow Wilson to win as president. But in 1920, the Republican Party came back to again win the presidency until 1932.

D. The New Deal Democratic Party: The stock market crash of 1929 and the Great Depression that followed resulted in a complete loss of confidence in the business and political leadership in place and the people voted for Democrat Franklin D. Roosevelt who promised the people a "New Deal."

The Depression saw major realignments of voters to the Democratic banner including working class and union members, white ethnic groups who had previously aligned themselves with the Republicans, Catholics and Jews, African Americans, poor people, and southern whites.

The New Deal passed a great deal of social legislation--welfare and Social Security. This legislation provided support for workers, the aged, disabled, widows and children, and farmers.

E. A New Republican Majority: The Vietnam War and turmoil of civil rights convoluted the Democratic Party,,,, and the 1968 convention in Chicago saw police attacking unruly demonstrators and the party changing its rules to allow more minority and women representation in future conventions.

By the 1972 convention, the party convention represented the views of antiwar protestors, civil rights advocates, feminist organizations, and liberal activists. The Republicans painted the Democrats as ultraliberal, soft on crime, tolerant of disorder, and committed to racial and gender quotas. These positions were far to the left of many in the Democratic Party and the American electorate as a whole. Republican Richard Nixon won reelection in 1972. The Watergate burglary and its aftermath resulted in Nixon's resignation (the first president to do so) and the entry of Gerald Ford as president. Ford's pardon of Nixon resulted in Democrat Jimmy Carter winning by a narrow margin in 1976.

F. The Reagan Coalition: Under the leadership of Ronald Reagan, the Republicans were able to assemble a majority coalition and win the presidencies of 1980, 1984, and with Bush in 1988. This coalition was represented by (1) economic conservatives, who worried about high taxes and excessive government regulation; (2) social conservatives, who were concerned about crime, drugs, and racial conflict; (3) religious fundamentalists who were concerned with abortion and school prayer; (4) southern whites, who were concerned about racial issues such as affirmative action, and; (5) internationalists, who wanted the U.S. to maintain a strong military force in the world.

Reagan was popular and the "Great Communicator." In addition, the Republicans gained control of the Senate, and southern Democrats in the House voted for some Republican proposals to cut taxes. Reagan was successful his first two years. But increased defense spending and failure to cut social spending saw an increase of the deficit. Middle-class Americans began to identify with the Republican Party while the Democratic Party still was labeled as representing only special interests. Republicans portrayed the Democrats as liberals when the mood of the country was swinging in a more conservative direction. Reagan won reelection in 1984, and Bush was elected as president in 1988.

G.   Clinton and the "New Democrats": The increasing alienation of the Democratic Party from mainstream voters caused many Democratic governors and senators to form the Democratic Leadership Council led by the Governor of Arkansas--William Clinton. The council concluded that the party's traditional support for social justice and welfare overshadowed its commitment to economic prosperity.

As the party's nominee in 1992, Clinton attacked Bush for a faltering economy (the central theme of his campaign was: "It's the economy, stupid!"). He also downplayed the traditional liberal special interests in the party, but they supported his candidacy nonetheless (they could not support Bush). The Perot factor made it a three-man race, and Clinton won the most votes, capturing 43 percent. But this meant he was a minority winner.

H.   Republican Resurgence: The resurgence of the Republicans in 1994 confounded all the experts. Not only did the Republicans regain control of the Senate (lost in 1986), but they also captured the House for the first time in 40 years. They also captured a majority of state governorships. Not one single Republican incumbent lost a race for Senator, the House, or governor.

I.   Clinton Holds On: The Republicans were not able to make much use of their political opportunity. They made numerous promises in their "Contract with America" that went unfulfilled. When President Clinton took a hard line approach in the budget conflict and eventually shut down the federal government, his poll ratings soared. Despite his popularity, Clinton has not been able to rejuvenate the Democratic Party. The GOP still controls both houses of Congress.

III.   POLITICAL PARTIES AND DEMOCRATIC GOVERNMENT: Political parties are essential to one of the main functions of a democracy--the contesting of elections to control the government. Political parties in the U.S. have grown weak as other organizations and structures have replaced traditional party activities: special interest groups, the mass media, independent candidates and organizations, primary elections, social welfare programs, and the career civil service.

A. "Responsible" Parties in Theory: In theory, political parties organize people around broad principles of government in order to win office and enact these principles into law. A "responsible" party should:

1. Adopt a platform outlining its principle and policy positions.
2. **FILL IN**
3. **FILL IN**
4. **FILL IN**
5. Organize the legislature to ensure party control to carry out it policies.
6. **FILL IN**

If responsible, disciplined parties offered clear policy proposal to voters who would cast their ballots based on this information, then the winning party would have a "popular mandate" to act.

B. Winning Wins over Principle: American political parties have never resembled the responsible party model (the closest resemblance are political parties in parliamentary democracies). American parties stress winning over principles. To win requires voting coalitions and thus it is virtually impossible to have a unifying platform that would appeal to every member of the coalition. Thus, party platforms are mushy and try to appeal to a broad cross-section of society. Both parties try to position themselves in the middle of the voter spectrum because this is where most of the voters lie. Hence, there is little substantial policy difference between the two major parties.

C. Erosion of Traditional Party Functions: In the areas of campaign organization and finance, parties play only a limited role. Candidates are often self-seeking, not selected by party elders. Campaigns are financed by contributions solicited by the candidate's organization, not the party.

Today, campaigning is a professional operation media, polling, campaign material. Party nominees are selected in primary election by the party's registered voters, not by party bosses. Normally, the party does not even endorse a candidate in the primary election. Once nominated, the candidate relies mostly on his organization, friends, etc. If elected, the party has no way to maintain party discipline--there are some sanctions available--committee assignments, pet project denial, but these are exercised rarely.

Parties no longer have the capability to perform social services--like public jobs, pot hole filling, housing, etc. These are now done by government. Formerly, these were done by political machines, especially for newly arrived immigrants. In return, they asked for the vote of whom they aided. This system was called patronage.

IV.   PARTIES AS ORGANIZERS OF ELECTIONS: Political parties remain the primary institution for organizing elections. Party nominations organize electoral choice. There are two types of elections: <u>partisan</u>, where a candidate is identified on the ballot as belonging to a particular party, and <u>nonpartisan</u>, where candidates are not identified by party. State and national government offices are normally partisan elections. Some local government offices are nonpartisan-county commissioners or school boards are some examples.

   A.   Party Conventions: **DEFINE CAUCUS. DEFINE CONVENTION**.

   B.   Party Primaries and Types of Primaries: Today, the majority of states use party primary elections to chose their party's candidates. The primary election was a result of the progressive era's goal of minimizing the influence of party bosses. This change has succeeded in weakening the power of party leaders to chose party candidates. **DEFINE CLOSED PRIMARIES. DEFINE OPEN PRIMARIES. DEFINE RAIDING. DEFINE BLANKET PRIMARY. DEFINE RUNOFF PRIMARY.**

   C.   General Elections: This election determines who will hold office. Winners of the Democratic and Republican primaries face each other as well as any independent or write-in candidates. Registered voters can vote here as they choose, either by voting a straight party ticket or splitting their vote among the various candidates. State laws make it difficult for independent or write-in candidates to get on the ballot.

V.   WHERE'S THE PARTY? The political parties can be found in three very different arenas. They are the: (1) Party-in-the-Electorate. These are essentially the party voters. Here party activity has declined as more voters register as independents and even party voters split their vote. (2) Party-in-the-Government. Essentially party elected or appointed officials. The lack of party discipline has weakened party activity in this area as well. (3) Party as Organization. This includes party leaders, workers, delegates, etc. In this area, party activity has strengthened, primarily because of technology-computers and communications.

   A.   National Party Structure: The party conventions held every four years possess the formal authority of the party. They not only choose the presidential and vice presidential nominees, but approve party platforms, approve party rules, etc. Because the convention is large and only meets for a short time, they essentially rubber-stamp decisions made by party leaders. The National Democratic and Republican committees nominally act for the party between conventions. These committees are composed of members from all the states. However, the day-to-day work of the party is undertaken by the party chairperson and national committee staff. The chair is normally chosen by the party's nominee for president. His/her principal mission is to raise campaign funds and assist the party's candidates.

B.   State Party Organizations: Each party in the state has a state committee and state chairperson. Most have full-time staffs for public relations, research, fund raising, and voter registration. They sometimes also seek out candidates for difficult races, i.e., challenging a well-entrenched incumbent.

C.   Legislative Party Structures: The U.S. and state legislatures are organized by parties. The majority party meets in a party caucus to select leadership positions--Speaker, whips, etc. The minority party also caucuses to elect its leaders. Committee chairs and membership is determined by party affiliation. Committee assignments in both the House and Senate are allocated on a party basis.

D.   County Committees: In most of the 3,000 counties in the U.S., both major parties have a county committee which works with city and county candidates.

VI.   NATIONAL PARTY CONVENTIONS: The national conventions occur every four years. The main event is ratification of a party presidential nominee who really was previously selected in party primaries and caucuses. Last contested nomination was in 1952 when the Democratic Party convention took three ballots to select Adlai Stevenson, who lost to Eisenhower in the general election. The convention is really a media event. A lot of hoopla, carefully selected speakers to extol the party faithful, selection of the VP nominee, etc.

A.   Convention Delegates: The delegates to the national convention are selected by states. About 80 percent are selected as a result of primaries. Generally, the number of delegates a state has corresponds to the strength of the party in the state. Most delegates are party activists, ideologically motivated, and strongly committed to the presidential candidate.

B.   Making Party Rules: The rules governing the party are ratified at the national convention and often concern delegate selection rules and voting procedures in state delegations. The Democratic Party rules now allow for superdelegates. **DEFINE SUPERDELEGATES. DEFINE UNIT VOTE.**

C.   Party Platforms: The national convention is also where the party platform is written. This document outlines the party's goals and policy preferences, but is not binding on the candidates.

D.   Selecting a Running Mate: The selection of the vice-presidential candidate is always made by the presidential candidate and dutifully ratified by the convention. Sometimes this is the only suspense in the convention--who will get the nod?

E.   Campaign Kickoff: The national convention is used as a kickoff for the general election campaign.

VII.   THE PARTY VOTERS: Traditionally more people have self-identified as Democrats, but this identification has been eroding recently because of an increase in independent identification and an increase in Republican identification.

A.   Growing Numbers of Independents: As voters become disillusioned with the two major parties, they register as nonaffiliated or independent.

B.   Dealignment: **DEFINE DEALIGNMENT**.

C.   Party Loyalty in Voting: Despite the decline in party identification, it remains a strong influence on voter choice.

D.   Realignment? A massive shift of voters to one party that results in party control of government for a lengthy period of time is called a realignment. Political scientists agree that realignments occurred in 1824, 1860, 1896, and 1932. This results in a cycle of about every 36 years. According to this schedule, the next should have happened in 1968. While Nixon was elected as a Republican, the Democrats still controlled the Congress and state governments. Thus, the case for realignment is murky. The Democrats remain the dominant party and receive disproportionate support (more support than average) from Catholics, Jews, African Americans, less educated, lower income groups, blue-collar workers, union members, and big city residents.

The Republicans have made major inroads with one social group--southern whites who have shifted their allegiance from the Democratic Party primarily over the issue of civil rights. Other than that, the Republican Party receives disproportionate support from Protestants, whites, more educated and higher income groups, white-collar workers, nonunion workers, and suburban and small town dwellers.

VIII.   THIRD PARTIES IN THE U.S. SYSTEM: In spite of our fascination with the major parties, there are some third or minor parties in American politics. These can be grouped as:

A.   Ideological: These parties exist to promote an ideology rather than to win elections. They use the electoral process to further their ideals.

B.   Protest Parties: These parties usually involve an unsolved issue ignored by the major parties.

C.   Single Issue Parties: **DEFINE SINGLE ISSUE PARTIES.**

D. Splinter Parties: Many third parties are really splinter parties which develop when there is dissatisfaction with one of the major parties and a group splits off from the major party.

E. Third Party Prospects: In recent years, polls show that a majority of American's favor the idea of a third party.

IX. THE REFORM PARTY: There is widespread disillusionment with politics in America.

A. Creating a New Party: It takes a lot of money to create a new party. Ross Perot, a billionaire, created a grass-roots effort, "United We Stand." He won 19 percent of the vote in 1992, but not a single electoral vote. The Reform Party was created. The party qualified for federal campaign matching funds in 1996, but Perot only gained 9 percent of the vote.

B. A Party Without a Platform? Perot's support came mainly from independents and moderates. The Reform Party is best explained as a "protest party," but it seems to protest party politics generally, rather than any specific condition in society.

X. WHY THE TWO-PARTY SYSTEM PERSISTS: No third party candidate has won the presidency and few have won congressional seats. Why not?

A. Cultural Consensus: The values of democracy, capitalism, free enterprise, individual liberty, religious freedom, and equality of opportunity are widely shared. There is little support for fascist or authoritarian parties. Because of the separation of church and state, there is no political party with a religious identification, such as in Europe. Likewise, socialist parties have existed but not attracted much support, primarily because the Democratic Party was home for union members and workers. Most Americans are grouped at the political center. Radical or fringe groups do not attract much support. For a review of political parties in other parts of the world see Compared to What: Political parties of the World.

B. Winner-Take-All Electoral System: **DEFINE WINNER-TAKE ALL SYSTEM. DEFINE PROPORTIONAL REPRESENTATION.**

C. Legal Access to the Ballot: The Democratic and Republican Party candidates are automatically listed on the ballots in all states, but that is not the case for third party candidates. Significant barriers such as requiring petitions signed by 5 to 10 percent of the registered voters in a state are placed in the way of third party candidates.

CHAPTER SEVEN SAMPLE QUESTIONS

TRUE-FALSE:

1. A special interest group is more concerned with public policies than who wins political office.

2. The framers of the Constitution considered political parties to be a vital aspect of democracy.

3. The principle motivation for the formation of the Republican Party was to support big business.

4. The New Deal Coalition refers to the group of voters brought together by the Democratic Party in light of the Great Depression.

5. American parties fit the "responsible" party theory.

6. For American political parties, winning the election is more important than standing on principles.

7. There is no reason for vote-maximizing parties to take strong policy positions in opposition to each other.

8. Most state and national elections are nonpartisan.

9. Independents are allowed to vote in most primary elections.

10. Ticket-splitting is voting for candidates of different political parties on the same ballot.

MULTIPLE-CHOICE :

11. The first political parties included one of the following:
    a. Republican Party　　　　b. Whig Party
    c. Federalist Party　　　　d. Populist Party

12. The Reagan coalition consisted of all but one of the following groups:
    a. Religious fundamentalists　　b. Southern whites
    c. Social conservatives　　d. Social progressives

13. Elections in which voters must register their party affiliation sometime prior to election day when they will select their party's candidate for office are called:
    a. General elections
    b. Closed primaries
    c. Open primaries
    d. None of the above

14. The New Deal Democrat Party coalition consisted of all but one of the following groups:
    a. Working class and union members
    b. Protestants
    c. Catholics and Jews
    d. Black Americans

15. National party conventions normally do all but one of the following:
    a. Nominate the presidential candidate
    b. Approve the party platform
    c. Approve party rules
    d. Elect the national committee chair

16. The process that describes the increasing number of independents is called:
    a. Realignment
    b. Dealignment
    c. Critical election
    d. Split-ticket voting

17. All but one of the following conditions would describe the "responsible party" model:
    a. A general, vague party platform
    b. Recruitment of candidates
    c. Educating the public about the issues
    d. Enact the party platform

18. The Republican Party draws disproportionate support from all groups except one of the following:
    a. High income groups
    b. Whites
    c. White-collar workers
    d. Union members

19. Raiding is most likely to take place in:
    a. caucuses
    b. closed primary
    c. conventions
    d. open primary

20. Public officials would best describe:
    a. Party-in-the-Electorate
    b. Party-in-government
    c. Party as organization
    d. National party committee

CHAPTER SEVEN SAMPLE QUESTION ANSWERS

TRUE-FALSE:

1. **TRUE.** While special interest groups support candidates with money, they are more concerned with who will support their issues rather than which party will govern. And they themselves are not interested in governing. See page 187.

2. **FALSE.** The framers considered parties to be dangerous factions. See page 188.

3. **FALSE.** While the Republican Party is often associated with big business today, its original purpose was to prevent the spread of slavery into the Western territories. See page 191.

4. **TRUE**. See page 193.

5. **FALSE**. American political parties do not fulfill the criteria of the "Responsible" party theory. See page 200.

6. **TRUE.** With the multi-dimensional coalitions necessary to win elections, American parties must broaden their appeal to win, and standing on principles could offend some of the coalition members. See page 202.

7. **TRUE.** If the majority of voters lie in the middle of the political spectrum and both parties are trying to win their votes, their policy appeals will be very similar. See page 200.

8. **FALSE**. Most state and national elections are partisan. See page 204.

9. **FALSE.** One of the disadvantages of registering as an independent is that the voter forfeits their participation to chose the majority party candidates. See pages 204-205.

10. **TRUE**. See page 206.

MULTIPLE-CHOICE:

11. **C**. The Federalist and Democrat-Republicans were the first organized political parties in the U.S. See page 189.

12. **D**. Social progressives were not part of the Reagan coalition. See page 196.

13. **B**. Elections in which voters must register their party affiliation some time prior to election day when they will select their party's candidate for office are called closed primaries. See page 204.

14. **B**. By and large, Protestant groups have remained with the Republican Party. See page 193.

15. **D**. The National committee chair is normally selected by the presidential candidate, not the convention. See page 207.

16. **B**. A growing number of independents would certainly fit under the definition of dealignment. Refer to page 212.

17. **A**. Parties would be expected to write clear, specific party platforms under this model. See page 200.

18. **D**. Union members are still in the Democratic camp, but many did support Reagan. See pages 214-215.

19. **D**. Open primaries permit voter cross-over which would facilitate raiding. See page 204.

20. **B**. Public officials would be most likely found in the government. See page 206.

CHAPTER EIGHT: CAMPAIGNS AND ELECTIONS: DECIDING WHO GOVERNS

I. ELECTIONS IN A DEMOCRACY: If democracy is government by consent of the governed, then elections are the way that consent is given. Elections allow the governed to choose and pass judgment on officeholders who theoretically represent the governed.

   A. Elections as mandate? Since parties do not follow the responsible party model, it is difficult to support the idea that an election is a popular, majority mandate. Elections can only provide policy mandates if the competing candidates offer clear policy alternatives, the voters vote on the basis of these alternatives, the election results clearly indicate the voters' policy preferences, and elected officials are bound by their campaign promises. These conditions are rarely met in U.S. elections.

   B. Retrospective Voting: Voting can be either prospective (what the candidate will do--this is often determined from campaign promises) or retrospective (what the candidate did in office). Retrospective voting is probably more important for presidential elections than congressional elections because while the president stands out (the buck stops here!), Congress is a large body and most voters have no idea how their senator or representative voted on issues. Retrospective voting seems more important on economic issues.

   C. Protection of rights: Elections provide a remedy from official abuse. The vote is our most important peaceful weapon in protecting our rights.

II. POWER AND AMBITION: Personal ambition is the driving force in politics. Political ambition is the most distinguishing characteristic of public office holders. They are not necessarily the most intelligent, richest, or most successful, but they do have ambition for power and celebrity. Most politicians would deny this ambition. Yet if there were no personal rewards in politics aside from money, few would run for office (few get rich from public service). The following are some characteristics of office holders:

   A. Constitutional Requirements for National Office: The requirements to hold national office are relatively few:

      1. President. A natural-born citizen of the U.S., a resident for 14 years, and at least 35 years old.
      2. U.S. Senate. Citizen for 9 years, at least 30 years old, and a resident of the state.
      3. U.S. Representative. Citizen for 7 years, at least 25 years old, and a resident of the state.

B. Political Entrepreneurship: Political entrepreneurship is the ability to sell oneself and raise money from contributors, organize people to work for the campaign, and be media savvy. Candidates recruit themselves; they seek out interest groups for money.

C. Political Temperament: Perhaps most important is the willingness to work long hours, live and breathe politics, sacrifice family life, etc. To be successful, one must like politics--the meetings, the handshakes, speeches, interviews, etc.

D. Communication Skills: The ability to communicate in a variety of venues and formats and look good doing it is critical.

E. Professionalism: The idea of the citizen-officeholder is becoming less viable. Today, more office holders see politics as a full-time occupation. It is more demanding to run for office and hold office.

F. Careerism: Most professional political careers start early in life. Politicians start by working on the campaigns or in the legislative offices of others to gain experience and knowledge.

G. Lawyers in Politics: The legal profession is well represented in political office holders. Some might say that the law lends itself to politics. Lawyers represent clients, politicians represent voters. Laws are statutes, and lawyers interpret statutes. But more likely is that law and politics mix very well. Politics brings name recognition and contacts that can help the law office. Also many federal offices require a law degree--judgeships, federal attorneys,and the justice department. Since politics is often a full-time occupation, most politicians cannot practice law and politics at the same time. But upon defeat or retirement, most often a job is waiting in a law office.

III. THE ADVANTAGES OF INCUMBENCY: An incumbent is one already holding office. Incumbents seeking reelection have a very high success rate. This is ironic since people have such a low opinion of government in general. Voters apparently distinguish between the institution and the officeholder. There are several reasons that incumbents have the advantage when running for office.

A. Name Recognition: **DEFINE NAME RECOGNITION**.

B. Campaign Contributions: Incumbents have an easier time raising funds. They are already in office and can do favors. A challenger is often an unknown. Individuals and organizations, including political action committees (PACs) prefer incumbents. It is safer. Contributing to an opponent could make an enemy of the incumbent who could retaliate. Only when an incumbent has been very uncooperative or if the incumbent appears particularly vulnerable to defeat will a PAC contribute to their opponent.

C.   Resources of Office: Successful politicians can use their office to help them win re-election. They can make special appearances in order to keep their name and face in the minds of the voters. They can also use their staff to make sure any special needs of the people in their district are met. **DEFINE FRANKING PRIVILEGE**.

IV.   CAMPAIGN STRATEGIES: Campaigns for national office are largely media oriented and in the hands of professionals--public relation and advertising experts, pollsters, professional fund raisers, and media and political consultants. Marketing a commercial product strongly resembles a modern political campaign. Advertising is used to sell the product and the politician.   The campaign strategy includes collecting mailing lists for mail outs, fund raising and invitations to fundraiser functions--cocktail, barbecue, developing a campaign theme and candidate image, continual polling to monitor progress, production of TV tapes, newspaper ads, signs, bumper stickers, radio spots, writing speeches, and scheduling appearances.

A.   Selecting a Theme: Selecting a theme is a lot like launching an advertising campaign. It should not be controversial. It should be catchy and it should package the candidate.

B.   Negative Campaigning--"Defining" the Opponent: A media campaign seeks to "define the opponent" in essentially negative terms. The weaknesses of opponents are identified and dramatized in cleverly commercials. Opposition research and personal background investigations are undertaken by professional individuals or companies. They seek "dirt" and voting records. They look at tax records, court records, insurance claims, and even seek medical reports. Campaign managers believe negative ads are more effective than positive ads, but political scientists disagree.

C.   Using Focus Groups and Polling: **DEFINE FOCUS GROUP.**

D.   Incumbent versus Challenger Strategies: Campaign strategies are influenced by the status of the candidates. Challengers attack the incumbent's record, conditions of the status quo, and stress the need for change. They frequently portray themselves as "outsiders" (not part of the Washington crowd) to appeal to voters turned off by government. The incumbent is a captive of current conditions. If the economy is sour, they may have a problem.

E.   News Management: News management is the key to a successful campaign. Since people give greater credibility to news programs than to paid advertising, maximum "free" coverage of the news media is sought.

Campaigns will endeavor to have their candidate in the "right spot" at the "right moment" doing something newsworthy in order to gain coverage. Photo opportunities are highly prized. Since coverage of the candidate will be short and his words allotted an even shorter period (7 seconds), what is said must be short and powerful. Thus, each day is a programmed activity of photo-ops and sound bites interspersed with dinners and meeting with campaign financial contributors who pay for the TV campaign.

F. Paid advertising: Television ads are expensive to produce and expensive to air. They are also often the key to success.

G. Free Air time: **DEFINE FREE AIR TIME.**

H. Money and Message Win Elections: The quality of the campaign theme and funding mean electoral victory.

V. HOW MUCH DOES IT COST TO GET ELECTED? Getting elected to public office has never been more expensive. The average House race cost nearly $700,000. The typical winning campaign for a Senate seat costs over $5 million.

VI. RAISING CAMPAIGN CASH: The professionalization of campaigning and heavy costs of a media campaign have driven up the costs of office seeking. In sum, in a presidential year, the costs of the presidential and congressional candidates to their political parties and independent political organizations tops $2 billion. To raise these kinds of funds requires much time and dedication.

A. Paying for Campaigns: Campaign funds come from a wide range of sources: small donors, big donors, interest groups, corporations, and even tax payers.

B. Public Money: All taxpayers have the option of helping fund presidential elections by checking the appropriate box on their income tax form, very few do however. Despite the lack of public support, this fund provided over $61 million to the two major presidential candidates in 1996.

C. Small Donations: Millions of Americans finance campaigns either by directly giving to the candidate or giving to political action committees. Small donors account for approximately 20 percent to 25 percent of campaign funds for members of Congress, and the percentage is even higher for Presidential candidates. Under federal law, donations under $200 need not be itemized.

D. Large Individual Donors: The single most important source of funding for presidential and senatorial candidates as well as political parties is large individual donors. Large donors are those who give $1,000 or more.

E.   Political Action Committees: **DEFINE POLITICAL ACTION COMMITTEES. WHAT PERCENTAGE OF CONGRESSIONAL CONTRIBUTIONS DO THEY GIVE?**

F.   Soft Money: **DEFINE SOFT MONEY.**

G.   Candidate Self-Financing: Candidates also use vast sums of their own money to finance their campaigns.   Members of the House and Senate typically spend from $50,000-100,000 of their own money on their campaign.

VII.   WHAT DO CONTRIBUTORS "BUY"? It is illegal to buy a vote. So there is no direct trade-off of a campaign contribution for a vote. Still, the contributor expects something for his money. A liberal or conservative contributor expects the candidate to support their respective views on policy.

A.   The Big-Money Contributors: **FILL IN.**

B.   Buying Access to Policy Makers: Money opens the door so that the contributor has a chance to present his/her view directly to the politician. While most cannot legitimately expect to knock on the door of the president, contact with key staff members is a possibility. Contributors have expectations of a personal meeting with their congressional representative; constituents get a letter.

C.   Buying Government Assistance: Contributors often with business connections expect some help with the federal bureaucracy. Politicians are asked to intervene, and their interest can expedite the case or cause. Congressional interest tags are placed on files. These get more attention than a normal file. The bending of rules or regulations can often backfire if the opposition party learns of them.

D.   Individual Contributors: **FILL IN.**

E.   Fund-Raising Chores: Fund-raising takes more of the candidate's time and energy than any other activity.

VIII.   Regulating Campaign Finance: The Federal Election Commission oversees all individual and organizational campaign contributions and expenditures in federal elections. Composed of six members, appointed by the president to serve staggered six-year terms, traditionally, the six members are split equally between the Republican and Democratic Parties.

A.   Limits on Contributions: Individuals can contribute up to $1,000 per candidate per race. Organization limits are $5,000 per candidate per race. However, there are legal ways to contribute more. Each member of a family can give $1,000/candidate/election. Organizations can "bundle" individual donations of $1,000 and thereby exceed the normal $5,000 limit. Both individuals and organizations can give money to parties for "party building" and "voter registration drives" as long as this "soft money" is not directly spent on the presidential campaign. Independent organizations can spend unlimited money so long as it is not coordinated with the candidate's campaign. Finally, individuals can spend as much of their money as they wish. Every candidate must file periodic reports listing contributions and expenditures. Individual contributors who give $200 or more must be listed by name, address, occupation, and employer. All PAC and organization contributions must be listed whatever the amount.

B.   Federal Funding of Presidential Elections. Federal funds are available for primary and general elections. Candidates can qualify if they raise $5,000 from private donors of contributions no more than $250 from at least twenty states. To receive federal funds, candidates agree to FEC limits on campaign spending. Generally, Republican and Democratic candidates receive the same amount of funds. Federal funding covers one-third of primary costs and all of the official presidential campaign organization costs. Parties also receive federal funds for their nominating conventions and general election activities. Third party candidates can receive matching funds <u>after</u> an election in which they receive at least 5 percent of the vote. If they fail to receive this margin, they get nothing. These federal funds are generated by the one dollar/taxpayer check-off on the income tax form.

IX.   THE PRESIDENTIAL CAMPAIGN: THE PRIMARY RACE. Presidential fever refers to the willingness to endure a grueling, physically, mentally, and emotionally exhausting campaign. Every aspect of one's life--family, friends, etc., is under the microscope.

A.   Media Mentions: **FILL IN.**

B.   Presidential Credentials: Despite the fact that virtually all presidential candidates testify that the presidential arena is far more challenging than any other, the traditional credentials for running for president have been holding the office of vice president, governor, U.S. senator, and/or member of the House.

C.   Decision to Run: The decision to run for president involves complex personal and political consideration. Serious planning and organizing must begin about two years before the general election.

D.   Primary Strategy: The primary strategy differs from that of the general election. It involves an appeal to party activists and ideologically motivated voters in key states.

E.   The New Hampshire Primary: New Hampshire is the first state to hold its primary. While it is relatively unimportant for delegate strength, it receives unusual media coverage. It begins the winnowing process of candidate elimination. A good showing in New Hampshire receives favorable media coverage and encourages financial contributions. A poor showing does just the opposite.

F.   The Front-End Strategy: **DEFINE FRONT-END STRATEGY**.

G.   Super Tuesday Southern Strategy: **DEFINE SUPER TUESDAY SOUTHERN STRATEGY.**

H.   Big State Strategy: **DEFINE BIG STATE STRATEGY**.

I.   Convention Showplace: Once a candidate has enough votes to assure nomination, the party convention should be used to provide the maximum exposure for the candidate.

X.   THE PRESIDENTIAL CAMPAIGN: THE GENERAL ELECTION BATTLE:

A.   General Election Strategies: Presidential election campaigns must concentrate on the electoral college count. Presidents are not popularly elected. State electoral votes are determined, in most cases, by a winner-take-all policy. A narrow plurality, say 51 percent of the vote, wins 100 percent of the electoral votes. The winning candidate must win at least 270 electoral votes--California has 54, New York 33, Texas 32, Florida 25. Winning just these four states would give a candidate over 50 percent of the electoral votes needed to become president. Refer to Up Close-Understanding the Electoral College.

B.   Targeting the Swing States: A candidate must identify which large electoral college vote states are winnable and concentrate his efforts there. States that are in his win column need some attention, just to show interest. States that are a definite loss can be ignored. Marginal states are targets, but more attention will be given to those with large numbers of electoral votes.

C.   Regional Alignments: The Republicans have relied on the southern and mountain states for their electoral college support, while the Democrats have gained their support from the northeast and upper midwest.

D.   The Presidential Debates: More people watch these debates than any other campaign event. The candidates can appeal to their supporters and undecided voters. These are "image" more than issue debates. How well does the candidate communicate? Hold up under pressure? Candidates are "prepped" for the event. Dress rehearsals are used with stand-ins for the opponents. Anticipated questions are pre-answered. Short, one-liner "zingers" are written and rehearsed. Media interpretation is very important, and the candidates' "spin doctors" try to convince the media that their candidate came out on top.

XI. THE VOTER DECIDES: There are many factors which explain why voters cast their ballot for a particular presidential candidate.

A. Party Affiliation: Party affiliation remains one of the most important explanations of voting. Since Democrats still outnumber Republicans, Republicans must receive independent and Democrat split-ticket votes to be successful.

B. Group Voting: Certain groups appear to identify disproportionately with one party or the other. The same pattern exists in voting. Democratic presidential candidates receive more support from African Americans, Catholics, Jews, less-educated, and lower income voters. Republican candidates receive more support from whites, Protestants, and better educated and high income voters. **DEFINE GENDER GAP**.

C. Race and Gender Gap: Women and African Americans have supported Democrats in recent years.

D. Candidate Image: Image is extremely important in presidential elections. It is crucial and has been characterized by warmth, compassion, strength, confidence, honesty, sincerity, good humor, appearance, and "character," which can be interpreted as moral. In communications, there are verbal and nonverbal aspects. Many studies show that nonverbal makes a more lasting impression than verbal. If a candidate appears to be uneasy, voters are likely to be uneasy about the candidate.

E. The Economy: People have a tendency to vote their pocketbooks or wallet. If they are unemployed, if disposable income is down, the party in power normally pays the price. It appears that a voter's perception of economic conditions may be more important than his/her own particular economic condition.

F. Issue Voting: Most voters do not cast their ballot based on an issue. However, some do. For example, pro-choice voters would be careful to see if the Republican platform was anti-abortion, and many would cast their vote on this issue alone. Gay rights advocates might so the same. But these would still be a minority of voters.

CHAPTER EIGHT SAMPLE QUESTIONS

TRUE-FALSE:

1. In a representative democracy, the people directly vote on policy proposals.

2. Most elections can be interpreted by successful candidates as a mandate from the voters.

3. Elections are intended in part to protect individual rights.

4. Personal ambition is the driving force in politics.

5. In order to be president of the United States, an individual must be a natural-born American.

6. Political temperament is the ability to sell oneself to others as a candidate.

7. A well-managed campaign will coordinate themes and images for both free news coverage and paid commercials.

8. For presidential and congressional races, the majority of campaign funds are spent for television production and advertising.

9. Soft money is the fastest growing source of campaign funds.

10. Virtually all major party nominees for the office of president have had previous high public elected office.

MULTIPLE-CHOICE:

11. All but one of the following are conditions for an election to be considered a mandate:
    a. Competing candidate offer clear policy alternatives
    b. Voters cast their ballots based on these policy alternatives
    c. Election results indicate voter policy preferences
    d. Elected officials ignore their campaign promises

12. John Jones has carefully analyzed the candidates for president. Noting that the economy is sluggish, Jones decides to cast his ballot for the challenger. This type of voting would be characterized as:
    a. Mandate voting   b. Retrospective voting
    c. Image voting   d. Prospective voting

13. All of the following are important sources of campaign fund EXCEPT:
    a. Public funds   b. Soft money
    c. Illegal contributions   d. Small donations

14. All but one of the following are important talents or skills of persons running for office:
    a. Political entrepreneurship b. Political temperament
    c. Communication skills   d. Citizen officeholder

15. Which of the following is not an advantage of incumbents?
    a. Name recognition   b. Campaign finances
    c. Franking privilege   d. Status of an insider

16. Which of the following is not part of a campaign strategy?
    a. Polling the marketplace   b. Rejecting a campaign theme
    c. Planning a victory party   d. Compiling computerized mailing lists

17. Which of the following is not a common strategy for winning the presidency?
    a. Big state strategy   b. Swing state strategy
    c. Front-end strategy   d. Super Tuesday strategy
    e. All of the above are strategies used to win the presidency

18. A focus group would be associated with:
    a. Group voting   b. Media advertising
    c. "Hot-button" issues   d. Ethnic voters

19. In which state is the nation's first primary for president?
    a. Vermont   b. California   c. New Hampshire   d. New York

20. How many total electoral votes are there?
    a. 200   b. 538   c. 435   d. 535

CHAPTER EIGHT SAMPLE QUESTION ANSWERS

TRUE-FALSE:

1.   **FALSE**. In a representative democracy the people decide who governs, but only indirectly influence policy. See page 229.

2.   **FALSE.** Considering the conditions necessary for an election to be mandated, very few elections if any can be considered a mandate. See page 229.

3.   **TRUE**. See page 231.

4.   **TRUE.** Whether for beliefs or celebrity status, the motivating force for political office is ambition. See page 231.

5.   **TRUE**. See page 232.

6.   **FALSE**. Political entrepreneurship is the ability to sell oneself as a political candidate. See page 232.

7.   **TRUE.** This is the essence of news management. See page 240.

8.   **TRUE.** Both types of campaigns must make heavy use of the media, and TV is where the action is. See page 241.

9.   **TRUE**. See page 246.

10.   **TRUE.** The only exception is Dwight Eisenhower, and one could argue that he held high public office--Supreme Commander during World War II and the first commander of NATO forces. He did not have any previous elected office experience. See page 254.

MULTIPLE-CHOICE:

11. **D**. Candidates must be bound by their promises to meet the condition for a voter mandate. See page 230.

12. **B**. Voters that look at the performance of the incumbent which they evaluate as poor, and then cast their vote for the challenger have retrospectively voted. See page 230.

13. **C**. Illegal contributions are not common nor are they an important source of campaign funds. See pages 241-246.

14. **D**. The increasing professionalization of politics and careerism make it increasingly unlikely that Jefferson's concept of the "citizen officeholder" is viable today. See page 234.

15. **D**. Many challengers try to tag the incumbent as a member of the <u>status quo</u>, especially if voters are turned off by government. Incumbents will sometimes campaign against the "<u>status quo</u>." All the other choices are definite advantages of incumbency. See pages 235-237.

16. **B**. Selecting a campaign theme is a part of the strategy. The theme should become the paradigm of the campaign. See page 237.

17. **E**. The big state, swing state, and front-end strategies are all used to win the presidency. See page 258-259.

18 **C**. Focus groups are used to identify "hot button" issues which can then be used to frame campaign issues and themes. See page 238.

19. **C**. The small New Hampshire is where the official presidential race kicks off. See page 258.

20. **B**. See page 262

CHAPTER NINE: INTEREST GROUPS:
GETTING THEIR SHARE AND MORE

I. INTEREST GROUP POWER: Organization concentrates power and concentrated power prevails over unorganized interests. INTEREST GROUPS <u>ARE</u> <u>INTERESTED</u> IN POWER TO INFLUENCE PUBLIC POLICY; THEY ARE <u>NOT</u> <u>INTERESTED</u> IN EXERCISING POWER. POLITICAL PARTIES ARE INTERESTED IN EXERCISING POWER AND IN SO DOING MAKE PUBLIC POLICIES. The First Amendment gives us the right to organize to influence the government.

   A. Electoral versus Interest Group Systems: The electoral system is organized geographically--by state and congressional districts. The interest group system is organized to represent specific constituencies--economic, ideological, religious, racial, gender, and specific issues, e.g., abortion. Both systems provide the individual with an avenue for participation in the political process. Interest group activity provides a more direct representation of policy preferences than electoral politics. Interest groups provide a concentrated focus on issues, while voters can only indirectly act through elected representatives.

   B. Checking Majoritarianism: Parties and the electoral system cater to majoritarian interests, while interest groups are much more narrow. In effect, they can help check the impulse of majoritarian politics. However, these special interests can obstruct the majority from exercising its will and can also be attacked as not representing the public interest, but rather a sectarian interest.

   C. Concentrating Benefits while Dispersing Costs: Interest groups often seek special benefits, subsidies, privileges, and protections and also seek to pass the cost of these on to the taxpayers. When the cost is distributed so widely, it is rarely worth the time and effort of an individual taxpayer to organize to oppose the benefit. But if the benefit, etc. is odious enough, some groups may organize to act against it. The diffusion of so many special favors over time results in <u>organizational sclerosis</u>--work, productivity, and investment are discouraged which, in effect, lowers everyone's standard of living.

II. ORIGINS OF INTEREST GROUPS: James Madison's "factions" are today called special interests. Madison viewed them as a necessary evil--they would compete against each other and prevent one interest from becoming all-powerful and thus help to preserve democracy.

   A. Protecting Economic Interests: Madison felt the cause of most factions was an unequal distribution of property. He therefore identified economic interests as the most prevalent in society. Indeed, business interests organized from his day to today to protect their interests.

B.   Advancing Social Movements: **FILL-IN**

C.   Seeking Government Benefits: Expanded government activity creates more interest groups. The growth of the welfare state spawned more interest groups such as the American Association of Retired Persons (AARP). The Professionalization of state and local governments and the expanded role of the federal government in state/local affairs created interest groups to lobby the federal government, i.e., one government level lobbies the other level of government.

D.   Responding to Government Regulation: As more businesses come under government regulation, more and more interest groups arise to protect their interests. Examples include the American Medical Association and the American Bar Association.

III.   THE ORGANIZED INTERESTS IN WASHINGTON: Thousands of groups, associations, nonprofit organizations, and professions are represented in Washington by some professional interests.

A.   Business and Trade Organizations: Economic organizations dominate special interest group politics in Washington. Business interests are represented by large umbrella organizations, such as the U.S. Chamber of Commerce, the National Association of Manufacturers, and other such groups. **DEFINE TRADE ASSOCIATIONS**.

Many individual corporations and firms also open their own lobbying offices or hire experienced lobbying or law firms.

B.   Professional Associations: These rival business and trade organizations for influence in Washington. Some of the more prominent are the American Bar Association (ABA) and the American Medical Association (AMA).

C.   Organized Labor: Union membership has declined over the years from 35 percent of the labor force to 15 percent. The American Federation of Labor-Congress of Industrial Organizations (AFL-CIO) is an umbrella group which represents more than 100 separate unions. The AFL-CIO has influence in Congress and the Democratic Party.

D.   Farm Organizations: Farm population has decreased from 25 percent in the 1930s to about 3 percent today. Still, large producers remain a very strong force in Washington. The most powerful include The American Farm Bureau and National Grange and specialized groups, such as the National Milk Producers and National Cattlemen's Association. Small and low income farmers are represented by the National Farmers Union.

E.   Women's Organizations: **FILL-IN**

F.   Religious Groups: **FILL-IN**.

G.   Public Interest Groups: These groups claim to represent a broad section of society and act to balance the narrow selfish interests of business, trade, and professional organizations and unions. They are frequently allied with liberal ideological groups, civil rights organizations, and environmental groups. Their interests include government regulation of consumer products, public safety, and campaign finance. Among the most influential are Common Cause and Ralph Nader's organizations.

H.   Single-Interest Groups: **FILL-IN**

I.   Ideological Groups: These groups pursue conservative or liberal agendas, often with great passion and considerable financial resources. They are heavy users of computerized mailing lists. Some notable organizations include the liberal Americans for Democratic Action (ADA) and conservative American Conservative Union (ACU).

J.   Government Lobbies: Federal grant-in-aid programs have led states to compete and thus lobby for federal funds. Some lobbying groups include: National Governor's Association, The National Council of State Legislators, The National League of Cities, the National Association of Counties, and the U.S. Conference of Mayors.

IV.   LEADERS AND FOLLOWERS: Every group needs a leader. The question often is: How well does organization leadership reflect the views of the membership?

A.   Interest Group Entrepreneurs: Many recent interest groups of late have been started by entrepreneurs. Ralph Nader is a good example. Sometimes these groups can overcome a perennial problem--that of the free rider. **EXPLAIN THE FREE-RIDER PROBLEM**.

B.   Marketing Membership: Some entrepreneurs appeal to passion or emotion, especially ideological, public interest, and single-issue organizations. An appeal is made to sense of duty and commitment to cause rather than material benefits. Business, trade, and professional organizations usually offer members more tangible benefits, such as information, journals, and newsletters. It is generally easier to organize small, specialized economic interest groups than larger, general, noneconomic ones. Larger organizations must rely on material benefits to attract members. For example, the AARP offers discount drugs, magazines, discounts for travel and lodging, etc., as an inducement for membership. Members of large organizations often join for these benefits and rarely even know or care what policy positions the organization is pushing.

C.   Organizational Democracy and Leader/Member Agreement: Most special interest organizations are run by a group of leaders and activists. Few are governed democratically. Relatively few members take an active part in meetings, etc. Leaders may or may not reflect members' views. An exception to this rule are single-interest groups which, because of the intensity of the member's views, require leaders to adhere closely to these views.

D.   Class Bias in Membership: Special interest group membership is closely tied to professional and managerial, college-educated, and high-income persons. The class bias of membership varies with the organization. Unions obviously recruit workers. Public interest groups draw heavily from the university educated. The same statement could be made about environmental groups. Business, trade, and professional memberships obviously have a high socio-economic status (SES). Usually, leaders and activists have an even higher SES than members.

V.   THE WASHINGTON LOBBYISTS: Washington is awash with firms and individuals lobbying the federal government--law firms and lawyers, private consultants, public and governmental relations firms, business, trade and professional associations, and advocates of special causes.

A.   Who Are the Lobbyists? **DEFINE LOBBYIST.**

Most lobbyists now use more benign titles--"government relations," "public affairs," "regulatory liaison," legislative counseling," or merely "representation." Many are "fixers" who try to influence government policies for a price. Many are insiders--former Congress members, cabinet secretaries, White House aides who "know their way around." They help to open doors for their clients, and they are usually well paid for the service.

B.   Regulation of Lobbies: While the First Amendment protects lobbying, the government can regulate lobbying activities. The Regulation of Lobbying Act requires lobbyists to register and report how much they spend, but enforcement is weak. Some groups clearly engaged in lobbying have never registered, e.g., National Bankers Association. The law requires disclosure for lobbying Congress; it does not cover lobbying efforts in the executive branch or administrative agencies. Nonprofit agencies cannot engage in direct lobbying. Individual donors can deduct any contributions to a nonprofit, from their taxes and the income of the nonprofit, is tax free. If a substantial part of their activity is lobbying, they may risk losing their tax free status.

VI.   THE FINE ART OF LOBBYING: Any activity directed at a government decision maker with the hope of influencing the decision is lobbying. Lobbying is a continuous activity--congressional committees, congressional staff offices, White House staff offices, executive agencies, and Washington cocktail parties. If a group loses a battle, it does not necessarily lose the war. Losing in Congress, the lobbyist can try to influence the agency or executive department administering the law, or it can challenge the law in court. The following year, it can try to repeal the law, weaken it with amendments, or reduce the agency's budget that administers the law. The fight goes on! The following are typical lobbying activities:

A.   Public Relations: **FILL-IN**

B.   Access: **FILL-IN**

C.   Information: Lobbyists provide technical and political information about pending legislation. They gather detailed information from various sources and provide the information to legislators who do not have the time or staff to become fully conversant with every piece of legislation. In this activity, honesty is critical. Providing false or slanted information could backfire and access would be lost.

D.   Grass Roots Mobilization: This is an "outside" activity. Organized interests can often mobilize their members to contact their legislator by providing preaddressed post cards or even telephone numbers. The hope is to deluge the legislator's office and show public interest in a particular piece of legislation. However, legislators are aware of these tactics and while they must be sensitive to the callers, etc., they know it is an orchestrated effort. Lobbyists can also try to mobilize the media by providing news clips, articles, etc. They may even buy advertising in the newspaper.

E.   Protests and Demonstrations: **FILL-IN**

F.   Coalition Building: Frequently interest groups form coalitions groups that have similar interests. They may often band together to influence legislation. For example, veteran groups work together—officer, and enlisted--to influence legislation affecting retired military personnel.

G.   Campaign Support: Interest group contributions help lobbyists gain access as well as elect candidates who are sympathetic to the groups' goals. Most experienced lobbyists avoid making threats--support my bill or we'll help your next opponent. Irritating a legislator is not a way to gain support, and besides, the threat is largely an empty one and the legislator knows it. Bribery is not only against the law, it is rare.

VII.   PAC POWER: Organized groups funnel their campaign contributions through PACs. **DEFINE PACs.**

A.   Origins: PACs were initially started by labor unions as a means of getting around the prohibition against using union dues to finance elections. The Federal Election Campaign Act of 1974 gave encouragement to corporations to form their PACs,, and since then there has been a deluge of PACs of corporations, trade, and professional, etc. Candidates soon learned to like PACs because it was like one-stop shopping--that is, it is easier to collect $5,000 from a PAC than $1,000 in individual donations.

B.   Regulation: **FILL-IN**

C.   Distributing PAC Money: PAC contributions go overwhelmingly to incumbents of either party. Nevertheless, ideological and issue, based PACs make contributions based on policy stances. PAC money is less important in the Senate than House. Note EMILY's List.

VIII.   LOBBYING THE BUREAUCRACY: Lobbying does not cease after a bill is passed and signed into law by the president. The law still has to be implemented by the bureaucracy.   Interest groups try to influence the bureaucracy by monitoring regulatory agencies for notices of new rules and changes, providing reports, testimony, and evidence in administrative hearings, submitting contracts and grant applications and lobby for their acceptance, monitoring the performance of executive agencies, influencing the selection of personnel in the agency, and arguing for strict or loose interpretation or enforcement of the law.

A.   Iron Triangles: The mutual interest of congressional committee members, organized groups, and bureaucratic agencies come together to form what has been called "The Iron Triangle."   Each feeds the other.   The congressional committee approves budgets for the bureaucracy and makes the laws. It in turn is treated with deference by the bureaucracy and the group provides the finances for the committee member's reelection. The bureaucratic agency works closely with the special group. It is a cozy relationship. This triangle works best in specialized policy areas. Conflict is more apparent when powerful, diverse interests are at stake, e.g., environment.

B.   Policy Networks: In place of cozy iron triangles, many observers see networks of interested parties developing. The parties can include interest group leaders and lobbyists, members of Congress and their staffs, executive agency officials, lawyers and consultants, foundations and think tank personnel, and even media personnel.

These networks involve people normally working in the same policy area. They interact and communicate frequently. They know each other. They depend on each other. In short, it is a marriage of mutual convenience.

C.   Revolving Doors: This term is normally used to describe people who move from a government job to the private sector as a consultant, lobbyist or salesperson. They have a commodity that the private sector is willing to pay for--technical expertise, contacts, and knowledge of the inner workings of the government agency. The down side is the suspicion that as they get closer to retirement or departure, they may make decisions favorable to their next employer. The Ethics in Government Act prohibits former members of Congress from lobbying Congress for one year. Former executive agency members cannot lobby their agency for one year nor lobby for two years on a matter in their former area of responsibility.

IX.   LOBBYING THE COURTS: Litigation has become a favorite instrument of interest groups. These groups bring issues to the court by furnishing lawyers to individuals who are parties to the case, initiating class action suits, and filing amicus curiae (friend of the court) briefs. **DEFINE AMICUS CURIAE.**

Some of the interest groups have specialized legal staffs that concentrate on certain issues--e.g., the American Civil Liberties Union (ACLU) on First Amendment cases or the Environmental Defense Fund, etc. Direct lobbying of judges is forbidden. Lobbying about the selection of judges is not, and interest groups are very active, especially when a Supreme Court vacancy occurs.

X.   POLITICS AS INTEREST-GROUP CONFLICT: Pluralists argue that interest-group politics is a natural extension of the democratic ideals of popular participation in government, freedom of association, and promotes competition over public policy.

A.   Pluralism as Democratic Politics: Pluralism is the idea that democracy can be achieved through the competition among groups to which citizens belong. Pluralists argue that interest groups are simply an extension of the idea of participation. It also states that public policy is an equilibrium among various interest groups. The relative influence of the interest group changes over time and is dependent on the issue. Accordingly, the government is passive and only referees the squabble between interest groups. Government acts as an honest broker.

B.   Balancing Group Power: According to pluralists, interest groups act to check each other and that no one group will ever become so dominant as to prevent compromise between groups. This assumption is based on the belief that:

1. <u>Countervailing power</u> will protect everyone's interests.
2. <u>Overlapping</u> group membership will moderate demands and lead to compromise.
3. <u>Latent interest groups</u> will check the more radical ones.

C. Interest-Group Politics: How Democratic? Democratic theory looks at public policy as the rational choice of individuals with equal influence who evaluate their needs and reach a majority decision with due regard for the rights of others. This traditional theory does not view public policy as a product of interest-group pressures. If there were true competition between interest groups it might be more acceptable, but accommodation is the rule rather than competition. Further, interest groups are not democratically governed but rather led by a small elite. Nor are interest groups at all equal--some are more powerful than others.

D. Interest Group Politics--Gridlock and Paralysis: Democracies require a sense of community and common purpose. If the demands of special interest groups displace the public interest, government cannot function well. Uncompromising claims by conflicting interest groups equal gridlock.

CHAPTER NINE SAMPLE QUESTIONS

TRUE-FALSE:

1. Interest groups act as a check on Majoritarianism.

2. Interest group activity is more of an indirect representation of policy preferences compared to electoral politics.

3. Organizational sclerosis refers to a society with so many special interest benefits that the standard of living for all individuals is lowered.

4. Government activities spawn creation of new interest groups.

5. Public Interest groups really represent big business.

6. Interest groups can usually rely on the ideological beliefs of the people to attract membership.

7. The Federal government's grant-in-aid programs to state and local governments have resulted in one government body lobbying another government body.

8. Because of the larger membership, it is easier to organize large groups than small groups.

9. The socio-economic status of group membership shows a bias toward professional, managerial, college-educated, and high-income persons.

10. Probably the most important strategy for interest group success is coalition building.

MULTIPLE-CHOICE:

11. The mutually supportive relationship among interest groups, government agencies, and congressional committees is known as:
   a. Policy networks
   b. Revolving doors
   c. Iron triangles
   d. None of the above

12. If an interest group meets with other groups which have similar interests in order to increase their power, the strategy is called:
   a. Building policy networks
   b. Coalition building
   c. Gaining access
   d. All of the above

13. Madison believed that the primary cause of factions was:
    a. Unequal distribution of property b. Human nature
    c. Competition   d. Government

14. All but one of the following explains the origin of interest groups:
    a. Protecting economic interests
    b. Response to government regulations
    c. Advancing social movements
    d. Media pressure

15. The American Medical Association (AMA) would be best identified as a:
    a. Business organization   b. Trade organization
    c. Professional organization   d. Public interest group

16. Which of the following is/are commonly used by interest groups?
    a. Grass roots mobilization
    b. Public relations
    c. Protests and demonstrations
    d. All of the above

17. The Americans for Democratic Action (ADA) would be classified as:
    a. Ideological group   b. Single-issue group
    c. Professional organization   d. Public interest group

18. The purpose of government in pluralist theory is to:
    a. Promote interest groups
    b. Act contra to the elite
    c. Serve as an honest broker among competing interest groups
    d. Control the impulsive nature of man

19. A person who enjoys the benefit of group membership, but refuses to contribute anything to the costs to obtain the benefit is called a(n):
    a. Scoundrel   b. Free rider
    c. Elite leader   d. Entrepreneur

20. If an interest group cannot compel paid membership, then it must rely on:
    a. Material incentives   b. Union shop
    c. Appeal to patriotism   d. Free riders

CHAPTER NINE SAMPLE QUESTION ANSWERS

TRUE-FALSE:

1.   **TRUE**. See page 280.

2.   **FALSE.** Election politics means we elect representatives who may or may not act according to our wishes regarding public policies. Our influence is through this representative and thus is indirect. In fact, the representative has to be concerned with many issues. In an interest group, we could be a more active participant and the interest group normally concentrates on an issue and directly represent the group to the government. See page 279.

3.   **TRUE**. See page 280.

4.   **TRUE**. The expansion of government into veteran affairs, welfare, education, etc., helped to create special interest groups in these areas. See page 283.

5.   **FALSE.** Public interest groups represent broad classes of people and seek to balance the narrow self-interests of business and trade lobbies. See page 288.

6.   **FALSE.** Because of the free-rider problem, interest groups are forced to attract members by offering material benefits. See page 292.

7.   **TRUE.** State and local governments lobby the federal government, and local governments lobby state governments. See page 291.

8.   **FALSE.** Just the opposite. In a smaller group, people recognize their importance to the group and are more willing to support it. See page 293.

9.   **TRUE.** Although 90 percent of Americans belong to some group, for most it is their local church. Membership in most other groups shows a class bias. The only exception are labor unions, which are supposed to represent the working class. See page 293.

10.   **FALSE.** Probably the most important strategy for interest group success is providing campaign support for candidates. See page 302.

MULTIPLE-CHOICE:

11. **C.** The mutually supportive relationship among interest groups, government agencies, and congressional committees is known as iron triangles. See page 306.

12. **B.** If an interest group meets with other groups which have similar interests in order to increase their power, the strategy is called Coalition building. See page 302.

13. **A.** Economic interests then as well as now largely explain the existence of factions. Human nature explains the origin of factions but not the cause. See page 280.

14. **D.** Media pressure is scarce in covering interest groups, and we could not claim that the media played any role in creating interest groups except in their own area of communications. See pages 280-283.

15. **C.** Medical doctors are professionals. See page 286.

16. **D.** Grass roots mobilization, public relations and demonstrations are all used by interest groups. See pages 296-301.

17. **A.** The Americans for Democratic Action (ADA) is an ideological group. See page 291.

18. **C.** Government's role as seen by the pluralists is to act as a referee to help promote a point of equilibrium in public policy. See page 310.

19. **B.** While a free rider may be regarded as a scoundrel, the proper terminology is free rider. See page 292.

20. **A.** While ideological, single-interest, and public interest groups may base appeals for paid members on commitment and sense of duty, most have to offer material incentives for membership. This would include most trade and professional organizations and many business ones as well. See page 293.

CHAPTER TEN: CONGRESS: POLITICS ON CAPITAL HILL

I. THE POWERS OF CONGRESS: Madison argued that one task of legislators was to control "factions."

   A. Constitutional Powers: The founding fathers saw the legislature as the first and most powerful branch of government. Article I, Section 8 of the Constitution laid out very specific areas of responsibility of the Congress. In addition to legislation, the House of Representatives will elect the president if no candidate obtains a majority in the electoral college. The Senate is called upon for "advice and consent" for treaties and presidential nominations to the judicial and executive branches. The House has the power to impeach executive or judicial officials and the Senate tries the charges. Each chamber can conduct investigations, discipline its members, and regulate its internal affairs.

   B. Institutional Conflict: The Constitution was designed with "checks and balances" so that conflict among the branches of government was not only foreseen, but encouraged so that no branch would become too powerful at the expense of the others. Indeed, over our two hundred year plus history, power has flowed and ebbed among the branches. However, in this century, we have seen a steady, if not undramatic, shift of power toward the executive branch. Normally, it is easier for Congress to play an obstructionist rule than be the source of policy initiatives. Thus, Congress defeats or modifies presidential proposals, tinkers with the budget, delays or rejects nominees, etc. Very recently, the Congress has tried to seize the initiative in policy initiatives, especially in the Contract with America, but many of these policy initiatives were watered down or vetoed.

   C. Dividing Congressional Power: House and Senate. **DEFINE BICAMERAL.** No law can be passed or money spent without the approval of both chambers. The House has 435 members elected to two-year terms, and the Senate has 100 members who serve six-year overlapping terms. Representation in the House is based on population while in the Senate all states are given two seats.

   D. Domestic versus Foreign and Defense Policy: Congress is more powerful in the domestic policy area, and usually defers to the president in the foreign and defense policy areas. The president is "commander in chief" but only the Congress can declare war.

   E. The Power of the Purse: Congress's real power lies in its ability to control the budget--the power of the purse. Only Congress can levy and collect taxes and only they can appropriate funds. These powers give Congress the ability to control all aspects of the federal government.

F. Oversight of the Bureaucracy: **FILL-IN. WHAT IS THE DIFFERENCE BETWEEN THE FORMAL AND REAL RATIONALE OF OVERSIGHT? HOW DOES CONGRESS CARRY OUT ITS OVERSIGHT RESPONSIBILITY? HOW DOES OVERSIGHT SOMETIME BEGIN?**

G. Agenda Setting and Media Attention: Congressional hearings and investigations often involve agenda setting or bringing issues to the public's attention. However, without the media, this effort would not be very successful. Hearings are usually on a specific bill whereas investigations are usually into alleged misdeeds or scandals. The formal reason for congressional investigations is to seek information to assist in lawmaking, but often the investigations are used for political purposes.

Congress has many powers to assist it in hearings or investigations: Subpoena witnesses (compel them to appear), administer oaths, cross-examine witnesses, bring criminal contempt charges (refusing to cooperate), and perjury (lying under oath). Congress cannot impose criminal penalties as a result of its investigations but can refer the matter to the Justice Department for prosecution.

H. Impeachment and Removal: A formidable power whereby the House brings charges and the Senate acts as a jury. President Clinton was the second president to be impeached.

II. CONGRESSIONAL APPORTIONMENT AND REDISTRICTING: While the Constitution requires a reapportionment every ten years in the House, it does not specify the number of representatives. This was done by Congress in 1910 when it fixed the membership at 435. It could be changed again tomorrow, but most likely will not.

A. Apportionment: This means that every 10 years in accordance with the latest census, the 435 seats must be divided up between the 50 states based on their population. This division is based on a formula devised in 1929 which has withstood court challenges and is still used today.

B. Malapportionment: The Constitution does not indicate how each state will apportion its number of representatives. Some states were notorious for malapportionment. **DEFINE MALAPPORTIONMENT.**

C.   Enter the Supreme Court: Prior to 1962, the Court had refused to intervene in malapportionment cases, holding that this was a problem of the states and the federal courts should avoid this "political thicket." The Supreme Court decision in *Baker v. Carr* (1962) was a surprise when the activist Warren Court ruled that population inequities violated the Fourtenth Amendment's equal protection clause.

D.   "Enumeration": The Constitution is very specific. It calls for the enumeration or actual counting of the population in the census and the determination of congressional districts. The census bureau has come under political fire of late for consideration of the use of samples and population estimates. Both those in favor and opposed are so for purely political reasons.

E.   Redistricting: After each decennial census, new congressional district lines may be redrawn based on the census. Some states because of population shift or growth may gain or lose House seats. State legislatures draw up the new boundaries subject to the governor's approval or override of his veto. Recently, the Justice Department and courts have been involved in redistricting issues, especially to determine whether redistricting disadvantages black or Hispanic minorities.

F.   Gerrymandering: **DEFINE GERRYMANDERING, SPLINTERING, AND PACKING**.

G.   Partisan Gerrymandering: The Supreme Court has upheld partisan gerrymandering unless it degrades a voter's or group of voters' influence in the political process. This is very vague and allows much leeway.

H.   The Politics of Redistricting: Party control of the legislature and governorship are the keys to redistricting. Since the Democratic Party had more control at the state level after the 1990 census, they were better positioned to protect Democratic House seats. The Republicans turned to the courts and championed efforts to create black majority-minority districts hoping to "pack" Democratic members in a few districts and help Republicans to win in the other districts.

I.   Racial Gerrymandering: The Voting Rights Act of 1965 (VRA) required states that had a past history of voter discrimination to clear redistricting plans with the Justice Department to ensure there was no intent to discriminate against black, Hispanic, American Indian, Alaskan Native, or Asian voters. A 1982 amendment to the VRA changed "intent" to "effect" minority voting. A 1986 decision of the Supreme Court *Thornburg v. Gingles* interpreted the "effect" test to require state legislatures to draw district lines that would maximize minority representation in Congress and state legislatures. These are called majority-minority districts. This has been called affirmative racial gerrymandering. Following the 1990 census, redistricting plans where there were large minorities were closely scrutinized by the Justice Department and the courts. The creation of new majority-minority districts resulted in a dramatic increase of Black American and Hispanic representatives in Congress. Yet in order to draw in a maximum number of minorities, the resulting districts in many cases were bizarre. A closely divided Supreme Court has recently voided majority-minority districts in Texas, North Carolina, and Georgia, and a federal court did the same in Florida, holding that using race as the predominant factor in drawing district lines was unconstitutional.

III. GETTING TO CAPITOL HILL: Most members of Congress are political entrepreneurs. They nominate themselves, raise their own campaign funds, and organize their own campaign staff.

A. Who Runs for Congress? Most members of Congress have backgrounds in law, business, or prior public service. Many of the lawyers have not practiced law but rather practiced politics instead. Increasingly, they are career politicians.

B. Competition for Seats: **DEFINE SAFE SEAT. DEFINE OPEN SEAT.**

C. Turnover: Despite the high reelection rate of incumbents, there has been a higher rate of turnover in recent years.

D. Congressional Term Limit: Explain the pros and cons of congressional term limits..

E. The Congressional Electorate: Congressional elections are not of high interest to many voters. Most people cannot even name both senators from their state. Voter turnout in congressional elections (nonpresidential) is only about 35 percent and voter turnout for congressional primary races is even lower at 15-20 percent. This low turnout normally favors incumbents.

F. Independence of Congressional Voting: Congressional voting is largely independent of presidential voting. Voters regularly cast their ballots for candidates from one party for president and another party for Congress. This demonstrates differing expectations.

G. Congressional Campaign Financing: In most incumbent versis challenger elections, the incumbent heavily outspends the challenger. In open elections,

Democratic and Republican candidates spend about the same. Raising over $700,000 for a House race or $5 million for a Senate race occupies much time of an incumbent. Even incumbents without opposition raise large amounts of money--just in case. An incumbent with a large campaign fund chest is less inviting for a challenger. By and large, incumbents receive the vast bulk of PAC contributions.

H. The Historic Democratic Party Dominance of Congress: For forty years the Democrats dominated the House. The election of 1994 when the Republicans took control was a bombshell. Democratic control of the Congress has been attributed to:

   1. Predominance of Democratic registered voters. Party affiliation is a large predictor of voting.
   2. Many voted Democratic locally, but Republican nationally.
   3. Many looked at their representative to "bring home the bacon" and Democrats were better at doing this.
   4. Democrats enjoyed the advantages of incumbency.

I. The Republican Revolution? The sweeping Republican victory in 1994 surprised most observers. Why did it happen?

   1. Gingrich and the House Republicans *nationalized* the election, focusing voter attention on discontentment with government and its performance.
   2. The Democrat tradition of bringing home the bacon backfired in the era of budget deficits.

   Republicans have succeeded in maintaining their control of Congress despite the reelection of a Democratic president. The American people seem to prefer divided government.

J. The Democratic Revival: Democrats gained House seats in the 1996 and 1998 elections.

IV. LIFE IN CONGRESS: Attention to your local constituency is the key to survival and success in Congress.

A. The "Representativeness" of Congress: A large majority of the Congress is still white. While African American, Hispanic, and women's representation has gone up significantly in the past years, they are still underrepresented as a percent of their respective group.

B.   Congressional Staff: Each representative has a staff of about 20 headed by an administrative assistant with legislative assistants, secretaries, etc. Senators usually have a staff of 30-50 people. All representatives have Washington offices and local offices; they receive more than $500,000 for office, travel, and staff expenses. Senators receive even more--about $2 million for expenses. Staff personnel have great influence over legislation. They move the legislative process. They keep track of bills and amendments. They even handle negotiations over legislation with special interest groups, and other staff members. They also handle much of the contact with interest groups and constituents. In addition to personal staffs, each committee and subcommittee have their own staff which range in size from 25 to 200 personnel. These are subject to the chairman's control; although some committee staff is reserved for the minority party. If there is a change in party control or chairperson control, some committee staff could be looking for a new position.

C.   Support Agencies: In addition to personal and committee staff, there are four congressional support agencies to provide assistance to the members of Congress.

1.   The Library of Congress and Congressional Research Service (CRS): The CRS provides Congress with references and information on virtually any topic.

2.   General Accounting Office: **FILL IN**.

3.   Congressional Budget Office: The CBO was created to strengthen Congress's role in the budget process. It supplies the House and Senate budget committees with its own budgetary analysis to counter that of the Office of Management and Budget which works for the president.

4.   Office of Technology Assessment (OTA): **FILL IN**.

5.   Government Printing Office (GPO): **FILL IN.**

The creation and growth of congressional support agencies is tied to the continuing struggle between the executive and congressional branches for power.

D.   Workload: Members of Congress put in 12 to 15 hour days and often take work home. Members introduce 10-50 bills/session. Co-sponsoring a bill is very popular. While thousands of bills are introduced, only 400-800 become law in any year. There are 900-1,000 recorded votes during a session, and each Representative is a member of two standing committees and four subcommittees; each Senator may be a member of 9-12 committees and subcommittees. Meetings of these committees and subcommittees are scheduled each month.

E. Pay and Perks: In 1991, after passing a 41 percent increase in pay to $129,000 in the name of reform (since Congress could no longer receive payments from interest groups for appearances and speeches), many taxpayers were outraged. In addition to the pay, Congress has voted itself perks--the House had its own bank which acted as a credit union and which members abused by overdrafts, travel and office expenses, free medical care, free parking at the capitol and airports, free media studios for making self-promotional materials, free mailing privileges, subsidized dining, gift shop and barber shop.

V. HOME STYLE: Home style refers to the activities of legislators in promoting their images among constituents and personally attending to constituent problems and interests.

A. Casework: This refers to winning one vote at a time. Members of Congress can win votes by helping constituents on a personal level--trace or obtain Social Security cards, Medicare problems, IRS problems, federal job applications, etc. The staff does most of the work, but the letter goes back with the member of Congress's signature. One study indicated House members processed 100 cases/week and senators 300 cases/week.

B. Pork Barrel: **DEFINE PORK BARREL.**

C. Pressing the Flesh: Members of Congress spend about 100 days/year in their state or district. While there, it is important to be seen and heard, so they go to dinners, civic affairs, etc. Congress normally handles legislation on a Tuesday-Thursday schedule giving members the opportunity for long weekends at home.

D. Puffing Images: **FILL IN.**

VI. ORGANIZING CONGRESS: PARTY AND LEADERSHIP:

A. Party Organization in Congress: The major party organizations in the Senate and House are the principal means for organizing Congress. Leadership positions, while nominally elected by the whole body, are really decided in party meetings. Party leadership can help an incumbent be reelected--the right committee assignment is very important. Each party also has a campaign organization which can help funnel funds to their incumbents. While calls are heard for party leaders to discipline their members more (and they have the means to do so--committee assignments, support for legislation, denial of campaign funds, etc), this is done only in rare instances. Members of Congress cherish their independence.

B. In the House: "Mr. Speaker": The Speaker serves as both the presiding officer of the House and his party leader in the House. In the event of the death of the president and vice-president, the Speaker would be next in line to assume the presidency. The Speaker has many powers:

1. Recognizes speakers on the floor and rules on points of order.
2. Rules whether a motion or amendment is germane (relevant).
3. Assigns new bills to committee.
4. Can delay or schedule votes on a bill.
5. Names members of select, special and conference committees.
6. Names the majority members to the Rules Committee.

Because the Speaker represents the whole body, he is expected to apply the rules fairly; however, as head of his party he is expected to advance the interests of his party.

C. House Leaders and Whips: The principal assistant of the Speaker in the House is the majority leader. He helps formulate the party's legislative program, helps steer it through the House, persuades committee chairs to support the program and helps arrange the legislative schedule. The minority party selects a minority leader. He essentially does the same as the majority leader except schedule legislation. Both parties have whips to keep track of party members, their vote, pressuring them to be present for roll-call votes, and try to determine how they will vote on bills. The whips are part of the power structure and are consulted on the legislative program and scheduling.

D. In the Senate: "Mr. President": The official presiding officer of the Senate is the vice-president. This is his only constitutional duty. However, the vice-president rarely presides over the Senate. The only power of the presiding officer is to cast the deciding vote when the Senators' vote is tied.

E. Senate Majority and Minority leaders: Real Senate leadership is in the hands of the majority leader; although he is not as powerful as the Speaker of the House. The Majority leader schedules the business of the Senate and is recognized as the first speaker in floor debates. He is also one of the chief media spokesmen for the party. The minority leader represents the opposition party in negotiations with the majority leader.

F.   Career Paths Within Congress: Leadership is normally achieved by movement up in the party hierarchy. Leadership positions are usually decided by elections and sometimes someone gains entrance into the hierarchy without a prior leadership position.

VII.   IN COMMITTEE: Much of the real work in Congress is done in committees. Usually, the chamber floor is deserted. Only during roll-call votes does everyone make an attempt to be on the floor.

A.   Standing Committees: These are permanent committees that specialize in some area of legislation. Committee sizes vary from 30-40 in the House to 15-20 in the Senate. Party membership is usually proportional to party strength in the chamber. Every committee is chaired by a member of the majority party. The minority party is represented by the ranking minority member. The principal function of the committees is to screen bills--they serve as gatekeepers. Usually, a bill that does not muster a majority vote in a committee is dead. Most bills die in committee by either receiving an unfavorable vote or simply by never being discussed. Committee staff and committee members also draft their own bills, offer amendments, and rewrite bills.

B.   Decentralization and Subcommittees: Congressional subcommittees further decentralize the legislative process. The House has about 90 and the Senate 70 subcommittees. They are largely independent of their parent committee. They have their own staffs and budget. They meet and schedule their own hearings. But any bill approved by a subcommittee still has to go to the full committee which normally also approves it. This decentralization of power occurred in the early 1970s as the result of younger Democratic House members who wanted more independence and power. Formerly, interest groups could concentrate on a few House leaders and chairpersons of standing committees. But now with power decentralized, interest groups must pay attention to virtually every subcommittee. Executive agencies must do likewise. The result has been a considerable increase of policy networks. Chairing a committee is an opportunity to exercise power, attract media attention, and improve reelection chances. The decentralization of power weakens responsible government because party leaders do not have the power to push their party's legislative agenda through.

C.   Committee Membership: Members strive for committee assignments that will give them influence, allow the exercise of power, and improve their reelection chances. Party leadership in each chamber largely determines committee assignments.

D.   Seniority: Although committee chairs are elected by the majority caucus, the seniority system is still largely followed. The seniority system has a long tradition in the Congress. **DEFINE SENIORITY SYSTEM.**

E.   Committee Hearings: The decision to hold public hearings on a bill signals congressional interest in a particular policy matter and sets the agenda. They allow interest groups and government bureaucrats to be heard for the record. Staff members plan the meeting under direction of the chair and contact favorite lobbyists and bureaucrats and schedule their appearances. The purpose of the hearing is not so much to inform Congress as it is to rally popular support via the media.

F.   Markup: Once hearings are completed, the committee staff usually writes a report and drafts a bill. The committee members can mark up the bill--that is consider it line by line and propose any changes they think necessary. Markup sessions are usually closed to the public and interest groups to expedite the process. This is where the detailed work of lawmaking takes place and this is where experience pays off. Consensus and deal making are the order of the day. **DEFINE DISCHARGE PETITION.**

VIII.   ON THE FLOOR: A favorable committee vote enables a bill to be placed on a calendar. Even this does not guarantee success, since many bills die on the calendar.

A.   House Rules Committee: In the House, prior to consideration by the full membership, the bill requires favorable action by the Rules Committee. This committee may refuse to issue a rule for the bill which effectively kills it, or it may attach a rule to the bill, which is simply when the bill will be considered by the full House, how long it will be debated, and whether any amendments will be allowed. A <u>closed</u> rule prohibits any amendments. A <u>restricted</u> rule allows a few, an <u>open</u> rule allows an unlimited amount. The bill comes to the floor with a proposed rule. Before debating the bill, the House must agree to accept the rule which it normally does with little debate. Most bills carry closed or restrictive rules. The House also has a <u>germane</u> rule--that is, a proposed amendment must be related to the bill.

B.   Senate Floor Traditions: The Senate has no comparable gatekeeper Rules Committee like the House, but instead relies on <u>unanimous consent agreements</u> negotiated between the majority and minority leader and their staffs. This agreement specifies when a bill will be considered, what amendment will be considered, and when a final vote will be taken. Any

Senator can object to the agreement, but this happens rarely. The Senate also has the tradition of the filibuster, which permits a determined minority to talk the bill to death. Senate rules also allow a Senator to place a hold on a bill--indicating their unwillingness to allow a unanimous consent agreement. To cut off a filibuster, sixteen senators can petition to cut off debate. Two days must elapse before the petition introduction and the cloture vote. If 60 Senators vote for the petition, each senator is allowed only one more hour of debate. The Senate does not have a germane rule, and any senator can propose an amendment to a bill which may be totally unconnected to the bill. The Senate traditions of unlimited debate and nongermane amendments gives senators more legislative power than representatives.

C.   Floor Voting: Key floor votes are usually on amendments. Sometimes "killer amendments" are proposed with the objective of killing the main bill if they are adopted. Votes are taken by voice (where there is no record of how each member voted) or recorded roll-call votes. In the House a roll-call vote is done electronically, in the Senate bound by tradition, roll-call votes are by voice.

D.   Conference Committees: The Constitution requires that both chambers of the Congress pass a bill with identical wording. Sometimes one chamber will just adopt the other chamber's bill. But sometimes the differences are so great that the bills must be assigned to a conference committee to be worked out. These are temporary committees and the leadership assigns the members, usually senior members of the standing committees that considered each bill. The task of the conference committee is to write a single compromise bill that will pass each house without amendments.

IX.   DECISION MAKING IN CONGRESS: There are various factors that have been used to analyze voting in Congress. Among them are:

A.   Party Voting: Party voting refers to the situation when the majority of one party votes one way and the majority of the opposition party the other way. About half the roll-call votes exhibit party voting and it appears more common in the House than the Senate. Party Unity is the percent of Republicans voting with Republicans and likewise for the Democrats. Over the past 20 years, Republican unity has been 75-85 percent. Democratic unity was less due to Southern Democrat defections, but now is less of a problem. One explanation of party unity is that the members in each party are ideologically like minded--the Democrats more liberal and the Republicans more conservative. On many policy issues, there is bipartisan support of the goal, but party disunity on the means. Since parties organize the legislature, members of these parties have a vested interest in their party's fortunes and policies.

B.   Rising Partisanship: **FILL IN.**

C.   Presidential Support or Opposition: Presidents always receive more support from his party members in the legislature. With divided government (where one party controls the presidency and the other the legislature), presidential support or opposition is less operable and becomes more obstructionist. Presidential influence then is reduced by the other party, the electoral independence of legislators, and the decentralization of Congress. When negotiations break down, the president can try to appeal directly to the people via the media or threaten a veto.

D.   Constituency Influence: If an issue has attracted media attention and generates intense feeling among the legislator's constituency, members of Congress almost always defer to constituents' views regardless of party, leadership, or even their own feeling. This even applies to representatives from safe seats. Economic issues are the most likely to generate constituency pressure. Also the member lives in the community and possibly grew up there--so he/she has absorbed and internalized the views of his/her community. On most issues, the constituents are not aware, and thus the legislator has considerable leeway as to his/her vote.

E.   Interest-Group Influence: **FILL-IN.**

F.   Personal Values: **FILL-IN. DEFINE TRUSTEE AND DELEGATE.**

X.   CUSTOMS AND NORMS: These are designed to help members work together, reduce interpersonal conflict, facilitate and promote compromise, and make life a little more pleasant in Congress.

A.   Civility: Traditionally members of Congress maintained an air of civility and avoided hostile or inflammatory language. It was felt that this type of behavior could undermine the lawmaking process. Individual ambition and the desire for celebrity have caused a decline in civility of late. Accordingly, it has also become more difficult to reach agreement on policy issues.

B.   The Demise of the Apprentice Norm: At one time the norm was for freshmen legislators to defer to more senior members--"be seen and not heard." This norm is dead! Freshmen are now "seen and heard".

C.   Specialization and Deference: The committee and subcommittee structure facilitates specialization in certain areas. Party members are expected to give deference to party experts in these specialized areas. When the issue is technical or complicated or outside the member's own area of policy specialization, the system works. On major public issues however, it does not work.

D. Bargaining: This is central to the legislative process as it facilitates compromise. A member is not expected to violate his/her conscience in a bargain, but normally there is much leeway available for bargaining. Most bargains take place in committee meeting and are thus largely out of the public view. This system has also been compared to "horse trading." Bargains may be implicit--you vote for my bill, I'll vote for yours"--or they may be explicit--"You support me now and I'll catch you later." Bargaining requires integrity. A deal is a deal. Members must stick to agreements.

E. Reciprocity: **DEFINE RECIPROCITY.**

F. Logrolling: This is a mutual agreement to support projects that primarily benefit individual members of Congress and their constituents.

G. Leader-Follower Relations: Since members are largely independent and the means of discipline relatively few, leaders have to rely on their bargaining skills to get cooperation. There are some tangible benefits that can be granted or withheld--to be recognized as a speaker, favorable treatment of a bill, including a favorable rule, good committee assignment, etc. In the long

run, alienating a party leader is not a path to a successful career in the legislature.

H. Gridlock: **FILL IN.**

XI. CONGRESSIONAL ETHICS: While some may consider "congressional ethics" to be an oxymoron, morality is a relative term in regards to Congress.

A. Ethics Rules: Congress over the years has established ethic committees as well as its own rules. These include:

1. Financial disclosure-All members must file annual personal financial statements.
2. Honoria-Now forbidden to accept fees for speeches or personal appearances.
3. Campaign funds-surplus funds cannot be for personal use.
4. Gifts-Representatives cannot accept any gift more than $200; Senators are allowed a $300 limit.

5. Free travel-members may not accept free travel from private corporations or individuals for more than four days of domestic travel or seven days of international travel.

6. Lobbying: **FILL IN**.

B. Gray Areas: Services and Contributions: The Keating scandal.

C. Expulsion: Each chamber under the Constitution has the power to discipline its members for "disorderly conduct," but the Constitution does not define this. Expulsion is the most severe penalty. It is not a criminal conviction. Only one member of the House was expelled--the first since the Civil War. Most members resign rather than face expulsion, which would cut off their pension. If they resign they may still get a pension.

D. Censure: A lesser form of punishment, but still humiliating. The chamber votes a motion of censure and the object of the censure has to stand in front of the chamber as the motion is read and voted upon. Sometimes censure can be used by an opponent in the next election--but even with censure, some are reelected.

CHAPTER TEN SAMPLE QUESTIONS

TRUE-FALSE:

1. Congress and the presidency have enjoyed a relatively peaceful relationship over the last two centuries.

2. House members face reelection every four years.

3. A House member must live in the district he/she represents.

4. Congress is more powerful in domestic than in foreign and military affairs.

5. The most important source of congressional power stems from its power of the purse.

6. Malapportionment is the drawing of congressional district lines for political advantage.

7. Congressional hearings and investigations often involve agenda setting.

8. Congressional district lines are drawn by the House of Representatives.

9. Congress regularly increases its own pay and benefits.

10. The party whips are responsible for helping to pressure party members to vote the way the party leadership wishes.

MULTIPLE-CHOICE:

11. The House has the sole constitutional power to:
    a. Appropriate money   b. Originate tax bills
    c. Declare war   d. Try impeachments

12. Which of the following is NOT a characteristic of Senators:
    a. Minimum age 25
    b. Six-year term of office
    c. U.S. citizen for 9 years
    d. Resident of state they represent

13. Which of the following influence the way members of Congress vote?
    a. Interest group influence
    b. Personal values
    c. Constituency influences
    d. All of the above

14. The real reasons for congressional oversight of executive agencies include all but one of the following:
    a. Secure favorable treatment for friends and constituents
    b. Lay the groundwork for increases/decreases of agency budgets
    c. Influence executive branch decisions
    d. Praise presidential appointees

15. When congressional or state districts have grossly unequal numbers of people, this is called:
    a. Apportionment
    b. Malapportionment
    c. Redistricting
    d. Gerrymandering

16. A member of Congress who feels obligated to use his/her own best judgment when making voting decisions could be classified as a:
    a. Trustee
    b. Delegate
    c. Politico
    d. All of the above

17. The Congressional tradition of mutually supporting projects that primarily benefit individual members of Congress or their constituents is called:
    a. Reciprocity   b. Bargaining   c. Logrolling   d. None of the above

18. The most common occupational background of representatives is:
    a. Law   b. Business   c. Public service   d. Journalism

19. All but one of the following is a congressional support agency:
    a. Office of Management and Budget
    b. General Accounting Office
    c. Library of Congress
    d. Congressional Budget Office

20. The presiding officer of the Senate is:
    a. Vice-president
    b. Majority leader
    c. President pro tempore
    d. Majority whip

CHAPTER TEN SAMPLE QUESTION ANSWERS

TRUE-FALSE:

1. **FALSE.** The Congress and Presidency have been engaged in an ongoing struggle for power for the last two centuries. See page 318.

2. **FALSE.** House members must run every two years. See to page 320.

3. **FALSE.** While most do live in their district, Article 1, Section 2 of the Constitution specifies that they need only be a resident of the state they represent. See page 338.

4. **TRUE.** This has been true since the very beginning because of the president's role as Commander in chief. See page 320.

5. **TRUE.** See page 321.

6. **FALSE.** Gerrymandering is the drawing of congressional district lines for political advantage. See pages 325-327.

7. **TRUE.** Bringing issues to the attention of the media and public can get them on the national agenda. See page 351.

8. **FALSE.** They are drawn by state legislatures and approved by state governors. See page 326.

9. **FALSE.** See pages 341-342.

10. **TRUE.** See page 347.

MULTIPLE-CHOICE:

11. **B.** The House has sole power to originate tax bills. See page 318.

12. **A.** The minimum age for a Senator is 30. See page 338.

13. **D.** Interest group influence, personal values, and constituency influences all effect the way members of Congress vote. See page 360-363.

14. **D.** Rarely if ever is a congressional oversight for praise, but rather for embarrassment. See to page 322.

15. **B**. When congress or state districts have grossly unequal numbers of people it is called malapportionment. See page 325.

16. **A**. A member of Congress who feels obligated to use his/her own best judgment when making voting decisions could be classified as a trustee. See page 363.

17. **C**. The congressional tradition of mutually supporting projects that primarily benefit individual members of Congress or their constituents is called logrolling. See page 368.

18. **A**. This is also true in the Senate. See page 330.

19. **A**. OMB is an executive agency, the rest belong to Congress. See pages 340-341.

20. **A**. The only constitutional duty of the vice-president is to preside over the Senate, which is rarely done. See page 348.

CHAPTER ELEVEN: THE PRESIDENT:
WHITE HOUSE POLITICS

I. PRESIDENTIAL POWER: There are many aspects to presidential power. Some are:

   A. The Symbolic President: The president is seen as the symbol of the nation. As the nation's leading celebrity, the office is the focus of public and world attention. The President also gives expression to the nation's pride in victories, whether it be the national champion football team or 2000 Olympians.

   B. Managing Crises: In times of crisis, Americans look to the president to take action, express the sadness of the nation, etc.

   C. Providing Policy Leadership: The president is expected to set priorities for policies since most originate with the executive branch. As a political leader, the president must rally support for these policies, both with Congress and the general public.

   D. Managing the Economy: The American people hold the president responsible for a healthy economy. If it falters, he will be blamed rightly or wrongly. If the economy is good, the president will take credit for its performance. Public expectation of the president's power far exceeds his actual power. In most cases, government action does not immediately correct the ills in the economy as there is a lag time.

   E. Managing the Government: As chief executive of the federal bureaucracy, the president is responsible for implementing policy.

   F. The Global President: The president is the single voice in international affairs. The president is the commander in chief and it is this office that orders the armed forces into combat.

II. CONSTITUTIONAL POWERS OF THE PRESIDENT: Compared to Congress, the office of the president has fewer specified powers. But the presidents over time have used these powers quite well and expanded them to the fullest.

   A. Who May be President? Any thirty-five-year-old, natural-born citizen who has been a resident in the U.S. for over 14 years is eligible. The original Constitution fixed the term of office as four years but did not specify how many terms a president could have. George Washington started the tradition of only serving two terms (eight years), which endured until Franklin

Roosevelt ran for a third and fourth term. In reaction, the Republican controlled Congress in 1947 proposed the Twenty-second Amendment which was ratified in 1951. This amendment formally limits the president to two terms.

B.   Presidential Succession: Although the original Constitution provided for the replacement of the President for death, resignation, removal, or inability with the vice-president, there was no provision for a serious presidential illness nor any procedure to replace the vice-president who might have to take the President's place. The Twenty-fifth Amendment allows the vice-president and a majority of the cabinet to notify congressional leaders in writing that the president is unable to discharge his powers and duties. The vice-president becomes _acting_ president. The president may inform Congress in writing that no inability exists. If the VP and majority of the cabinet disagree, Congress must decide the issue within 21 days. A two-thirds vote in each chamber is required to replace the president by the vice-president. This procedure has never been used to date.

C.   Impeachment: The House of Representatives has the power to impeach the president, other executive officials and judicial personnel for reasons of treason, bribery or other high crimes or misdemeanors. Political disagreements are not a cause. Once impeached, the accused would stand trial in the Senate, which could vote to remove the official by at least a two-thirds majority. Once removed, the official is barred from ever holding federal office again.

D.   President Pardons: The Constitution gives the president the power to grant reprieves and pardons. This is an absolute power, not subject to congressional review or judicial action. The most modern controversial pardon was when President Ford granted former President Nixon a full, blanket pardon.

E.   Executive Power: Is this executive power broad or limited? This is an ongoing debate between liberals and conservatives.

F.   Some Historical Examples: U.S. history is filled with examples of presidents acting independently.

G.   Checking Presidential Power: President Truman's seizure of the nation's steel mills during the Korean War was declared unconstitutional by the Supreme Court. In doing so, they stated that the president must follow the law.

H.   Executive Privilege: Through the ages, the presidents have claimed the right to confidentiality to protect national security and sensitive discussions within the White House. Congress has never recognized this executive privilege. The courts have generally refrained from interfering, but did so in *U.S. v. Nixon* (1974) when it said the executive privilege did not cover criminal acts. The Supreme Court did allow that this privilege might be invoked to cover military or diplomatic matters.

I. Presidential Impoundments: While the Constitution forbids the president to spend money not appropriated, it is silent whether the president has to spend money appropriated. Various presidents refused to spend certain appropriations, but in 1974 Congress passed the Budget and Impoundment Act which requires the president to spend appropriated money. He can propose deferrals--postpone spending or recessions--canceling the spending. Congress by resolution (not subject to presidential veto) may vote to restore the deferrals, and a recession cannot proceed unless both chambers approve the recession.

J. The Constitution's Congressional Tilt: The Constitution gives Congress the upper hand:
   1. Override of presidential veto by two-thirds majority in each chamber.
   2. Impeach and remove the president.
   3. Only Congress can appropriate money.
   4. Major presidential appointments require Senate confirmation.
   5. President must faithfully execute the laws.

Congress constitutionally dominates the American government, but the president politically dominates the nation's public affairs.

III. POLITICAL RESOURCES OF THE PRESIDENT: The principle tool is the power to persuade. The president is the center of focus and attention and can communicate directly to the American people.

A. Reputation for Power: To be effective, the president must be perceived as powerful. One seen as weak will not be very effective.

B. Presidential Popularity: Popularity is a resource in that popular Presidents usually have greater success in their dealings with Congress. National opinion polls regularly track presidential popularity. This is usually very high at the beginning of the president's term of office, but drops off over time. Presidents usually recover some popularity if they run for reelection. Presidential popularity rises during periods of crisis, especially facing an international threat or military conflict. On the other hand, major scandals hurt popularity and approval e.g., Nixon and Reagan. Economic recessions hurt the incumbent president.

C.   Access to the Media: The president dominates the news. The most skilled reporters are assigned to the White House. Presidential press secretaries brief reporters daily. The president can use press conferences to advance his agenda. Presidents can also make a national address during television prime time. In addition, the president can use addresses at national meetings, college and university commencements, etc., to maintain contact with the American people.

D.   Party Leadership: **FILL-IN**

IV.   CHIEF EXECUTIVE: The president presides over a huge enterprise--2.8 million employees, 60 independent agencies, 14 departments, and the large Executive Office of the President. Yet the president cannot command this bureaucracy like a military officer or corporation president. Instead he has to persuade, negotiate, bargain, and compromise to achieve his goals.

A.   The Constitutional Executive: The Constitution is rather vague about presidential power. It grants executive power to the president, and gives authority for the president to appoint principal officers with advice and consent of the Senate, and allows the president to require opinions in writing from these principal officers on subject matter in their departments. Most importantly it also charges the president to faithfully execute the laws. But Congress also has great constitutional power over the executive branch--the power of the purse and impeachment. It can also establish or abolish executive departments, agencies, etc., and perform oversight over these executive departments, agencies, etc.

B.   Executive Orders: Presidents issue about 50-100 such orders every year. They usually direct specific federal agencies to pursue the president's wishes or desired course of action. These orders may be based on the president's constitutional powers or powers delegated to the president by laws passed by Congress. While most are somewhat mundane, some stand out: President Truman's E.O. 9981 in 1948 ordering desegregation of the armed forces, and President Johnson's E.O. 11246 requiring private firms with federal contracts to institute affirmative action programs.

C.   Appointments: The President can appoint only about 3,000 of the 2.8 millioncivilian employees of the federal government. These are top officials such as cabinet secretaries, agency heads, and White House staff. These people are selected because they share the president's policy views. However, a great many factors influence their selection: interest group support; unifying various parts of the party; rewarding political loyalty; finding jobs for unsuccessful candidates; seeking a balance of gender, ethnic and racial representatives. Presidents have very limited power to remove independent regulatory agency members. Having a loyal follower at the head of an agency does not guarantee presidential control over the agency. Career bureaucrats have the knowledge, skill, and experience to frustrate directives they do not like.

D. Budget: The Constitution makes no mention of the President in reference to the budget, but the Budget and Accounting Act of 1921 provided the president a role in the budget process. This act required the President to submit a budget for all executive departments and created the Office of Management and Budget.

E. The Cabinet: **FILL-IN.**

F. The National Security Council (NSC): Sometimes called the "inner cabinet," the NSC is chaired by the president. Statutory members are the vice-president, and secretaries of state and defense. The director of the CIA and the chairman of the Joint Chiefs of Staff are statutory advisors to the NSC. This body advises the president in matters involving foreign, defense and intelligence activities.

G. White House Staff (WHS): Today the president exercises his power primarily through the White House staff. The WHS contains the closest allies and advisors of the president. None of the staff are subject to Senate confirmation, and their loyalty is to the president. Staff positions include: Chief of staff, senior advisors, press secretary, national security advisor, counsel to the president, director of personnel, etc.

V. CHIEF LEGISLATOR AND LOBBYIST: About 80 percent of the bills considered by Congress are originated in the executive branch.

A. Policy Initiation: The president uses the annual State of the Union address before a joint session of Congress as the principal opportunity to make a policy statement and address necessary legislation. This is followed by the president's recommended budget which contains the president's programs with price tags. While Congress will not rubber stamp the budget, it still sets the agenda for debate and further congressional action. During the year, many other executive departments will draft legislation and transmit it to the White House for review and approval, after which it will be sent to Congress for further action.

B. White House Lobbying: The White House employs a legislative liaison section which tracks bills, attends committee hearings, arranges executive branch witnesses, and advises the president as to legislative status and which bills need help by the president. The White House is not without resources. They have many favors at their disposal. Support for projects in congressional districts or states, invitations to state dinners and ceremonies, speeches in one's district with an invitation to accompany the president on Air Force One. In addition, the president can "twist arms" of individual, representatives or senators by personally calling them and appealing to party loyalty, etc.

C.   The Honeymoon: **FILL-IN.**

D.   Presidential "Box Scores": Of legislation in which there was a clear presidential interest, how did the president fare? The most important determinant is whether the president's party controls Congress. Where this is true, the presidential success rate is very high. Where the opposition party controls Congress, the president's success rate falls dramatically.

E.   Veto Power: **FILL-IN. DEFINE POCKET VETO.**

F.   Line-Item Veto: Commencing in 1997, the president now has a line-item veto. Potentially this new power could dramatically increase the president's power over Congress. Opponents argue however that the line-item veto is unconstitutional, so it will not alter the balance of power in the long run.

VI.   GLOBAL LEADER: The president of the United States is the leader of the world's largest and most powerful democracy. In the new global order, the U.S. can no longer dictate its will, it must still must provide necessary leadership. This leadership is based on the president's power of persuasion. This is enhanced by a strong economy, military forces, and support of the American people and Congress.

A.   Foreign Policy: The president has the power to make treaties (subject to Senate ratification), appoints U.S. diplomatic personnel (subject to Senate confirmation), and receives foreign ambassadors. The president exercises the power of diplomatic recognition which is the granting of legitimacy to a foreign government. The president's role in foreign policy is strengthened by his role as commander in chief because military force is the ultimate diplomatic language. The president is the official spokesman for the United States in the world community of nations.

B.   Treaties: **FILL-IN.**

C.   Executive Agreements: These agreements made by the president with another head of state do not require Senate ratification. They are based on the president's constitutional power to execute the laws, command the armed forces, and determine foreign policy. They cannot supersede laws of the U.S. or any state. Congress is not fond of executive agreements, and in 1972 passed the Case Act which requires the president to notify Congress of any executive agreement within 60 days.

D. Intelligence: The president is responsible for the intelligence activities of the U.S. The director of Central Intelligence is appointed by the president and confirmed by the Senate. The DCI directly supervises the Central Intelligence Agency (CIA) and coordinates the activities of the National Security Agency (NSA)-electronic surveillance and the National Reconnaissance Office (NRO)-satellite surveillance.

VII. COMMANDER IN CHIEF: The global power of the president stems from his role as commander-in-chief. As commander in chief, the president can issue orders to the military.

A. War-making Power: The Constitution splits the war-making power between the president who is commander in chief and Congress who can declare war. The president has sent troops into combat many times, but Congress has only declared war five times.

B. War Powers Act: Passed in 1973 at the height of the anti-Vietnam war movement in this country, it was an attempt by Congress to control presidential use of the armed forces. The Act has four provisions:

   1. In the absence of a congressional declaration of war, the president can use armed forces only:

      a. To repel an attack on the U.S. or imminent threat of attack
      b. To repel an attack on U.S. armed forces outside the country or forestall such an attack
      c. Protect and evacuate U.S. citizens and nationals in another country if their lives are endangered.

   2. President must promptly report the use of force to the Congress.
   3. Involvement must be no longer than 60 days unless Congress authorizes more time.
   4. Congress can terminate a presidential use of force by a resolution, not subject to presidential veto.

C. Presidential Noncompliance: There is some question as to the legality of the War Powers Act and presidents, both Democratic and Republican, have largely ignored it. For example, President Clinton's sending of troops to Haiti and Bosnia were not reported under the War Powers Act.

D. Presidential Use of Military Force in Domestic Affairs: The Constitution contemplates the use of federal armed forces in states facing domestic violence only when the state legislature is not in session, or the governor requests the help of federal troops. But what happens when states violate federal laws, court orders, or constitutional guarantees? Presidents have, in the history of our country, used federal troops--Pullman strike in 1894, and in Little Rock in 1957 to enforce a federal court order for desegregation are two good examples.

VIII.   VICE PRESIDENTIAL WAITING GAME: The principal responsibility of the vice president is to be prepared to step into the president's shoes. Eight VPs have had to do so.

   A.   Political Selection Process: Candidates were selected to give geographical balance to the ticket. Some effort is made for ideological balance. Obviously, one consideration in selecting the VP is finding a candidate who can help the ticket win the White House.

   B.   Vice President Roles: Largely determined by the president. The only official duty of the VP is to preside over the Senate. The political function of the VP is more important than the government function. The VP can serve as a "lightening rod" while the president can remain above the fight. VPs can help with fund raising. Lately, presidents have given their VP more responsibility and view them now as senior policy advisors.

   C.   The Waiting Game: Most vice presidents have further ambitions-the Oval Office. Yet they have to be very discreet. They have to support the administration, yet develop an independent organization and agenda. Only four VPs have successfully advanced to the White House. Counting four VPs who entered office upon the death of a president and Nixon who lost in 1960, but came back in 1972, in all only nine VPs have made it to the White House,or less than 20 percent. Obviously, VP is not the best route to the White House.

CHAPTER ELEVEN SAMPLE QUESTIONS

TRUE-FALSE:

1.   Popular expectations of presidential leadership far exceed the office's constitutional powers.

2.   Most policy initiatives originate in the White House.

3.   Presidents have rarely attempted to go beyond their constitutional powers.

4.   The president and other high executive officials can be impeached by the Senate.

5.   Executive privilege is the power of the president to withhold appropriated funds.

6.   The president is constitutionally required to seek the advice of the cabinet.

7.   Congress is constitutionally positioned to dominate the American government.

8.   Presidential popularity with the American people is a political resource.

9.   The president's ability to appoint executive branch officials gives the president firm control of the bureaucracy.

10.   The honeymoon period of the presidency starts about midterm.

MULTIPLE-CHOICE:

11.   All of the following are formal powers given to the President in the Constitution EXCEPT:
a. Pardons
b. Access to the media
c. Execute the laws passed by Congress
d. Appointment of ambassadors

12.   The American public expects the President to:
a. Manage crises
b. Provide policy leadership
c. Manage the economy
d. All of the above

13.   Which Executive office agency gives the president good control of the budget process?
a. CBO
b. OMB
c. Department of the Treasury
d. Council of Economic Advisors

14. The president attends a meeting of the Group of Seven in Paris. This would be in his role as:
   a. Crisis management
   b. Policy leadership
   c. Managing the economy
   d. Global president

15. Which of the following is <u>not</u> a full member of the National Security Council?
   a. Vice-president
   b. Secretary of State
   c. Chairman of the Joint Chiefs of Staff
   d. President

16. The presidential appointment of federal judges is part of the constitutional powers of the presidency, specifically:
   a. Chief administrator
   b. Chief legislator
   c. Chief diplomat
   d. Chief of state

17. The president receives a bill and Congress adjourns six days later. If the president does not sign the bill it:
   a. is null and void
   b. b. becomes law automatically
   c. can be kept until Congress comes back
   d. must be sent back to the Congress

18. What is the term of office of the president?
   a. 4 years   b. 8 years   c. 10 years   d. Unlimited

19. Which action seeks to cancel an appropriation?
   a. impoundment   b. deferral   c. rescission   d. miscue

20. All but one of the following help to explain the president's reputation for political power.
   a. Presidential popularity
   b. Access to the media
   c. Party leadership
   d. Presidential impeachment

CHAPTER ELEVEN SAMPLE QUESTION ANSWERS

TRUE-FALSE:

1.   **TRUE.** Our expectations frequently exceed reality. See page 378.

2.   **TRUE**. Most policy initiatives originate in the White House. See page 376.

3.   **FALSE.**   Presidents have frequently attempted to go beyond their constitutional powers. See page 384.

4.   **FALSE.** Impeachment is an action of the House, not the Senate. See page 380.

5.   **FALSE**. Impoundment is the power of the President to withhold appropriated funds. See page 385.

6.   **FALSE**. There is no mention of the Cabinet in the Constitution. See page 396.

7.   **TRUE.** But the President is better positioned to politically dominate the nation's public affairs. See page 386.

8.   **TRUE.** An incumbent president popular in the polls is very hard to defeat for reelection. See page 387.

9.   **FALSE.** Most people the president cannot fire and as political appointees, they can be captured by career bureaucrats and "go native." See page 396.

10.   **FALSE.** The period actually is very early in the term, usually the first 60 days or so. See page 387.

MULTIPLE-CHOICE:

11. **B**. Access to the media is not one of the formal powers of the President. See page 388.

12. **D**. The American public expects the president to manage crises, provide policy leadership, and manage the economy. See pages 376-378.

13. **B**. Office of Management and Budget (OMB) is the answer. See page 396.

14. **D.** While managing the economy would be a close second, since this is a meeting of the heads of the leading industrialized nations, it is the president acting as a global leader. See page 403.

15. **C.** The chairman of the JCS is a statutory advisor but not a participating member of the NSC. See page 387.

16. **D.** Although chief administrator seems appropriate, the correct answer is chief of state. See page 395.

17. **A.** A pocket veto essentially kills the bill-it is null and void. Congress can reintroduce the bill when it reconvenes. See page 402.

18. **A.** The term of office is four years. The number of terms was not limited until passage of the Twenty-second Amendment in 1947. See page 379.

19. **C.** Rescission is an attempt to cancel spending; unless both branches concur, the money must be spent according to the Budget and Impoundment Act of 1974. See page 385.

20. **D.** Presidential impeachment is a weakness not a strength. See page 380.

CHAPTER TWELVE: THE BUREAUCRACY: BUREAUCRATIC POLITICS

I.   BUREAUCRATIC POWER. Once a bill is passed by Congress and signed into law by the president, the journey does not end here. For then the law passes to the bureaucracy which has to interpret and implement the law.

    A.   Nature of Bureaucracy: Bureaucracy is often associated with red tape, paperwork, duplication of effort, waste and inefficiency, yet government is not the only organization with a bureaucracy--churches, businesses, armed forces, etc., all have established bureaucracies, Max Weber rationalized bureaucracy as having these features:

        1.   Chain of Command-hierarchial and command flows downward.
        2.   Division of Labor--work is divided among specialized workers.
        3.   Specification of authority-**FILL-IN**.
        4.   Goal orientation-**FILL-IN**.
        5.   Impersonality-equal treatment based on merit and rules.

    B.   The Growth of Bureaucratic Power: Due to advances in technology and increase in size and complexity of society, the president and Congress do not have the time nor expertise to concern themselves with the myriad of details involved in legislation. Thus, "technocrats" are necessary to carry out the intent of the law. However, Congress is also to blame when they pass vague and ambiguous laws requiring bureaucratic interpretation. They can show symbolic support for the law, but if it works out badly, they can blame the bureaucracy. Also vague laws play into the hands of special interest groups who can help shape the law like they desire. Another factor is that a growing bureaucracy becomes a power in itself. A growing budget and more personnel is a sign of power.

    C.   Bureaucratic Power: Implementation: Implementation is the development of procedures and activities to carry out policies legislated by Congress. This may involve creating new agencies or assigning new responsibilities to established agencies, translate laws into operational rules and regulations, and allocation of resources--money, personnel, offices, and supplies. In some cases, bureaucracies act rapidly to implement the law; in other cases, they seek to delay by holding hearings, failing to allocate sufficient resources, etc.

    D.   Bureaucratic Power: Regulation: Regulation is the writing of formal rules for implementing legislation. Congress has established procedures for writing rules because, once published in the Federal Registrer, the rules have the same weight as law.

E. Bureaucratic Power: Adjudication: **FILL-IN.**

F. Bureaucratic Power: Administrative Discretion: Most of the work of bureaucrats is routine, but some cases may not fit the law, or rules may conflict. In these cases the bureaucrats become powerful in that the decision making is left up to their discretion.

G. Bureaucratic Power and Budget Maximization: Most bureaucrats strongly believe in the value of their programs and their importance. Like everyone else, they also seek higher pay, increased benefits, etc. These public and private motives lead to bureaucrats seeking to increase the size, scope, and budget of their agency.

II. THE FEDERAL BUREAUCRACY: The federal bureaucracy, which is concentrated in the executive branch, consists of 2.8 million civilian employees and 1.4 million members of the armed forces. It is organized into 14 cabinet departments, 60 independent agencies, and the executive office of the president. All government spending--federal, state and local--equals about $2.7 trillion.

A. Cabinet Departments: These employ about 60 percent of federal workers. Each of the 14 departments is headed by a secretary (except the Justice department which is headed by the attorney general) who is appointed by the president and confirmed by the Senate. The departments vary greatly in the size of their budgets and personnel. The cabinet status of these departments makes them (and their secretaries) particularly influential in the policy making process.

B. Cabinet Department Functions: The importance of the cabinet departments does not come solely from the size of the personnel or budget. The importance of their functions also provides power.

C. Cabinet Appointments: The Constitution requires that cabinet officers are confirmed by the Senate, and in the past it was the tradition of the Senate to rarely interfere with a president's choices for Cabinet secretaries. This tradition seems to be in decline.

D. Independent Regulatory Commissions: Regulatory commissions are designed to regulate some sector of society or the economy. They both make, enforce, and adjudicate rules. The design of these commissions is to differ them from the cabinet in their organization and accountability to the president. Most organizations are headed by commissions of 5-10 members. They are appointed by the president and confirmed by the Senate. Usually membership is balanced by partisan identification. The president cannot remove a commissioner.

E. Independent Agencies: These are outside any cabinet department and are headed by an administrator (not a commission). Administrators are appointed by the president and confirmed by the Senate, but can be dismissed by the president. Thus, they are not truly independent, but report directly to the president. The intent of their independence is to ensure that the budgets and missions of these agencies do not become subject of other concerns which might be the case if they were located within some other cabinet department. The Environmental Protection Agency is an example.

F. Government Corporations: These are created by Congress to undertake independent commercial enterprises which are valued, but are also considered a public service. Compared to most other countries, the U.S. has very few of these. Amtrak and the Postal Service are examples.

G. Contractors and Consultants: While government employee levels have been relatively constant, the growth of government spending has been in this area. Roughly one-fifth of all federal government spending flows through private contractors for supplies, equipment, services, leases, and R&D.

III. BUREAUCRACY AND DEMOCRACY: Should the federal bureaucracy be staffed by people loyal to the president or by nonpartisan people selected on the basis of merit and protected from political influence?

A. The Spoils System: To the victor goes the spoils--so said Senator William Marcy in 1832. The spoils system is closely associated with the administration of Andrew Jackson, elected in 1828. From what started as a policy of rewarding loyal party members, it grew to the bartering and selling of government jobs with attendant scandal. The assassination of President James Garfield by a disgruntled office seeker set the stage for reform of the spoils system.

B. The Merit System: Passage of the Pendleton Act of 1883 initiated the career federal service and established the Civil Service Commission. Based on competitive examinations, the system initially covered only 10 percent of federal government employees. By 1978, more than 90 percent of federal workers were covered by civil service or other merit systems. The civil service general service system consists of two types of levels-general level with grades from GS-1 to GS-15. College graduates normally enter at the GS-5 level. GS-9 through GS-12 are technical and supervisory positions. GS-13 troough GS-15 are middle management and highly specialized positions. When an opening occurs, the three highest testing individuals are sent to the agency with the opening. The agency is supposed to hire one of the three, with the other two going on a waiting list. By defining the job with every particular requirements, the agency can give special preferences to the chosen few. Once hired and successfully completing a probationary period, an employee can only be fired for "cause."

C. Political Involvement: Note changes in Hatch Act.

D. The Problem of Responsiveness: **FILL-IN.**

E. The Problem of Productivity: Most federal workers receive pay raises almost automatically. Poor performance seldom is punished. Only 1/10 of 1 percent of federal employees are fired. Given this situation, there is little incentive to become more productive.

F. Civil Service Reform: President Carter in 1977 pushed through the Civil Service Reform Act of 1978 which abolished the Civil Service Commission and replaced it with the Office of Personnel Management (OPM). The act also streamlined dismissal procedures, established merit pay for middle managers, and created a Senior Executive Service (SES) for the 8,000 top managers. The SES might be given salary bonuses, transferred among different agencies, or demoted if performance was lacking. Top civilian managers were often seen by their political appointee bosses as impediments to change, and the idea of the reform was to move them around, so they could not become an immovable fixture in the agency. Like many reforms, intentions did not become reality. Congress never appropriated any money for merit pay increases. SES personnel have not been transferred, and dismissal rates have not essentially changed.

G. Bureaucracy and Representation: In general, the federal bureaucracy mirrors the American population. However, as Table 12-4 shows, top management positions are <u>unrepresentative</u> of the general American population.

IV. BUREAUCRATIC POLITICS: Who does the bureaucracy really work for?

A. Presidential Plums: About 3,000 jobs are directly controlled by the president. Some 700 of these positions are considered "policy making." These include cabinet and subcabinet officials, judges, U.S. attorneys, U.S. marshals, ambassadors, and various commissions and boards. There are also "Schedule C" jobs, which are described as "confidential or policy determining."

B. Room At the Top: Cabinet departments have become top heavy with administrators.

C. Whistle blowers: **FILL-IN.**

D.   Agency Cultures: **FILL-IN.**

E.   Friends and Neighbors: Most bureaucratic hirings take place through the "old boy" network of personal friends and professional associates. The inside candidate learns of the position and can tailor his resume. Sometimes the individual is requested by name; other times the personal request is tailor made for the applicant.

V.   THE BUDGETARY PROCESS: The annual budget battle is the heart of the federal government. The budget is the single most important policy statement of any government. The president's proposed budget frames the issues. While Congress occasionally frets and fumes, the reality is that final congressional appropriations rarely deviate more than 2 or 3 percent from the president's proposed budget. Thus, the president and the OMB in the executive office have real budgetary power.

A.   Office of Management and Budget (OMB).   This office has several responsibilities:

1.   Preparation of the budget.
2.   Improve the organization and management of executive agencies.
3.   Coordination of the extensive statistical services of the federal government.
4.   Analyze and review proposed legislation.

Budget preparation begins 16-18 months before the beginning of the fiscal year. The government's fiscal year begins October 1st and ends the following September. The specific fiscal year is keyed to the September year, i.e., the FY 2002 budget would end on September 30, 2002. OMB, after consultation with the president and his staff, develops spending targets or ceilings. Agencies are then instructed to prepare budget submissions in accordance with these targets. After internal coordination, the proposals are sent to OMB which performs its own analysis.

B.   The President's Budget: By December, the president and OMB spend considerable time looking over the budget submissions, making last minute changes, etc. By late January, the president sends his proposed budget to the Congress. This gives the Congress about nine months to finish the budget before the beginning of the fiscal year in October.

C.   House and Senate Budget Committees: The president's budget is sent to these committees, which rely on the Congressional Budget Office (CBO) to review the president's budget, especially the revenue assumptions. These committees draft a first budget resolution (due May 15th) which sets forth goals or targets to specific committees for their use in the authorization process. If proposed spending by these committees exceeds these targets, the first budget resolution comes back as a reconciliation measure and a second budget resolution (due September 15th) sets binding budget figures for committees.

D.   Congressional Appropriations Committees: Congressional approval of the budget takes the form of 13 separate appropriations bills covering broad areas--defense, commerce, etc. These are first started in subcommittees of the appropriations committees where agency witnesses, lobbyists, etc., get a chance to discuss the bills.

E.   Appropriations Acts: An authorization bill establishes a program and how much money it requires. It does not actually allocate any money. Authorizations for programs may be for a single year or multiple years. The appropriations bill is for a single year and actually allocates money for the programs. The allocation is frequently less than the authorization. These acts include obligational authority (permission to enter into contracts that require government payments over several years, e.g., aircraft carrier) and outlays (which must be spent in the fiscal year in which they are appropriated).

F.   Continuing Resolutions (CRA) and "Shutdowns": Since the fiscal year begins in October, all 13 appropriations bills should be finished before that date. This rarely happens. Constitutionally, no government agency may spend money which has not been appropriated. Thus, if an appropriation bill is not finished, the agency faces a shutdown. To prevent this from happening, Congress normally passes a CRA to provide money for a specified period of time at roughly the same level as the last fiscal year. Sometimes the heat of the budget battle results in a CRA expiration with the executive and legislative branches still engaged in combat. In the FY 1996 budget battles between President Clinton and the Republican Congress, the government shut down a number of times. It really never shuts down completely, so temporary layoffs are for "nonessential or noncritical personnel."

VI.   THE POLITICS OF BUDGETING: Being a good bureaucratic politician involves building support for one's agency in the public at large as well as among the groups that the agency serves, stimulating interest and enthusiasm for agency programs, obtaining media coverage for agency programs, and exploiting opportunities for the agency.

A.   Budgeting is "Incremental": The most important factor in determining this year's budget is last year's budget. Usually, last year's is used as a base and only changes and increases are really looked at. The result of this incremental budgeting is that many programs and expenditures continue long after there is no need for them. **DEFINE ZERO-BASED BUDGETING**.

B.   Budgeting is Nonprogrammatic: **DEFINE PROGRAM AND NON-PROGRAMMATIC BUDGETING.**

VII. REGULATORY BATTLES: Virtually every aspect of American life is regulated by some bureaucracy--whether it be interest rates by the Federal Reserve, automobile and airline safety, racial and sexual discrimination in the workplace, etc. Federal regulatory agencies have quasi-executive, legislative and judicial powers, all wrapped into one. They make the rules, investigate complaints and conduct inspections, hold hearings, issue corrective orders, levy fines and penalties.

A.   Traditional Agencies: Capture Theory: **DEFINE CAPTURE THEORY.**

B.   The Newer Regulators: The Activists: New activist regulatory agencies were created by Congress in the civil rights, environmental, and consumer protection areas. Unlike other agencies, these do not concentrate on one industry, but rather regulate activities over a broad spectrum. Examples include the EPA, Equal Employment Opportunity Commission (EEOC), and Occupational Safety and Health Administration (OSHA).

C.   Deregulation: In the 1980s, there was much public pressure to deregulate based on the heavy costs of compliance with regulations, the burdens these placed on innovation and productivity, and the adverse impact on global competitiveness. One of the first industries to be deregulated was the airline industry. While there is little doubt that this deregulation led to lower prices and more travelers, it also resulted in less service to outlying areas and the loss of some airlines. The Interstate Commerce Commission established in 1887 was abolished in 1995. Thus, the first regulatory agency was also the first to be abolished.

D.   Reregulation: **FILL-IN.**

VIII. Regulating America: Federal regulatory agencies add about 5000 rules to American life each year. From 1996-1999, $22.2 billion of new costs of regulation were imposed on American society.
A.   Multiplying Regulations: Both the Federal Register and the Code of Federal Regulations have expanded.
B.   The Cost of Regulation: There are both direct and indirect costs.

IX. CONGRESSIONAL CONSTRAINTS ON THE BUREAUCRACY: Bureaucracies are unelected hierarchical organizations and in a democracy must be responsive to the people. Although the president is the nominal boss of executive agencies, Congress has its power also in the budget and its power to establish or abolish agencies. Congress can expand or contract the authority of an agency. In addition, Congress has passed specific legislation which governs the bureaucracy:

1.   Administrative Procedures Act (1946): requires notification of proposed rules, publication in the Federal Register and the holding of public hearings.

2. Freedom of Information Act (1966): allows private inspection of public records, with some exceptions.

3. Privacy Act (1974): requires agencies to observe confidentiality regarding personnel records of individuals.

A. Senate Confirmation of Appointments: The Senate has the opportunity to scrutinize appointees and ascertain their views. If in disagreement, they can refuse to confirm or delay the confirmation indefinitely.

B. Congressional Oversight: **FILL-IN**

C. Congressional Appropriations: **FILL-IN**

D. Congressional Investigations: **FILL-IN**

E. Casework: Responding to calls, letters, faxes, telegrams, etc., from constituents in their state or district requesting information or action, legislators frequently contact regulatory agencies for their assistance. Congressional requests are handled expeditiously, and when possible every effort is made to respond favorably to the congressional inquiry.

X. INTEREST GROUPS AND BUREAUCRATIC DECISION MAKING: Interest groups pay more attention to the bureaucracy than the president or Congress because their interests are often directly impacted by the bureaucracy. These interest groups focus on the agency in their particular policy field. Some bureaucracies were created by the pressure of interest groups--the EPA and EEOC are examples. Interest groups lobby the bureaucracy directly or through Congress. Sometimes they try to influence the bureaucracy through appeals in federal courts.

XI. JUDICIAL CONSTRAINTS ON THE BUREAUCRACY: Judicial oversight is another check on bureaucracy.

A. Judicial Standards of Bureaucratic Behavior: Judicial review of bureaucratic actions normally focuses on two issues: 1. Did the agency exceed the authority given by Congress? 2. Did the agency abide by procedural fairness--given proper notice of hearings, etc.?

If the answer is NO to the first question and YES to the second question, the courts will normally not interfere.

B. Bureaucrats' Success in Court: Overall, bureaucracies have been very successful in defending their actions in court. Independent agencies enjoy greater success than departments. This success is explained by the battery of attorneys employed by the agencies who are paid by public funds and are specialized in an area of law. It is very expensive for individual citizens to undertake litigation, and businesses and special interest groups must use a cost/benefit analysis to determine whether it would be useful to litigate. The long delay in court proceedings might cost more than a victory.

CHAPTER TWELVE SAMPLE QUESTIONS

TRUE-FALSE:

1. Bureaucracies are characterized by a division of labor and goal orientation.

2. Bureaucracy is a form of social organization found not only in government but also in corporations, churches, military forces, etc.

3. Bureaucratic power has grown with advances in technology and increases in the size and complexity of society.

4. Regulatory rules that appear in the Federal Register are advisory only.

5. Discretionary funds are those which bureaucrats have flexibility in determining how to spend.

6. The administrators of independent agencies are not subject to senatorial confirmation.

7. The merit system is the selection of government employees based on political loyalty.

8. Independent regulatory agencies differ from cabinet departments because only cabinet secretaries are political appointees.

9. Compared to other countries, the U.S. has a great number of government corporations.

10. Reformers have been successful in implementing zero-based budgeting.

MULTIPLE CHOICE:

11. An agency that is created to be outside the cabinet and the usual political considerations is a(n) :
    a. Government corporation
    c. Regulatory commission
    b. Independent agency
    d. None of the above

12. Max Weber indicated that a rational bureaucracy would have certain characteristics. Which of the following is NOT one of these characteristics?
    a. Generalized labor
    b. Chain of command
    c. Specification of authority
    d. Impersonality

13. All but one of the following factors explain the growth of the federal bureaucracy:
    a. Neither the president nor Congress has the necessary time to be concerned details
    b. The increasing complexity and sophistication of technology requires technical experts
    c. Congress writes specific and detailed laws
    d. Bureaucracy is its own source of power and growth

14. When an agency develops its own set of beliefs and values about its programs it is called:
    a. Agency society
    b. Agency norms
    c. Agency culture
    d. All of the above

15. The growth of government has been explained by many factors including all but one of the following:
    a. Incrementalism
    b. Citizen pressures
    c. Wagner's Law of Societal Demands
    d. Wars and crisis

16. Which of the following statements is correct regarding government workers and the general population?
    a. Blacks are under represented in the federal work force
    b. Hispanics are over represented in the federal work force
    c. Females are over represented in the lowest pay grades
    d. Both females and minorities are under represented in executive levels in the federal work force

17. Which of the following is responsible for the preparation of the president's budget?
    a. Department of the Treasury b. OMB c. Council of Economic Advisors d. CBO

18. What is the principal difference between a regulatory commission and an independent agency?
    a. Members of the former are appointed by the president while the latter are designed by Congress
    b. Independent agency heads can be fired by the president
    c. Only regulatory commission members are confirmed by the Senate
    d. Regulatory commissions are more important

19. The spoils system selected persons based on all but one of the following:
    a. Party loyalty
    b. Merit
    c. Electoral support
    d. Political influence

20. All but one of the following are bureaucratic budget strategies:
    a. Spend it all b. Always ask for more c. Cut vital programs d. Avoid new programs

CHAPTER TWELVE SAMPLE QUESTION ANSWERS

TRUE-FALSE:

1.   **TRUE**. Bureaucracies are characterized by a division of labor and goal orientation as well as a chain of command, specification of labor, and impersonality. See page 421.

2.   **TRUE.** Any hierarchy is indicative of a bureaucracy. See page 421.

3.   **TRUE.** See page 421.

4.   **FALSE.** These published rules have the effect of law and the regulatory agencies have the power to ensure compliance. See page 423.

5.   **TRUE**. See page 424.

6.   **FALSE**. The administrators of independent agencies are appointed by the president and confirmed by the Senate. See page 431.

7.   **FALSE**. The spoils system is the selection of government employees based on political loyalty. See page 436.

8.   **FALSE**. Both cabinet secretaries and regulatory commissions and heads are politically appointed. The main difference is that the president can remove a cabinet secretary but cannot remove a regulatory commission member or head. See page 431.

9.   **FALSE.** In reality, we have very few-three in total. See page 443.

10.   **FALSE**. See page 447.

MULTIPLE-CHOICE:

11. **B**. An agency that is created to be outside the cabinet and the usual political considerations is an Independent agency. See page 431.

12. **A**. A bureaucracy would stress specialized workers to improve productivity. See page 421.

13. **C**. The fact that Congress writes vague and ambiguous laws requires a bureaucracy to interpret and implement these laws. See page 419.

14. **C**. When an agency develops its own set of beliefs and values about its programs it is called agency culture. See page 442.

15. **B**. Interest group pressures are a cause but not individual citizen pressures. See page 457.

16. **D**. At the highest level of the federal work force there are not many women or minorities. See page 441.

17. **B**. The Office of Management and Budget (OMB) has the key responsibility. See page 443.

18. **B**. Like cabinet secretaries, agency heads serve at the pleasure of the president. Answer D may appear to be correct, except that the EPA is extremely powerful, arguably more so than any regulatory commission. See page 436.

19. **B** Merit was a secondary consideration. See pages 437.

20. **D**. Bureaucrats do not avoid suggesting new programs, but present them in an incremental fashion so as to not arouse opposition. See page 446.

CHAPTER THIRTEEN
COURTS: FEDERAL POLITICS

I. JUDICIAL POWER: Many political questions are eventually turned into judicial questions. For example, the courts have taken the lead in deciding many contentious political issues, such as:

1. Elimination of racial segregation and decisions about affirmative action.
2. Ensure separation of church and state.
3. Determine personal liberties on the issue of abortion.
4. Defining free speech and press and deciding such issues as obscenity, censorship and pornography.
5. Ensure equality of representation in legislative districts.
6. Defining the rights of criminal defendants and preventing unlawful searches.
7. Decisions about capital punishment.

A. Constitutional Power of the Courts: The Constitution grants judicial power to the Supreme Court and other courts as established by Congress. These courts are independent. Judges are appointed, not elected. Their term is for life, barring any impeachable offense. Their salary may be increased but not cut during their time in office to prevent political punishments by Congress.

B. Interpreting the Constitution: Judicial Review: Since the Constitution is the supreme law of the land and takes precedence over federal and state laws, and since the interpreters of the Constitution are the courts, this gives the judiciary great authority. Judicial review--the power to invalidate congressional or state laws--is not mentioned in the Constitution but was discussed in the Federalist Papers. It was the historic decision in the case of Marbury v. Madison (1803) that officially established the power of judicial review. The legal reasoning of Marshall is outlined on page 465. The power of an unelected body to overturn the decisions of democratically elected officials is troubling to some observers who view this power of the Court as undemocratic.

C. Arguments over Judicial Review: The power of the Supreme Court to interpret the Constitution and the supremacy of the Constitution over state and federal laws is widely accepted today. But one could still ask why the opinions of appointed judges should take precedence over the actions of elected members of Congress or the president.

D. Judicial Review of Laws of Congress: Judicial review is the most powerful of the Supreme Court's weapons, yet they have been restrained in its use.

Prior to the Civil War the court struck down very few laws of any kind. Since then, they have been more likely to declare state laws (as opposed to national) unconstitutional. This restraint should not be interpreted to mean that when the Court has used this power it has only been aimed at trivial or unimportant laws. Quite the contrary, some of the most significant cases of judicial review have been used on the most important issues of our time. Over two centuries, the Court has struck down fewer that 150 of the more than 60,000 laws passed by Congress.

E. Judicial Review of Presidential Affairs: The Supreme Court has only rarely challenged presidential power. Examples include cases involving Lincoln, Truman, Nixon, and Clinton.

F. Judicial Review of State Laws: Key examples here are the *Brown* desegregation and *Roe v. Wade* abortion decisions.

G. Interpreting Federal Laws: Not only do the courts interpret the Constitution, but they also are called upon to interpret statutory laws written by Congress. Sometimes vague or ambiguous language is used--such as fairness, good faith, probable cause, etc., and the courts are called upon to give specific meaning to these phrases.

H. The Supreme Court's Policy Agenda: The federal courts deal with a wide variety of policy areas. The Supreme Court dominated policy-making in three areas:

1. Civil rights and treatment of minorities and women.
2. Procedural rights of criminal defendants.
3. The First Amendment-especially freedom of religion and speech.

The Court is also active in determining the meaning of American federalism. Finally, the Court gives considerable attention to governmental regulatory activities--environmental, banking and securities, and labor-management issues. The Court has been noticeably absent in areas of national defense and international affairs, leaving these areas for the Congress and president to resolve.

II. ACTIVISM VERSUS SELF-RESTRAINT: Justice Felix Frankfurter once said that the only check on judicial power was the sense of self-restraint.

A. Judicial Self-Restraint: This doctrine holds that judges should not read their own philosophy into the Constitution and should avoid confrontations with the other branches of government where possible since federal judges are elected.

B.   Wisdom versus Constitutionality: A law may be unwise or even stupid, but that doesn't mean it is unconstitutional. Yet there is the suggestion that the Supreme Court indeed often equates wisdom with constitutionality.

C.   Original Intent: Should the Constitution be interpreted in terms of the values of the founders or should the Constitution be considered a "living document" which must be interpreted by today's standards and values? If the latter, whose interpretation and values should prevail? Those favoring original intent suggest that the Constitution should be interpreted using the values of the founders.

D.   Judicial Activism: **FILL-IN.**

E.   Stare Decisis: The rule of precedence is very important in the law. This rule provides continuity and stability in the law. It essentially means that a previous decision should stand in a present case, the facts and issue being essentially the same. Thus, if the Supreme Court decided an issue 20 years ago, and the same issue is before the Court again with different justices, these justices are bound to observe the previous ruling. Those favoring judicial activism do not give much credibility to <u>state</u> <u>decisis</u>. The Supreme Court has overturned some of its previous rulings, i.e., violated precedence, e.g., *Brown v. Board of Education*.

F.   Rules of Restraint: Even an activist Supreme Court does exercise some self-restraint:

1.   It does not issue advisory opinions to Congress or the president; it only rules on actual cases of legislation.
2.   It does not decide hypothetical cases or issues.
3.   The Court tries to apply the narrowest interpretation possible.
4.   The Court will not decide a constitutional question if the case can be disposed of using some other means, procedural or structural.
5.   A plaintiff must show injury to have standing.
6.   A plaintiff must exhaust all other remedies at lower levels before the Supreme Court will accept the case for review.
7.   **FILL-IN.**
8.   **FILL-IN.**
9.   **FILL-IN.**
10.   **FILL-IN.**

III.   STRUCTURE AND JURISDICTION OF FEDERAL COURTS: The federal court system consists of three levels: the Supreme Court, the Court of Appeals, and the district courts.

A.   Federal District Courts: There are 89 federal district courts in the 50 states and one each in Puerto Rico and the District of Columbia. There are over 600 federal judges that serve in these courts who were appointed by the president, confirmed by the Senate, and serve for life. There is also a U.S. marshall for each district whose staff carries out the orders of the court and provides order in the courtroom. District courts serve as the entry point for a federal case, that is, they have <u>original jurisdiction.</u> They handle both criminal and civil cases. Each district also has a U.S. attorney and staff representing the Department of Justice.

B.   Courts of Appeal: There are 12 regional federal Courts of Appeals and one for the District of Columbia. They have <u>appellate jurisdiction</u> only. That is, they hear appeals from district court decisions. They do not hold another trial, but consider only the written record of the district court and oral or written arguments (briefs) submitted by attorneys. Federal law grants everyone the right of appeal. Appellate judges estimate that 80 percent of the appeals are without merit. There are more that 100 federal appellate judges, again appointed by the president, confirmed by the Senate and serving for life. Generally, appeals are heard by a panel of three judges. More than 90 percent of cases end at this level. Appeal to the Supreme Court is not guaranteed.

C.   Supreme Court: The Court is the final interpreter of all matters involving the Constitution and federal laws and treaties. The Court can reject an appeal without explanation.

D.   Appeals from State Courts: The Supreme Court has appellate jurisdiction over state supreme courts as well as the lower federal courts, therefore it oversees the national court system.   Nevertheless, the great bulk of cases begin and end at the state level and never see any federal action.

E.   Federal Cases: About 10 million civil and criminal cases are begun every year. Of these, fewer than 300,000 begin in federal courts. There are about 7,000 cases appealed to the Supreme Court, but it accepts only about 100. Thus, the vast bulk of cases are heard in state/local courts. Federal caseloads have risen over the past years. This has been caused by greater activity of the FBI, DEA, ATF, and IRS as well as Congress expanding the list of federal crimes.

IV.   THE SPECIAL RULES OF JUDICIAL DECISION MAKING: Unlike the other branches, the courts employ highly specialized rules for decision making.

A. Cases and Controversies: Courts do not initiate action on cases; someone must bring the case to them. A case must involve two disputing parties and must involve real damage. The vast majority of cases do not involve important policy decisions, but rather determinations of guilt or innocence, contract claims, and negligence civil suits. Federal courts do not render advisory opinions or policy declarations, they must wait until a case is brought to them for them to interpret the meaning of law or determine constitutionality.

B. Adversarial Proceedings: **FILL-IN.**

C. Standing: To bring an issue to court, one party must have standing, that is, they must be directly harmed by a law or action. Anyone prosecuted by the government automatically has standing. Federal courts in recent years have liberalized the definition of standing. The party suffering the damage is the plaintiff. The party against whom the suit is filed becomes the defendant. The doctrine of sovereign immunity means that one cannot sue the government without its consent. By law, the U.S. government has granted this consent in contract and negligence cases. Citizens can also sue to force a government official to perform his/her duty or for acting contrary to the law.

D. Class Action Suits: Suits that are filed not only by an individual but for a whole group of people similarly situated in being damaged by the same defendant. One of the earliest class action suits was *Brown v. Board of Education*. Class suits mushroomed in popularity, especially fed by lawyers.

E. Legal Fees: It costs money to go to court. Criminal defendants are guaranteed services of an attorney without charge if they are poor. But if you have money you have to pay the bill. In civil cases, both parties must pay legal fees. The most common arrangement for the plaintiff is the contingency fee--plaintiffs will pay the expenses of the lawyer and share one-third to one-half of any award for damages if the case is won or settled out of court. If the case is lost, the attorney gets zero. Lawyers will not accept contingency fee cases unless they think they have a good chance of winning.

F. Remedies and Relief: Judicial power has greatly expanded through court determinations of remedies and relief that go beyond a prison sentence, fine, or cash judgment. Federal judges have supervised the operation of schools, ordered forced busing, local authorities to build low-cost housing in a specific area, supervision of a state prison system, and ordered a school board to raise taxes to pay for a desegregation plan.

G. Appointments of Independent Councils: **FILL-IN.**

V.   THE POLITICS OF SELECTING JUDGES: All federal judges are appointed by the president and confirmed by the Senate. Judicial recruitment is a political process. Almost always presidents appoint judges of their own party. More than 80 percent of federal judges held some political office prior to appointment. Political philosophy also is now an important criteria.

      A.   The Politics of Presidential Selection: Since judicial appointments are made for life, presidents have a strong motivation to select judges that share their political philosophy. However, presidents have been surprised about 25 percent of the time when their appointees deviated from their expected judicial philosophy.

      B.   Political Litmus Test: In general, Democratic presidents and senators prefer more liberal activist judges while Republicans prefer more conservative judges who profess judicial self-restraint. A litmus test refers to the judicial candidate's position on a single issue. More recently, this has been the abortion issue. Another issue could be capital punishment.

      C.   Competence and Ethics: **FILL-IN.**

      D.   The Politics of Senate Confirmation: Presidential nominations are sent to the Senate Judiciary Committee which holds hearings, votes on the nomination and then reports it to the full Senate. The custom of <u>senatorial</u> <u>courtesy</u> has been used to screen nominees. If a senator from the same party as the president objects to the nomination of a judge for his state, normally his colleagues in the Senate would disapprove the nomination. Note that this courtesy applies only to judges in a state-it would not apply to appellate judges or Supreme Court justices. Supreme Court nominations receive unusually strict scrutiny. Over the first two centuries, the Senate refused to confirm or rejected 20 percent of the president's nominations. In this century, only five nominations have been defeated. The general rule is to respect the president's nomination and unless some extraordinary circumstance exists, e.g., financial scandal, racial or religious bias, etc., the Senate usually concurs with the nomination.

      E.   The Bork Battle: The Senate's rejection of President Reagan's Supreme Court nominee Robert Bork set a new precedent for the confirmation process. The confirmation process was conducted on TV, and he was eventually rejected for his views and "conservative activism" as opposed to any qualification question. This battle set the stage for future confirmations.

VI.   WHO IS SELECTED: In spite of differing views on the law, the Constitution and its interpretation, the background of Supreme Court justices is remarkably similar.

      A.   Law Degrees: While there is no constitutional requirement that Supreme

Court justices be lawyers, every one has been one. Moreover, the majority have attended the most prestigious law schools--Harvard, Yale and Stanford.

B. Judicial Experience: About half of the justices have been federal or state judges prior to appointment to the Court. About one-quarter have come from private practices. Many have served as U.S. Attorneys. Relatively few have been elected politicians--two notable exceptions are Sandra Day O'Connor who served in the Arizona legislature, and William Howard Taft, who was president before taking his place on the court.

C. Age: Most of the justices are in their fifties when they are appointed to the Supreme Court.

D. Race and Gender: Until President Johnson appointed Thurgood Marshall in 1967, no black American had been a justice. Until President Reagan appointed Justice O'Connor in 1981, no woman served on the court. When Marshall retired, President Bush decided to appoint another black American to the court who proved to be very controversial--Justice Clarence Thomas. President Clinton added another woman to the bench when he appointed Ruth Bader Ginsburg.

VII. SUPREME COURT DECISION MAKING: Except for original jurisdiction cases, the Supreme Court decides what cases it will hear. More than 5,000 cases come to the Court each year, yet the Court accepts for opinions only about 200 or, in other words, about 4 percent. In another 150 or so cases, the Court decides the case summarily (without opinion) either affirming or reversing the lower court decision. It is important to realize that by not agreeing to hear a case the Supreme Court creates law by allowing the decisions of the lower courts to stand.

A. Setting the Agenda: Granting Certiorari: The party losing a case at the appellate level may petition the Supreme Court for a writ of certiorari. In effect, this petition requests the Supreme Court to require the lower court to turn over its records for review. The decision to grant certiorari depends on the Rule of Four. Four justices have to agree to accept the case. While the Court rarely explains why it accepts or rejects a case, some patterns are observable.

1. The issue is one the justices are interested in--it may be abortion, or free speech.
2. When there is conflict in the court system. Two Courts of Appeals have decided cases exactly opposite.
3. A lower court has either ignored a Supreme Court decision or misinterpreted it.
4. The U.S. government is a party in the case.

B.   Hearing Arguments: Once the Supreme Court accepts a case and places it on its calendar, attorneys for both sides prepare written briefs citing applicable law and previous cases. The Court may also allow other interested parties to file <u>amicus</u> <u>curiae</u> (friend of the court) written briefs. This is the only opportunity for interest groups to influence a judicial decision. The U.S. government will frequently submit these briefs when it is not a party to the case. Oral arguments are scheduled after the justices have had time to read the written materials. Usually attorneys for the parties are allowed from one-half hour to one hour for the oral presentation, which is strictly controlled. Judges can interrupt at any time with questions-some of which may be friendly and others hostile. Some court observers try to guess the eventual decision in the case by the tenor and identity of the justice asking the questions.

C.   In Conference: The justices meet in private conference (no public, reporters, or law clerks) on Wednesday and Friday afternoons and discuss the cases of the week. The chief justice presides. A vote is taken to determine who wins or loses the case or whether the lower court case is affirmed or reversed.

D.   Writing Opinions: **FILL-IN. WHAT IS A MAJORITY, CONCURRING AND DISSENTING OPINION?**

E.   Voting Blocs: The most prominent bloc involves the liberal-conservative axis. Sometimes an activist-judicial restraint axis is employed. Over time the composition of the Court has changed and the voting blocs have shifted.

VIII. POLITICS AND THE SUPREME COURT: Justices are influenced by their ideologies. But public opinion, interest groups, and the president influence cases as well.

A.   Liberal Conservative Voting Blocs: The most prominent bloc involves the liberal-conservative axis. Sometimes an activist-judicial restraint axis is employed. Over time the composition of the Court has changed and the voting blocs have shifted.

B.   Public Opinion: Supreme Court decisions have generally followed shifts in American public opinion. But the Court appears to lag behind public opinion. Public opinion affects the Court indirectly, through the nomination and confirmation process.

C.   Presidential Influence: Influence is generated by the solicitor general, who wins about 75 percent of cases.

D.   Interest Group Influence: **FILL-IN.**

IX. CHECKING COURT POWER: As unelected members of a powerful branch of government, there is some concern about the possible abuse of power. There are, however, some checks on this power:

A. Legitimacy as a Restraint in the Judiciary: The courts do not have the power to enforce their decisions. With only a few thousand marshals, the court must depend on the executive for enforcement of its decisions. Although the courts decided that Mississippi, Arkansas, and Alabama schools had to integrate, federalized troops were required to accomplish the task. Most Americans feel that court decisions are authoritative and that citizens have a duty to obey the decisions whether they agree with them or not. Widespread opposition to a decision can delay its implementation as integration of schools and the banning of school prayer demonstrate.

B. Compliance with Court Policy: Lower federal judges and state courts are obliged to follow Supreme Court decisions in their courts. Sometimes courts will express their disapproval of the decision, but they still must follow it. Sometimes they will try to narrowly interpret the decision when they disagree with it. Public officials who defy Court rulings risk lawsuits and court ordered compliance. Failure to comply will result in fines and penalties. Even the president must comply with Court orders. Failure to do so could result in impeachment.

C. Presidential Influence on Court Policy: Presidents can influence the federal courts through their appointment powers. The opportunity to fill a vacancy on the Supreme Court is rare, but there are a large number of lower federal court positions to be filled by any president.

D. Congressional Checks on the Judiciary: Congress has the power to establish or disestablish inferior courts. Congress can increase or decrease the number of Supreme Court justices. Congress can increase or decrease the number of federal district or appellate judges. Congress can limit the jurisdiction of the courts and can specify in legislation how many appeals will be made. Were it used too often, the Court might proclaim the limitation to be unconstitutional. Often the Court is called upon to interpret the meaning of a law. If the Court interprets the law to Congress's disliking, Congress can always amend the statutory law. In terms of the Court interpreting the Constitution to Congress's dislike, the only remedy is to amend the Constitution. Attempts by Congress to amend the Constitution to overturn a Supreme Court decision are rarely successful, e.g., school prayer, prohibiting flag burning, etc. In theory, Congress could impeach justices, but only for committing a crime, not for a decision. So in reality, the threat of impeachment has no real influence over judicial policy making.

CHAPTER THIRTEEN SAMPLE QUESTIONS

TRUE-FALSE:

1. Courts are "political" institutions.

2. The Supreme Court has hesitated to use judicial review in all but the smallest of cases.

3. The power of judicial review is contained in Article III of the Constitution.

4. Judicial self-restraint is the idea that judges should not read their own philosophy into the Constitution.

5. The Supreme Court has challenged legislation more than executive actions.

6. An unwise law is a prime candidate to be found unconstitutional.

7. Democrats pSee appoint judges who profess judicial restraint.

8. If Congress is in doubt about the constitutionality of a proposed law, the judiciary committees can ask the Supreme Court for an advisory opinion.

9. The background and education of the members of the Supreme Court are highly diverse.

10. An *amicus curiae* brief permits interest groups to influence the courts.

MULTIPLE CHOICE

11. The courts have decided issues in all the following areas EXCEPT:
    a. Civil rights
    b. Voting rights
    c. Reproductive rights
    d. Medical care rights

12. Which of the following is <u>not</u> one of the patterns explaining Supreme Court case acceptance?
    a. A lower court has ignored a Supreme Court ruling
    b. There is conflict within the court system
    c. The federal government is a party to the case
    d. The amount of damages in the case exceeds $1 million

13. Which of the following are a check(s) on the power of the Supreme Court?
    a. Presidential appointments
    b. Lower court compliance
    c. The perceived legitimacy of the decision
    d. All of the above

14. The Supreme Court has been most active in three of the following areas. Which area is <u>not</u> correct?
    a. Civil rights
    b. Rights of criminal defendants
    c. Rights of criminal victims
    d. First Amendment rights

15. What is the name of the doctrine that states that individuals may sue the government only with the latter's consent?
    a. Stare decisis   b. Class action
    c. Sovereign immunity   d. Amicus curiae

16. A justice believes that in making a ruling, he should avoid where possible confrontations with the Congress and president. This justice could be said to believe in:
    a. Judicial activism   b. Judicial restraint
    c. The living Constitution   d. Stare decisis

17. To grant a writ of certiorari requires the approval of:
    a. All justices   b. A minimum of four
    c. Two-thirds of the justices d. Three-quarters of the justices

18. The federal district courts are an example of:
    a. Original jurisdiction   b. Appellate jurisdiction
    c. Mixed jurisdiction   d. Petit juries

19. The U.S. Supreme Court is an example of:
    a. Original jurisdiction   b. Appellate jurisdiction
    c. Mixed jurisdiction   d. Grand jury

20. Most Supreme Court justices have been:
    a. Catholics   b. 51-60 when appointed
    c. Republicans   d. Females

CHAPTER THIRTEEN SAMPLE QUESTION ANSWERS

TRUE-FALSE:

1.   **TRUE.** The courts decide who gets what. See page 463.

2.   **FALSE**. The Court has exercised judicial review in some of the most important cases. See page 466.

3.   **FALSE.** The Supreme Court said it had this power in the case of *Marbury v. Madison*. See page 465.

4.   **TRUE**. See page 468.

5.   **TRUE.** The instances of challenges to the president have been very few. See page 467.

6.   **FALSE.** Wisdom does not equal constitutionality. Some think it does, but the court tries to avoid such a relationship. See page 469.

7.   **FALSE.**   Democrats usually prefer to appoint judges who are activists. See page 480.

8.   **FALSE.** This is an example of Supreme Court restraint. They will not rule on hypothetical questions. See page 471.

9.   **FALSE**. The members of the Supreme Court share a very similar background and education. See page 485.

10.   **TRUE**. See page 494.

MULTIPLE-CHOICE:

11. **D.** So far the Court has not found a right to medical care in the Constitution-in all the other areas it has. See page 463.

12. **D**. The amount of damages has <u>not</u> effect on the Court's acceptance of a case. See page 486.

13. **D**. Presidential appointments, lower court compliance, and the perceived legitimacy of the decision are all checks on the power of the Supreme Court. See page 495.

14. **C**. The Court has been active in protecting the rights of criminals. See page 468.

15. **C**. Sovereign immunity if the name of the doctrine. See page 478.

16. **B**. This would be a clear case of judicial restraint. See page 468.

17. **B**. The Rule of Four is applicable. See page 486.

18. **A** District courts are courts of first instance, i.e., original jurisdiction or where the rubber hits the road. See page 472.

19. **C**. The Supreme Court has both original and appellate jurisdiction or mixed. See page 473.

20. **B**. This is the magic age for most appointments. See Table 13-3 on p. 485.

CHAPTER FOURTEEN: POLITICS AND PERSONAL LIBERTY

I. **POWER AND INDIVIDUAL LIBERTY:** Liberty or freedom was the most sacred value to the founders of our country who saw government as a mechanism for preserving liberty.

   A. **Authority and Liberty:** In order to secure their liberty, citizens willingly give up some for a government that will protect the liberty of all. However, this sets up a dilemma--people must create laws and government to protect their liberty, but the laws and government restrict freedom.

   B. **Democracy and Personal Liberty:** If democracy is defined only as a decision-making process, there is little protection for liberty. It must also be defined to include substantive values--the dignity of the individual and equality under the law. The purpose of the Constitution and Bill of Rights was to limit government power over the individual and place personal liberty beyond the reach of government.

   C. **Nationalizing the Bill of Rights:** Originally, the provisions in the Bill of Rights applied only to the national government. Most state constitutions contained similar provisions, but these were enforceable in state courts only. With the passage of the Fourteenth Amendment and its due process and equal protection of the law provisions, there was a question whether these general phrases incorporated the Bill of Rights and made them applicable to states. At first, the Supreme Court did not agree with this idea. Gradually, beginning in 1925, case by case, the Supreme Court has incorporated almost all of the provisions of the Bill of Rights in making them applicable to both the federal government and lower governments.

II. **FREEDOM OF RELIGION:** Americans not only believe in freedom of religion, but they also practice their religion more than people in any other industrialized country. The First Amendment established two specific provisions regarding this freedom: government shall not establish a religion, nor prohibit the free exercise of religion.

   A. **Free Exercise of Religion:** Although the wording of this provision seems absolute: "Congress shall make no law...," Congress has passed laws that restrict the practice of religions and some of these have been upheld by the Supreme Court. One of the earliest was a law to ban polygamy in Utah. The Court distinguished between faith and behavior. Beliefs are absolutely protected, but religious practices are not. If government has a valid secular (nonreligious) reason for banning a religious practice, it may be upheld e.g.,. human sacrifice or ceremonial use of illegal drugs.

B.   No Establishment of Religion: Interpretations of this clause range from simply prohibiting the state from establishing an official religion to building a wall of separation between church and state. **DEFINE WALL-OF-SEPARATION DOCTRINE.**

C.   What Constitutes "Establishment"? This has proven to be one of the most vexing problems for the Supreme Court. The Supreme Court uses a test for establishment that it fashioned in the *Lemon v. Kurtzman* case. The three prongs of this test are:
1.   **FILL-IN**
2.
3.

D.   Prayer in School: The question of prayer and the reading of the <u>Bible</u> in school has been the most controversial involvement of the Supreme Court with freedom of religion. In spite of the long history of prayer in school, in 1962 the Court declared this practice to be unconstitutional. In 1963, they said the same about reading from the <u>Bible</u>. The majority opinion held that the <u>Bible</u> could be studied as part of a secular course, but not used in religious ceremonies. When Alabama mandated a moment of silence for meditation or silent prayer, the Court struck this down as well.

E.   Religious Freedom Restoration? Congress passed the Religious Freedom Act in 1993 which exempts persons from government laws or regulations that burden religious freedom, unless the government can prove the burden is the least restrictive means of furthering a compelling government interest. But the Supreme Court ruled the Act unconstitutional in 1997 (*Boerne v. Flores*).

III.   FREEDOM OF SPEECH: Again, although the First Amendment is absolute "Congress shall pass no law...," the Supreme Court has never agreed that all speech is protected by the First Amendment.

A.   Clear and Present Danger: If speech creates a serious and immediate danger such as crying out "FIRE" in a crowded theater, it is not protected speech.

B.   Preferred Position Doctrine: **FILL-IN.**

C.   The Cold War Challenge: The passage of the Smith Act made it unlawful to advocate the overthrow of the U.S. government. In 1949, the federal government prosecuted 11 members of the Communist Party of the U.S. They were convicted and the Supreme Court upheld their convictions. Since then, the Court has returned to more stringent clear and present danger position. In later cases, the Court held that mere advocacy of revolution without any unlawful action is protected speech. Later cases struck down federal laws requiring Communist organizations to register with the government, the requirement of loyalty oaths, prohibition of Communists working in defense plants, and laws stripping the passports from Communist leaders.

D.   Symbolic Speech: **FILL-IN.**

E.   Speech and Public Order: Can authorities ban a speech because the audience may become unruly? Generally, the Court says no. However, authorities can require sponsors to post a bond or to take out a permit, or even be charged for extra police protection.

F.   Hate Speech and Hate Crimes: **FILL-IN.**

G.   Commercial Speech: While allowing some protection of commercial speech, the Court is far more forceful in protecting political speech. States had banned advertising by professionals and listing of prices by pharmacies. These the Court banned. But the Court upheld federal laws banning or controlling liquor and cigarette advertising.

H.   Libel and Slander: These have never been considered protected speech. Libel is defined as damaging falsehood. If aimed at public officials, not only must it be shown that the speech was libelous but that it was made with actual malice.

IV.   OBSCENITY AND THE LAW: Although obscenity can be banned, the main problem is defining what is meant by obscenity. Is nudeness obscene? Pornography is simply a synonym for obscenity.

A.   Slackening Standards: *Roth v. United States*: The Court's first comprehensive effort to define obscenity came in the 1957 Roth case. The Court ruled that obscenity is that which an average person applying contemporary community standards would find obscene. This test became very difficult to use in cases. Community standard later became society at large. The work as a whole had to be obscene. There could be no redeeming social or literary merit.

B.   Tightening Standards: *Miller v. California*: Because of the difficulty in interpreting the standards developed under *Roth*, the Court again looked at this issue in 1973 in the case of *Miller versus. California*. Local community was now the determining mechanism, and they defined prurient as patently offensive representations or descriptions of various sexual acts. The effect of this decision was to make convictions in obscenity-pornography cases more likely.

C. Child Pornography: Generally, the Court has come down much harder on child porn. The mere possession of child porn material is evidence that a crime has been committed.

D. The Information Highway: New technologies continue to challenge the Court's application of the First Amendment principles. The Internet in particular has made the transferring of all kinds of information, pornographic and otherwise, much easier. Congress unsuccessfully tried to ban "indecent" communications from the Internet in 1996. The Supreme Court held that the Communication Decency Act was unconstitutional in that it violated the First Amendment.

V. FREEDOM OF THE PRESS: The idea of a free and independent press is deeply rooted in the evolution of democratic government.

A. No Prior Restraint Doctrine: Prior restraint is the censorship of written material by government authorities before publication. It was quite common in England before the American Revolution. In 1931, the Court struck down a Minnesota law that prohibited the publication of a muckraking publication, although it held that prior restraint might be applicable in time of war. This issue came to the court in *New York Times v. Sullivan*--the case of stolen top secret Pentagon papers. Could the government prevent *The New York Times* and *Washington Post* from publishing this stolen material? The Court majority said NO.

B. Film Censorship: The Supreme Court has not given the film industry the same prior restraint protection as the press. The Court approved government censorship for obscenity, but the industry adopted its own system of rating films to head off the government.

C. Radio and Television Censorship: Since radio and TV use the public airways, and there is a problem with frequency allocation and usage, the Federal Communication Commission has been given much more control over this medium. The Court upheld fairness and equal time requirements of the FCC, for example.

D. Media Claims for Special Rights: The news media argue that they would be ineffective as reporters unless they can provide sources confidentiality. The Supreme Court has rejected this argument, but news organizations have pressured state governments to pass shield laws which allow them this confidentiality at the state level.

E.   Conflicting Rights: In order to protect witnesses, a court places a gag order on attorneys and parties to the trial. This gag order is a restriction of free speech and press. Thus, there is a conflict between the right of a free and impartial trial and free speech and press.

VI.   FREEDOM OF ASSEMBLY AND PETITION: The right to organize political parties and interest groups is derived from freedom of assembly. Freedom to petition protects most lobbying activities.

A.   Right of Association: Freedom of assembly includes the right to join organizations and associations. The Court has included student organizations within this right.

B.   Protests, Parades, and Demonstrations: Also protected by the freedom of assembly is the right to protest and demonstrate. Authorities have the right, within reasonable limits, to make restrictions as to time, place, permits, and manner of assembly to protect public order, but must apply these restrictions in an impartial manner.

C.   Picketing: The Court has generally upheld the use of public property for assembly, but it has not required private property owners to do the same. Abortion demonstrators have been on the forefront of testing the freedom of assembly rulings.

VII.   THE RIGHT TO BEAR ARMS: This is certainly one of the most volatile issues in public policy today.

A.   Bearing Arms: One interpretation of the Second Amendment is that it is an individual right. This stems from the fear, prevalent when this amendment was adopted, that despotic governments would try to seize the arms of citizens.

B.   State Militias: An alternate interpretation is that the writers of this amendment were interested in the maintenance of well-regulated state militias. Thus, there is no right for private groups or individuals to bear arms, but rather it is a collective right.

C.   Citizen Militias: Recently there have been self-styled citizen militias that have formed which have an anti-government mentality, and engage in training in military tactics and small arms practice. They see themselves as modern-day descendents of American patriot militias who fought in the Revolutionary War. These units frequently come into conflict with various federal agencies like the ATF.

VIII.   RIGHTS OF CRIMINAL DEFENDANTS: While society needs protection by the police, also important is to protect society from the police.

A.   The Guarantee of the Writ of Habeas Corpus: Part of English common law, this is a court order requiring officials to deliver the prisoner to the court and explain the reasons for detention. If unlawful, or insufficient evidence exists, the judge can order the prisoner's release. The courts have been very diligent in protecting this right, declaring in *Ex Parte Milligan* that Lincoln acted unconstitutionally is suspending the writ during the Civil War.

B.   The Prohibition of Bills of Attainder and Ex Post Facto Laws: **FILL-IN. DEFINE BILL OF ATTAINER AND EX POST FACTO LAW.**

C.   Unreasonable Searches and Seizures: **FILL-IN. ARE SOME SEARCHES ALLOWED WITHOUT A WARRANT?**

D.   Wiretapping and Electronic Surveillance: **FILL-IN.**

E.   Drug Testing: Mandatory drug testing is constitutional in some occupations, but "suspicionless" testing of the public is not.

F.   Arrests: Generally warrants are not required for arrests, except in the case of entering the home of someone to arrest them. If the owner gives his consent, a warrant is not required.

G.   Indictment: The Fifth Amendment requires that an indictment be brought by a grand jury before a person may be tried for a felony offense. This was designed to protect against the potential of prosecution used as a means of harassment.

H.   Self-incrimination and the Right to Counsel: The right to avoid self-incrimination is predicated on the assumption of innocence and to prevent torture being used to obtain confessions. The Fifth Amendment covers this right. "Taking the Fifth" is when a witness refuses to testify. Failure to testify cannot be used to influence a jury regarding a verdict. Witnesses not the subject of criminal prosecution can be compelled to testify by a grant of immunity from prosecution. Nothing a witness says can be used against him/her; therefore, they cannot refuse to answer questions. The Warren Court greatly strengthened self-incrimination and right to counsel:

SUMMARIZE THESE RIGHTS IN THE FOLLOWING CASES:

1.   *Gideon v. Wainwright* (1963):
2.   *Escobedo v. Illinois* (1964):
3.   *Miranda v. Arizona* (1966):

It does not appear that the granting of these rights has hampered successful prosecutions.

I.   The Exclusionary Rule: Illegally obtained evidence may not be used in criminal trials. This protection is unique to the United States and has been the source of much controversy.

J.   Bail Requirements: While the Eighth Amendment does not establish the right to bail, the Supreme Court held that one should not be held until trial except in unusual circumstances. Pretrial bail can be denied for heinous crimes, the untrustworthiness of the defendant, or to protect the safety of the community. Most people do not have the cash for bail, so they have to use the services of a bail bondsman who charges a hefty fee for the service. If the defendant shows up, the bond is returned. If the defendant flees, the bondsman has the fee, but loses the bond. They then send out mercenaries to find the defendant.

K.   Fair Trial: The right to such a trial is guaranteed by the Sixth Amendment. Specifically guaranteed are:

1.   Right to a speedy and public trial.
2.   Right to an impartial jury.
3.   Right to confront witnesses against the accused.
4.   Right of the accused to compel favorable witnesses to appear.
5.   Right of the accused to be represented by counsel.

Trials follow a fairly regular format. The prosecution makes the opening statement, followed by the defense attorney. The prosecution then attempts to prove the crime by calling witnesses and presenting evidence. The accused is in the courtroom. His/her defense attorney will try to impeach the veracity of the witnesses or evidence. After the prosecution rests, the defense presents its case. To place the accused on the stand is a large decision. Once the defendant is sworn, he/she must answer questions not only of the defense attorney, but also the prosecution. After the defense presents its case, the attorneys have a chance to summarize their cases in concluding remarks. The defense attorney goes first and the prosecutor has the last word. After the judge issues his instructions to the jury regarding appropriate law, the jury retires to render its verdict. Federal trials have 12 jurors. A unanimous verdict is required. If the jury is deadlocked, a mistrial is declared, and it is up to the prosecution to decide to reprosecute the case.

L. Plea Bargaining: More than 90 percent of criminal cases are plea bargained. In return for concessions from the prosecutor, such as dropping the more serious charges or agreeing to a lighter sentence, the defendant pleads guilty and waives the right to a jury trial. The process has many critics who argue that it is a form of leniency and loses any deterrent effect. They also charge the process violates the right to self-incrimination and trial by jury. Supporters argue it saves the state money and any other policy would result in clogged courts.

M. Double Jeopardy: Some exceptions to the rule exist (see page 538).

IX. THE DEATH PENALTY: One of the key issues in the criminal justice system today is the death penalty. Does capital punishment violate the Eighth Amendment's prohibition of cruel and unusual punishment? There is little doubt that the death penalty is applied in a capricious way. A large percentage of those executed have been poor, uneducated, and black.

A. Prohibition Against Unfair Application: Prior to 1971, the death penalty was in use in about half of the states. Federal law also called for the death penalty in certain crimes. In *Furman v. Georgia* (1972) the Court declared the death penalty to be unconstitutional because it was not applied uniformly. After this decision, many states rewrote their laws to conform to the guidance in the Supreme Court decision. They called for its mandatory use for certain crimes of violence--murder committed during rape, robbery, hijacking, murder of prison guards, murder with torture, and multiple murders. Two trials were established--one to determine guilt and the other to present aggravating or mitigating circumstances to determine the sentence.

B. Death Penalty Reinstated: In 1976, the Court upheld the death penalty. They used many different rationales--framers of the Bill of Rights accepted it, most state legislatures rewrote their laws, and hundreds of juries have imposed the death penalty. It has social purposes of retribution and deterrence. The Court also called for the automatic review of any death sentence by the state supreme court and also disapproved of state laws that made the death penalty mandatory for all first-degree murders.

C. Racial Bias: **FILL-IN.**

D. Delays: Delayed justice is mislaid justice. The average time between sentence and execution is over seven years. Prisoners file appeal after appeal at the state level and federal level. Recent legislation will now limit appeals to one.

CHAPTER FOURTEEN SAMPLE QUESTIONS

TRUE-FALSE:

1. The proper meaning of the establishment clause has been clear since the writing of the Constitution.

2. Democracy is both a decision-making process and a system of government that includes substantive values.

3. Nationalizing the Bill of Rights refers to legislation passed by Congress that made it applicable in the 50 states.

4. Statistical discrepancies of racial bias can be used to challenge the death penalty.

5. Commercial speech has been given the same degree of protection by the Constitution as political speech.

6. Congress and the courts have successfully banned pornography on the Internet.

7. The exclusionary rule refers to the peremptory challenge to jurors in a trial.

8. The Bill of Rights protects a person's right to be released on bail.

9. Prior to trial in a federal felony case, one must be indicted by a grand jury.

10. Freedom of assembly is guaranteed even on private property.

MULTIPLE-CHOICE:

11. Which amendment protects a person from self-incrimination?
    a. First
    b. Fourth
    c. Fifth
    d. Sixth

12. Congress passes a criminal law and makes it retroactive. This would be an example of:
    a. Writ of Habeas Corpus
    b. Ex Post Facto law
    c. Bill of Attainder
    d. Stare Decisis

13. Regarding the establishment of religion, the current *Lemon* doctrine has all but one of the following tests:
   a. The law may be acceptable if the majority of those affected agree with the law
   b. As its primary effect, the law must neither advance nor inhibit religion
   c. The law must have a secular purpose
   d. The law must not foster an excessive government entanglement with religion

14. Which of the following is protected absolutely:
   a. Religious practices
   c. Freedom of press
   b. Freedom of speech
   d. Religious beliefs

15. A wall of separation between church and state would be interpreted as:
   a. Government cannot establish an official religion
   b. Government may not prefer one religion over another
   c. Government should not endorse, aid, sponsor, or encourage religious activities
   d. None of the above

16. All but one of the following are used to ensure a fair trial:
   a. Speedy and private trial
   b. Impartial jury
   c. Right to counsel
   d. Right to cross-examine witnesses

17. Which of the following best describes the Supreme Court's position on obscenity?
   a. A local community standard is allowed
   b. An average person standard is used
   c. The obscene piece must be without redeeming merit
   d. The Court looks at sex and obscenity the same

18. The prior restraint doctrine is most applicable to:
   a. The press
   c. Film
   b. Books
   d. Radio and television

19. Authorities may do all but one of the following in regulating protest, parades, and demonstrations:
   a. Specify the time when they will be allowed
   b. Require a permit for a parade
   c. Deny a permit to a group that is radical
   d. Specify the place for the activity

20. Freedom of assembly and petition is important to all but one of the following:
   a. Political parties
   c. Student organizations
   b. Interest groups
   d. Government organizations

CHAPTER FOURTEEN SAMPLE QUESTION ANSWERS

TRUE-FALSE:

1.	**FALSE**. The meaning of the establishment clause has changed over time. See page 509 .

2.	**TRUE.** If democracy is defined only as a decision-making process, there is little protection for personal liberty. See page 504.

3.	**FALSE.** The Bill of Rights was made applicable for the states, not by an act of Congress, but rather by a series of Supreme Court decisions. See pages 504-505.

4.	**FALSE.** Only racial bias against the defendant can be used to challenge. See page 539.

5.	**FALSE**. Commercial speech is not given the same level of protection as political speech. See page 539.

6.	**FALSE**. See page 528.

7.	**FALSE.** It refers to the exclusion of contaminated evidence in a trial. See page 533.

8.	**FALSE**. The Bill of Rights protects against excessive bail. See page 535.

9.	**TRUE.** This is a right guaranteed by the Fifth Amendment. See page 532.

10.	**FALSE**. The courts have not extended the right to free assembly to private property. See page 526.

MULTIPLE-CHOICE:

11. **C**. This was fairly easy--taking the Fifth Amendment--refusing to answer questions. See page 533.

12. **B**. See page 529.

13. **A**. The constitutionality of a law is not subject to a vote. See page 509.

14. **D**. Only beliefs are protected unconditionally. See page 505.

15. **C**. Jefferson used the words "wall of separation," and it was intended to mean barring any government assistance to religion. See page 509.

16. **A**. You have a right to a speedy and <u>public,</u> not private trial. See page 536.

17. **A**. From an average person standard, the Court retreated to a local community standard. See page 521.

18. **A**. The press enjoys the greatest protection under the no prior restraint rule. See page 522.

19. **C**. Authorities have to be even-handed in applying the same rules to all groups. See pages 525-526.

20. **D**. This freedom is not applicable to government organizations. See pages 525-526.

CHAPTER FIFTEEN:
POLITICS AND CIVIL RIGHTS

I.   THE POLITICS OF EQUALITY: Equality is the very essence of our democracy: "All men are created equal.." Traditionally equality meant "of opportunity"--to develop individual talents and abilities and to be rewarded for work, initiative, merit, and achievement. Over time, there has been a shift to equality of result--an equal sharing of income and material rewards. This requires government action to modify the effects of equality of opportunity, i.e., policies to redistribute income, wealth, jobs, promotions, admissions, etc. A related issue is whether equality applies to individuals or groups. Traditionally, equality was seen as fair treatment of all individuals, rather than treatment afforded to particular groups--racial and ethnic minorities, women, and the handicapped. Inequality as a member of a group takes on even greater political significance than inequality among individuals.

II.   SLAVERY, SEGREGATION, AND THE CONSTITUTION:

    A.   Slavery and the Constitution: The Constitution recognized and protected slavery. Article I stated that slaves were to be counted as three-fifths of a person for purposes of representation in Congress and taxation. Article IV guaranteed the return of escaped slaves to their owners. The majority opinion in the Dred Scott case clearly stated the inferiority of the negro, who could be treated as mere property.

    B.   Emancipation and Reconstruction: The abolition movement totally disagreed with the Dred Scott decision. The election of 1860 was a four-man race which was won by Lincoln. Although personally opposed to slavery, Lincoln promised during the campaign not to abolish slavery where it existed. Southerners were not convinced, and three months after Lincoln was inaugurated, South Carolina seceded from the Union and the Civil War began. This was to be our nation's bloodiest war. Northern Republicans joined the abolitionists in calling for the emancipation of the slaves to punish the South since its economy depended on slave labor. Lincoln also realized that if the war was being fought to free slaves, British intervention to help the South was less likely. So on September 22, 1862, Lincoln issued his famous "Emancipation Proclamation." While this freed the slaves in the seceding states, the Thirteenth Amendment freed slaves in all the country. The Fourteenth Amendment required states to "provide equal protection to all citizens," and the Fifteenth Amendment prohibited the federal and state governments from abridging the right to vote on account of race, color, or previous condition of servitude. These amendments and civil rights laws passed during the 1860s and 1870s guaranteed the newly freed slaves protection in the exercise of their constitutional rights. Between 1865 and the early 1880s blacks made much progress--holding federal and state offices, and admission to theaters, eating places, hotels, and public transportation.

C.   The Imposition of Segregation: Political support for Reconstruction was eroding. Because of the close, disputed election of 1876, a deal was struck. In return for southern support to elect the Republican Rutherford B. Hayes, the national government would withdraw its troops from the South. As white southerners regained political power and blacks lost the protection of federal forces, the Supreme Court also struck a blow by declaring federal civil rights laws preventing discrimination by private individuals to be unconstitutional. This essentially paved the way for the imposition of segregation as the prevailing social system in the South. During the 1880s and 1890s white southerners imposed segregation in public accommodations, housing, education, employment, and almost every other sector of public and private life. These laws came to be called Jim Crow laws.

D.   Early Court Approval of Segregation: In *Plessy v. Ferguson*, the Supreme Court held that segregation of the races did not violate the equal protection clause of the Fourteenth Amendment so long as people in each race were treated equally. Schools that were separate but equal were constitutional. In a lone dissent, Justice Harlan argued for a color-blind standard.

III. EQUAL PROTECTION OF THE LAWS: The initial goal of the civil rights movement was to eliminate segregated education and then fight against segregation and discrimination in all sectors of American life, both public and private.

A.   The NAACP and the Legal Battle: The NAACP and its Legal Defense and Education Fund fought to abolish lawful segregation. Led by chief legal counsel Thurgood Marshall, his strategy was to attack the separate but equal doctrine. The NAACP was able to win a series of court cases when they could prove facilities were not equal, but Marshall's goal was to attack the issue of segregation as unequal. His goal was a reversal of *Plessy v. Ferguson.* Marshall's task was to locate a school district that was segregated, but where there was equality between white and black schools. He found such a district in Topeka, Kansas, and in 1952, the NAACP filed a suit on behalf of Linda Brown. Marshall wanted a case where the court could not simply order measures to achieve equality and then wash their hands of the case. Rather, he wanted the courts to squarely face the issue of segregated education.

B.   *Brown v. Board of Education of Topeka*: In 1954, a unanimous Supreme Court held that separate education facilities are inherently unequal and reversed *Plessy v. Ferguson*. This decision was of critical importance to the civil rights movement.

C.   Enforcing Desegregation: The *Brown* ruling struck down the laws of 21 states and the District of Columbia. Such a far reaching ruling clashing with very strongly held social views was bound to meet resistance. For this reason the Supreme Court did not order immediate desegregation, but rather required state and local authorities operating under the supervision of federal judges to proceed with "deliberate speed." Still it was at least 15 years before segregated schools were on their way out.

D.   Busing and Racial Balancing: Federal judges have been given wide freedom to fashion remedies for past or present discriminatory practices caused by government action. However, in 1971, the Supreme Court pulled in the reins somewhat. In the case of *Swann v. Charlotte-Mecklenburg County Board of Education*, the Court held that forced busing of students was not required to integrate schools unless the racial imbalance was caused by past or present government action. In other words, in the absence of any government action contributing to racial imbalance, states and school districts are not required by the Fourteenth Amendment to integrate their schools.

E.   De Facto Segregation: **DEFINE DE FACTO SEGREGATION**.

IV.   THE CIVIL RIGHTS ACTS: The early civil rights movement effort was to eliminate <u>public</u> discrimination and segregation practiced by government. For this remedy, they turned to the courts. When <u>private</u> discrimination was faced from private owners of restaurants, hotels, motels, stores; private employers; landlords and real estate agents, the movement took its fight to Congress.

A.   Martin Luther King, Jr. and Nonviolent Direct Action: King was the leader of the fight in the streets--the tactic of nonviolent action--the breaking of "unjust" laws in an open, "loving," nonviolent fashion. Publicity was key to the success of this tactic. King picked the city of Birmingham, Alabama--the most rigidly segregated city in the South--as a test case. In the Spring of 1963, thousands of blacks led by King were met by Police Chief Eugene "Bull" Connor and police and firefighters who met the demonstrators with fire hoses, cattle prods, and police dogs. All on prime time media. The event was designed to touch the conscience of white Americans. Later in 1963, King led a march on Washington, D.C., which attracted 200,000 white and black participants where he gave his famous "I Have a Dream" speech. President Kennedy proposed a civil rights bill in 1963 but was killed before he could see it enacted. As a tribute to the fallen president, President Johnson pushed Kennedy's civil rights bill through Congress in 1964. King was honored by receipt of the Nobel Prize for Peace in the same year.

B.   The Civil Rights Act of 1964: This acts stands alongside the Emancipation Proclamation, the Fourteenth Amendment and the *Brown* case in importance to the civil rights movement.

1.   Title II-forbids discrimination in any facility serving the public.
2.   Title VI-every federal department or agency was to end discrimination in all programs or activities receiving federal support, which could include termination of financial assistance.
3.   Title VII- **FILL-IN.**

C.   Civil Rights Act of 1968: **FILL-IN.**

V.   EQUALITY: OPPORTUNITY VERSUS RESULTS: The gains of the civil rights movement in the 1960s were mostly in the area of opportunity; racial politics today concerns actual inequalities between whites and blacks in incomes, jobs, housing, health, education, etc.

A.   Continuing Inequalities: Table 15-2 shows that there is still a gulf of inequality between blacks, Hispanics, and whites. Blacks are less likely to hold prestigious executive jobs or many skilled craft jobs.

B.   Explaining Inequalities: One explanation may be continuing discrimination.

C.   Policy Choices? What should be done to achieve equality? Should color-blind standards be used or should the government take affirmative action to remedy the results of past unequal treatment of blacks by giving preferential treatment in university admissions and scholarships, jobs and promotions, etc.

D.   Shifting Goals in Civil Rights Policy: From equal opportunity, the goals shifted to affirmative action involving the establishment of "goals and timetables" to achieve greater equality. While avoiding use of the word "quota," the notion of affirmative action observes whether blacks achieve admissions, jobs, and promotions in proportion to their numbers in the population.

E.   Affirmative Action: These programs were initially developed in the federal bureaucracy. President Johnson signed Executive Order 11246 in 1965 which required all businesses that contracted with the federal government to implement affirmative action programs. In 1972, the U.S. Office of Education issued guidelines which mandated goals for university admissions and faculty hiring of minorities and women. Federal officials generally measure "progress" in terms of the number of disadvantaged group members hired, admitted, employed, etc. The pressure to show "progress" can result in a relaxation of traditional measures of qualification, such as test scores. Advocates of affirmative action argue that these are not valid since they are biased in favor of white culture.

VI.   AFFIRMATIVE ACTION IN THE COURTS: The Constitution question involved is whether affirmative action programs discriminate against whites in violation of the equal protection clause of the Fourteenth Amendment and the Civil Rights Act of 1964. The Court has not developed thus far any clear-cut answers.

A.　The Bakke Case: Allan Bakke applied for medical school at the University of California. For two years he was denied admission, even though minorities with lower GPAs and medical aptitude tests were admitted. A special program reserved 16 of the 100 annual admissions for minority students. The university argued that its programs were designed to help minorities. The Supreme Court in *University of California Regents v. Bakke* ruled that while race could be a factor, it could not be the sole factor and ordered Bakke's admission. To use race as a sole factor would be a violation of the equal protection clause of the Fourteenth Amendment. Both opponents and supporters of affirmative action claimed victory: race was upheld as a legitimate factor in affirmative action. Bakke was admitted.

B.　Affirmative Action as a Remedy for Past Discrimination: The Court has continued to approve affirmative action programs designed to remedy past discrimination. The Court upheld in 1979 a training plan designed to help minorities into skilled technical jobs. Weber, who was white, was denied this training opportunity while blacks with less seniority and fewer qualifications were accepted. In 1987, the Court upheld a rigid 50 percent quota system for promotions in the Alabama Department of Safety. The court felt that whatever burdens were placed on innocent parties were out weighed by the need to correct the effects of past discrimination.

C.　Cases Questioning Affirmative Action: The Court has never adopted the color-blind standard which would claim that the Constitution makes no recognition of color. To do this would mean that there would be no room for any racial considerations. However the Court has said that any racial classifications must be subject to "strict scrutiny."

D.　Affirmative Action in Universities: The *Hopwood* case has inspired court challenges to admission policies.

E.　Identifying a Clear Constitutional Principle: There is no clear rule of law, or legal test, or constitutional principle that tells us what is permissible and what is prohibited in racially conscious laws and practices. Still, over time some general tendencies have appeared. Policies are more likely to be found constitutional when they are:

1.　Response to a past proven history of discrimination.
2.　Narrowly tailored.
3.　No absolute bar to white competition or participation.

4. Serve clearly identified, compelling, and legitimate government objectives.

VII. BATTLES OVER AFFIRMATIVE ACTION: Congress has also played a role in affirmative action. Mindful of the public's support of affirmative action in the abstract, but resistance to "quotas and preferences," Congress has tried to steer a middle course.

A. Affirmative Action in the Workplace: The CRA of 1964 bars racial or sexual discrimination in employment. Can statistical underrepresentation of minorities or women prove discrimination absent any specific concrete evidence of direct discrimination? If an employer uses a job requirement or test that has a disparate effect on minorities or women, who has the burden of proof to show that the requirement or test is relevant to effective job performance? In 1989, a closely divided Court held that statistical imbalance by itself was insufficient and that plaintiffs had the burden of proof.

B. Civil Rights and Women's Equity Act of 1991: Civil rights groups alarmed at the Supreme Court's narrowing of the CRA sought help from Congress to rewrite the section of the CRA to restore these protections. Businesses fought to avoid quotas. Congress in writing the bill specifically outlawed the use of quotas. Other important provisions include:

1. Statistical imbalances **FILL-IN**.
2. Disparate Employment Practices **FILL-IN**.

C. Public Opinion and Affirmative Action: Most Americans agree that discrimination still exists today, even if they do not agree on what to do about it. There is, however, significant differences across racial and ethnic groups in the degree to which they believe it exists.

D. The California Civil Rights Initiative: **FILL-IN.**

VIII. GENDER EQUALITY AND THE FOURTEENTH AMENDMENT: The Supreme Court has never interpreted the equal protection clause to give the same level of protection to gender as to racial equality. Indeed, in 1873, the Supreme Court specifically rejected arguments that this clause applied to women.

A. Early Feminist Politics: **FILL-IN**.

B. Judicial Scrutiny of Gender Classifications: Early in the 1970s, the Court became responsive to arguments that sex discrimination may violate the equal protection clause of the Fourteenth Amendment. In 1971, the Court ruled that sexual classification must be reasonable not arbitrary. Since then, the Court has also ruled:

1. The state cannot set different gender ages to become legal adults or purchase alcohol.
2. Women cannot be barred from police or firefighting jobs by arbitrary height and weight requirements.
3. Insurance and retirement plans for women must pay the same benefits.
4. Men and women coaches must receive the same pay in high school sports.

C. Continuing Gender Differences: The Court continues to grapple with the question of gender differences in the law. It has upheld statutory rape laws which make it a crime for an adult to have sex with a female under the age of 18, regardless of her consent. The Court upheld the draft registration of men only. Women in the military can serve in air and naval combat units, but remain excluded from combat infantry, armor, artillery, and special forces.

D. Aims of the Equal Rights Amendment: **FILL-IN.**

X. GENDER EQUALITY IN THE ECONOMY: As cultural views of women have changed and family budgets need two wage earners, women's participation in the work force has increased. With this, feminist political activity has shifted toward economic concerns--gender equality in education, employment, pay etc.

A. Gender Equality in Civil Rights Laws:

1. Title VII of the CRA of 1964 prohibits sexual discrimination in employment, pay, and promotions. The EEOC bars stereotyping of men's and women's jobs.
2. The Federal Equal Credit Opportunity Act of 1974 prohibits gender discrimination in credit transactions.
3. Title XI prohibits sex discrimination in education. This bars discrimination in admissions, housing, financial aid, faculty and staff recruitment and pay, and athletics.

B. The Earning Gap: Women earn on average 76 percent of what men earn. This wage difference is attributable to the labor market division of traditionally male and female jobs with the former paying more and not direct discrimination.

C. The Dual Labor Market and "Comparable Worth": The dual labor market with male-dominated "blue-collar" jobs distinguishable from female-dominated "pink-collar" jobs remains a major obstacle to pay equality between men and women. Women's choices of employment have been limited by cultural stereotyping, social conditioning, and training and education. Recognizing that wage equalities may be more a result of occupational differentiation rather than discrimination, some have called for <u>comparable</u> <u>worth</u> in the labor market. Advocates recommend that jobs should be evaluated by their responsibilities, effort, knowledge and skill requirements, and that jobs judged "comparable" should be paid the same wages. This approach raises many issues--who selects the standards? Who decides what wages should be equal? So far, the comparable worth has been rejected by the EEOC and federal courts, but has been accepted by a few state governments and employers.

D.   The "Glass Ceiling": **FILL-IN.**

XI.   HISPANICS IN AMERICA/HISPANIC POLITICS: The term Hispanic includes Mexican Americans, Puerto Ricans, Cubans, and others of Spanish-speaking ancestry and culture. Percentages follow the same order--the largest number of Hispanics are Mexican Americans, etc. Median family income for Hispanics is higher than blacks but lower than whites. The same is true of poverty levels and unemployment rates. The percentage of Hispanics completing high school is lower that blacks or whites. Yet the term Hispanic masks substantial differences among the various groups.

A.   Mexican Americans: **FILL-IN. WHY DOES MEXICAN AMERICAN POLITICAL POWER NOT MATCH THEIR POPULATION PERCENTAGE?**

B.   Puerto Ricans: **FILL-IN. WHAT EXPLANATION IS OFFERED TO EXPLAIN THE LOWER MEDIAN INCOME AND POVERTY OF PUERTO RICANS?**

C.   Cuban Americans: **FILL-IN. HOW DO CUBAN AMERICANS COMPARE ECONOMICALLY WITH OTHER HISPANIC GROUPS?**

D.   Organizing for Political Activity: **FILL-IN.**

E.   Hispanic Political Power: What was Proposition 187?

F.   Lower voter turnout among Mexican Americans is associated with language problems, low education level, and poverty. Most Hispanics identify with the Democratic Party.

G.   Hispanic Members of the House equal about 4 percent.

XII.   NATIVE AMERICANS: TRAILS OF TEARS: It is estimated that 7 to 13 million Native Americans lived in the U.S. and Canada before the arrival of the Spanish. Twenty-five more million lived in Mexico. There was not a single Indian nation, but rather hundreds of separate cultures and languages. The native population of the Americas was devastated by wars, disease, and famine. Overall, the population declined by 90 percent, the greatest disaster in human history. Diseases brought from Europe were the most effective killers--smallpox, measles, bubonic plague, influenza, typhus, etc. By 1910, there were only 210,000 Native Americans in the U.S. Since then, the population has climbed to 2.2 million, which is less than 1 percent of the American population.

A.   The Trail of Broken Treaties: In the Northwest Ordinance of 1787 and the Intercourse Act of 1790, the U.S. government promised to respect the territorial integrity of Indian lands, yet these promises were repeatedly violated by white invasions of these lands with subsequent wars that led to further loss of native lands.

B.   "Indian Territories": **FILL-IN. WHAT HAPPENED TO THE INDIAN TERRITORIES?**

C.   "Indian Wars": The continuing encroachment of Indian territories by white settles and hunters who decimated the buffalo herds led to malnutrition and demoralization of the Indian Plains peoples, which resulted in a long period of war. The most historic battle was that of the Little Bighorn River where Civil War hero General George Armstrong Custer and elements of the Seventh Calvary were destroyed by Sioux and Cheyenne Indians lead by Chief Crazy Horse. The Apaches under Geronimo also fought hard, but by 1890 Indian resistance was at an end.

D.   The Attempted Destruction of Traditional Life: The Dawes Act of 1887 governed federal policy toward Native Americans for decades. It broke up traditional Indian lands into homesteads to encourage the Native Americans to become farmers instead of hunters. Traditional native culture, traditions, and language were to be shed for English and traditional schooling. The net effect was the loss of 50 percent of native lands. The Bureau of Indian Affairs, which was supposed to look after the Native Americans, was corrupt and poorly managed. It encouraged dependency and interfered with native religious affairs and customs. The Native Americans suffered high infant mortality rates, poverty, and alcoholism.

E.   The New Deal: **FILL-IN.**

F.   The American Indian Movement: The civil rights movement in the 1960s inspired Indian activists. The American Indian Movement (AIM) was founded in 1968 and occupied Alcatraz Island and the site of the Wounded Knee battle. Several Indian nations pressed their claims in Congress and the federal courts to win back lands or compensation for lands taken in violation of treaties. Native culture was revitalized and best-selling books were written of the Indian's plight.

G.   Native Americans Today: **FILL-IN. WHAT IS THE STATUS OF NATIVE AMERICANS? ARE THEY ANY BETTER OFF TODAY?**

XIII.   THE RIGHTS OF DISABLED AMERICANS: Disabled Americans were not included in the landmark Civil Rights Act of 1964. Yet they have long suffered obstacles to participation in education, employment, and access to public accommodations. The Americans with Disabilities Act (ADA) of 1990 prohibits discrimination against disabled people in private employment, public accommodations, and telecommunications. The act is vague in many parts, providing lawyers and bureaucrats with much employment over the next several years. Specifically, the ADA provides:

A.   Employment: Employers should make reasonable accommodations for disabled employees, but are excused if these accommodations would cause undue hardship to the employer.

B.   Government Programs: The disabled cannot be denied access to government programs or benefits. New taxis, buses, and trains must be accessible.

C.   Public Accommodations: **FILL-IN. WHAT TYPE OF ALTERATIONS MUST BE DONE TO ACCOMMODATE THE HANDICAPPED?**

D.   Communications: Devices must be available for the hearing or speech impaired to the extent possible.

XIV.   INEQUALITY AND THE CONSTITUTION: Americans often claim rights that are not based on the Constitution--medical care, education, retirement benefits, and jobs. The Constitution is designed to limit the government, not mandate that it governs justly or wisely.

A.   Constitutional versus Legal Rights: All the benefits mentioned above come from laws passed by Congress, i.e. are legal rights as opposed to Constitutional rights.

B.   "Reasonable" Classifications: Government programs may classify people by income, age, illness, disability or any other "reasonable" standard. The equal protection clause of the Fourteenth Amendment has been interpreted by the Supreme Court to prohibit "invidious discrimination" by the government, but does not prohibit "reasonable classifications" of individuals. The equal protection clause does require that once such a classification is made, those meeting the eligibility must receive the same benefits. These benefits are legal requirements not constitutional. Therefore, Congress could change the benefits or eligibility as they desire.

C. Protections for Poor Americans: The Constitution does provide some protection for the poor's legal and political rights. Included among these rights are:

1. Free legal counsel in criminal cases.
2. No tax or financial requirement for voting.

But the poor cannot demand government funding as a constitutional right to exercise other rights. For example, the Hyde Amendment in 1977 denied government funding for Medicaid abortions. The Supreme Court recognized that abortions were a constitutional right, but that federal funding of them was not required by the Constitution.

D. Income Inequality: The government does not have any constitutional requirement to eliminate inequality of wealth or income. In fact, the founding fathers thought that any such requirement would violate the right to property. Minority groups have charged that unequal public school spending discriminates against poor children. But the Supreme Court disagreed, holding the spending differences based on dependence on property taxes and the value of property did not violate the equal protection clause. Some state courts have held that such inequalities do violate state constitutions.

CHAPTER FIFTEEN SAMPLE QUESTIONS

TRUE-FALSE:

1. The equal sharing of income and wealth would be described as equality of opportunity.

2. Traditionally equality was reserved for individuals rather than groups.

3. The court has adopted a color-blind standard for U.S. policy.

4. Racial imbalance in schools is grounds enough for the courts to require remedies.

5. Most Americans believe that the problem of discrimination has been overcome.

6. Once the Supreme Court in the *Brown* case announced that segregated schools were unconstitutional, integrated schools were rapidly operated in their place.

7. The Constitution does not govern the activities of private individuals. Only Congress at the national level could outlaw discrimination in the private sector.

8. The Comparable Worth doctrine was developed to help bridge the gap between white and black earnings.

9. Legal rights are those set forth by Congress.

10. Jim Crow laws were designed to overcome segregation in the south.

MULTIPLE-CHOICE:

11. Affirmative action programs are most likely to be upheld if:
    a. They are narrowly tailored
    b. They serve clearly defined, compelling government objectives
    c. They are adopted in response to a history of discrimination
    d. All of the above

12. What legislation prohibits discrimination in the rental or sale of housing?
    a. Civil Rights Act of 1957   b. Civil Rights Act of 1964
    c. Civil Rights Act of 1968   d. Civil Rights Act of 1871

13. Which of the following is included in the Constitution as protection for the poor?
    a. Free education
    b. Free legal counsel in criminal cases
    c. Health care funding
    d. All of the above

14. Which of the following Supreme Court cases upheld state segregation laws:
    a. Civil Rights cases of 1883   b. *Plessy v. Ferguson*
    c. *Brown v. Board of Education*   d. *South Carolina v. Kazenbach*

15. Among the more important provisions of the Civil Rights Act of 1991 are all but one of the following:
    a. Statistical workforce imbalance does not prove discrimination
    b. Quotas are permissible for certain industries
    c. Employers bear the burden of proving that a job's disparate impact bears some relationship to effective job performance
    d. Victims of discrimination can obtain both compensatory and punitive awards

16. Which of the following black leaders was influential in the founding of the NAACP?
    a. Booker T. Washington   b. W.E.B. Du Bois
    c. Oscar de Priest   d. Thurgood Marshall

17. In the important *Swann v. Charlotte-Mecklenburg County Board of Education*, the Supreme Court upheld all but one of the following:
    a. Racially balanced schools and assignment of pupils to schools based on race.
    b. Court ordered busing to achieve racial balance
    c. Close scrutiny by judges of schools that are of one race
    d. Using the above remedies when past or present government action did not contribute to racial unbalance

18. Since 1971, the Supreme Court has issued many rulings dealing with gender disparities. All but one of the following areas were included in such court rulings:
    a. Legal age to purchase alcohol
    b. Height and weight requirements for police or firefighters
    c. Monthly payments for insurance benefits
    d. Equal availability for the military draft

19. In most socio-economic measures, Blacks compared to Hispanics are less favorably placed except in one of the following measures:
    a. Percent completing college   b. Median family income
    c. Percent below poverty level   d. Unemployment rate

20. Which of the following Supreme Court cases addressed minority set-aside construction programs?
   a. *University of California v. Bakke*
   b. *United Steelworkers of America v. Weber*
   c. *United States v. Paradise*
   d. *City of Richmond v. Crosen Co.*

CHAPTER FIFTEEN SAMPLE QUESTION ANSWERS

TRUE-FALSE:

1.   **FALSE**. This would describe equality of result. See page 545.

2.   **TRUE**. Only recently have civil rights been extended to groups. See pages 545-546.

3.   **FALSE**. The court has never accepted the color-blind standard. See page 564.

4.   **FALSE.** See page 553.

5.   **FALSE**. Most Americans believe discrimination remains a problem, but they are divided on how to resolve the problem. See page 565.

6.   **FALSE**. Although the *Brown* ruling struck down segregated schools in 21 states and the District of Columbia, compliance was slow as molasses. See page 552.

7.   **TRUE**. Congress has the power to regulate interstate commerce. If discrimination, even private, interferes with this commerce, Congress has the power to pass corrective legislation. This was the basis of the 1964 Civil Rights Act. See pages 555-557.

8.   **FALSE**. Although logically it could apply, it was developed to close the gap between male and female earning. See page 571.

9.   **TRUE.** See page 585.

10.   **FALSE**. Jim Crow laws promoted segregation. See page 548.

MULTIPLE-CHOICE:

11. **D**. Affirmative action programs are most likely to be upheld if they are narrowly tailored, they serve clearly defined, compelling government objectives, and they are adopted in response to a history of discrimination. See page 563.

12. **C**. Sometimes called the Housing Act of 1968, it was amended in 1988 to cover the handicapped and families with children. See page 538.

13. **B**. Only free legal counsel is provided in the Constitution. See page 585.

14. **B**. It was in the infamous *Plessy v. Ferguson* decision that the lone dissenter, Justice John Marshall Harlan, stated that the Constitution is color blind. See page 549.

15. **B**. Quotas were specifically forbidden by the Act. See page 565.

16. **B**. Du Bois was on the original board of the NAACP when it was founded in 1909 on the 100th anniversary of the birth of Lincoln. See pages 550-551.

17. **D**. None of the remedies are allowed if government action did not contribute to the racial unbalance. See page 553.

18. **D**. Laws excluding women from the draft were upheld by the Supreme Court. See page 570.

19. **B**. More blacks complete college than Hispanics, but in the other categories Hispanics are more favorably placed than blacks. See page 575.

20. **D**. The Court voided a 30 percent set-aside program of the City of Richmond for minority contractors. See page 562.

CHAPTER SIXTEEN: POLITICS AND THE ECONOMY

I.   POLITICS AND ECONOMICS: Politics involves collective decisions and government coercion. A free market economic system involves individual decisions and relies on voluntary exchanges. Both politics and markets transform popular demands into goods and services. The proper relationship between politics and economics lies in the field of study called political economy.

II.   COMPETING ECONOMIC THEORIES: These competing theories attempt to explain the forces that generate demand--the purchase of goods and services and supply--the willingness and ability of firms to produce the goods and services. Macroeconomic theories also attempt to explain inflation--a general rise of prices; recession--a general decline in economic activity; and economic growth--an increase in the nation's total economic output, normally measured by the real (inflation adjusted) gross domestic product (GDP).

   A.   Classical Theory: In essence, this theory envisions minimal government intervention in the market which will be self-regulating by an invisible hand of the marketplace. Classical economists say that the normal forces of supply and demand will regulate the economy.

   B.   Keynesian Theory: The Great Depression of the 1930s shattered faith in classical economic theory. Unemployment averaged 18% for several years, reaching a high of 25 percent in 1933. John Maynard Keynes believed that economic instability was the fault of lowered demand. Unemployment and lower wages reduced demand for goods and services. Reduced demand led to further layoffs and cuts in production. These in turn led to further reductions in demand, and the spiral continued. Reduction of interest rates would not spur businesses to borrow money if production in demand was falling. Keynes saw that the economy would not turn around unless demand was increased. Therefore, government should spend more money to increase demand, and lower taxes to stimulate consumer and business spending, i.e., increased demand. In this situation, the government might have to run up a deficit. During inflationary periods, the government should take the opposite course--cut its spending, raise taxes, and run a budget surplus. The net effect of these actions would be to reduce demand and thus check inflation by stabilizing or lowering prices.

   C.   Employment Act of 1946: Keyne's ideas were codified into law in the Employment Act of 1946 which pledged that the federal government would promote maximum employment production and purchasing power through its taxing and spending policies. The act also created the Council of Economic Advisors to develop and recommend to the president national economic policies. The act also required the president to present an annual economic report to the Congress. While most economists endorse Keynesian theory, politicians have more of a problem with unemployment than inflation. Once in the habit of deficit spending, politicians are reluctant to raise taxes and cut spending to halt inflation and create a budget surplus. The Keynesian theory also had a problem in the 1970s when the U.S. economy experienced both high <u>unemployment</u> <u>and</u> <u>inflation</u> which should not occur simultaneously. This period also saw law economic growth and led to a new word-<u>stagflation</u>--a period of low economic growth and rising prices.

D.   Supply Side Economics: **FILL-IN.**

E.   Monetarist Economics: While Keynesian theory provided for the expansion of the money supply during a recession and the contraction of the money supply in inflationary periods, monetarist economic theory holds that the expansion of the money supply should be at the same rate as economic growth. They do not agree that manipulation of the money supply effectively influences economic activity. They argue that in the long run real income depends on actual economic output. In short, they feel government manipulation of the money supply is the problem, not the solution to economic inactivity.

F.   Politics and Economic Theory: Political liberals usually support Keynesian economics because it is consistent with the belief that government can/should be used to correct societal problems. Conservatives usually espouse classical supply-side economics because of its minimalist use of government.

III.   ECONOMIC DECISION MAKING: National fiscal policy focuses on taxing, spending, and borrowing by the federal government. The system of checks and balances functions in this area. Within the executive branch, responsibility for economic policy is divided among the White House, the Office of Management and Budget (OMB), the Treasury Department, the Council of Economic Advisors, and the powerful, yet independent, Federal Reserve Board.

A.   Congress and the President: The Constitution places all taxing, borrowing and spending powers in the hands of Congress. By terms of the pay all debts and provide for the common defense and general welfare clause in Article I, the Supreme Court held that any spending that serves the general welfare is allowed. Thus, there is no constitutional barrier to spending or borrowing by Congress. Efforts have been made to pass a balanced budget amendment to the Constitution, but these efforts have not been successful to date. While the president has little formal powers in this area, presidents have acquired leadership over national economic policy by virtue of submitting the budget of the U.S. government. In this document, the president lays out his proposals for spending, revenue estimates based on tax levels, and the estimates for projected deficits and the need for borrowing if this is necessary.

B. The President's Economic Team: There are three main players on the team:

1. The Office of Management and Budget: This office prepares the budget of the U.S. and also oversees the budget requests of every federal department and agency.
2. The Department of the Treasury: **FILL-IN.**
3. The Council of Economic Advisors: A small body of three eminent economists and staff, they prepare forecasts of economic conditions and make recommendations on economic policies, principally in its "Economic Report to the President."

C. The Federal Reserve Board: Most advanced nations have a central bank to regulate the supply of money and have found it best to remove this bank from direct control of elected politicians. These are tempted to pay for government programs by issuing more money rather than raising taxes. This results in inflation. The Federal Reserve is largely independent of the president and the Congress. It is governed by a seven member board of governors, nominated by the president and confirmed by the Senate for 14 year terms. While members can be removed for cause, none have ever been removed since its creation in 1913. The chairman of the board's term is four years, but it overlaps the term of the president, so new presidents cannot immediately name their own chair. The Fed regulates the supply of money to control inflation and recession. It also oversees the operation of the 12 federal reserve banks, which actually issue the nation's currency, which is called federal reserve notes. The federal reserve banks are bankers' banks; they do not serve the general public. They hold the deposits, or reserves of banks, lend money to banks at discount rates, and oversee the operation of the nation's banking system. They also act as a clearing house for checks throughout the banking system. The Fed influences the economy mainly through increasing or decreasing the nation's money supply. When inflation threatens, the Fed:

1. Raises the reserve requirement for member banks, thereby decreasing the amount of money in circulation.
2. Raises the discount rate for loans to member banks.
3. Sells off government bonds and notes in the market to withdraw money in circulation.

D. Politics and Monetary Policy: Although the Fed makes the nation's monetary policy, the voters hold the president accountable for the economy.

Accordingly, the president and often Congress try to influence Fed policy, especially in election years.

IV. **THE PERFORMANCE OF THE AMERICAN ECONOMY:** The U.S. economy produces about $10 trillion in goods and services annually for 275 million people or about $35,000 in output for every citizen.

A. Economic Growth: <u>Gross</u> <u>Domestic</u> <u>Product (GDP)</u> is a widely used measure of economic performance. It is the nation's total production of goods and services and counts only final purchase of goods and services. For example, it does not count the purchase of steel by an auto manufacturer, but does count the price of the car. This avoids double counting. GDP also excludes financial transactions and income transfers, such as Social Security. Although expressed in current dollars, GDP is also often calculated in constant dollars to reflect real values over time, adjusting for inflation. GDP estimates are prepared by the Commerce Department every quarter. Growth in constant dollars measures the overall performance of the economy. Economic recessions and recoveries are measured as fluctuations in GDP. For example, a recession is defined as negative GDP growth in two successive quarters. Economic growth has historically been followed by periods of contraction. In recent decades, the fluctuations have been more moderate suggesting to many economists that counter-cyclical government fiscal and monetary policies have succeeded in greater stability.

B. Unemployment: From a political viewpoint, unemployment may be the most important measure of the economy. Unemployment is different than not working. For example, retired persons are not unemployed, nor are those who are sick or attending school. Unemployed is defined as those looking for work or waiting to return to a job. The unemployed include those terminated from their last job, those temporarily laid off, those who voluntarily quit, those who entered the labor market for the first time, and 10 percent who have reentered the labor market. The unemployment rate is calculated monthly by the Labor Department by a random sampling of 50,000 households. The unemployment rate fluctuates with the business cycle, but generally lags GDP growth.

C. Inflation: Refers to the general rise of prices for all goods and services. Inflation erodes the value of the dollar, because it takes more money to purchase the same amount of goods. Since money has less value, savings are devalued as well, which reduces the incentive to save. Those living on fixed incomes, such as retired persons, are also hurt by inflation. When banks and investors anticipate inflation, they charge more interest for loans to offset the lower value of the inflated dollar. This, in turn, makes it harder to expand businesses, buy homes, or make credit purchases. Thus, inflation harms economic growth.

V.   "UNCONTROLLABLE" GOVERNMENT SPENDING AND FEDERAL BUDGET PRIORITIES: All government spending equaled 30 percent of GDP. The federal government alone spends $1.8 trillionor 18 percent of GDP.

A.   Much of the growth of the federal budget is attributed to uncontrollables:

1. Entitlement Programs: These are programs which provide legally enforceable rights to beneficiaries, and they account for over half of all federal spending. Some notable programs include Social Security, Medicare, federal retirements, and veterans benefits. These programs pay benefits regardless of the need of the recipient. Other entitlement programs are based on demonstrated need and these include welfare, Medicaid, and food stamps. Note that these are not constitutional entitlements, but rather legal ones. Congress could change the law modifying or eliminating a benefit and indeed has passed a welfare reform bill. Note that entitlement payments do not go only to the poor. Social Security, Medicare, federal retirements, and veterans benefits amount to two-thirds of these entitlements, while payments to the poor are only one-third of these payments.

2. Indexing of Benefits: Congress has indexed some benefits to automatically increase to match inflation. Indexing applies to programs such as Social Security, Supplemental Security Income, food stamps, and veterans pensions. This indexing pushes up the cost of these entitlement programs every year and contributes to inflation. Further, the Consumer Price Index used to calculate the index includes interest on homes and purchases of new appliances and cars. Older retirees may have already paid off their mortgages, and do not buy many new appliances and cars as working persons. Thus, the CPI and index may overestimate the needs of these older recipients for cost-of-living increases.

3. Increasing Cost of In-kind Benefits: **FILL-IN.**

4. Interest on the National Debt: **FILL-IN.**

5. Backdoor Spending and Loan Guarantees: Some federal spending does not appear in the budget, e.g., the U.S. Postal Service. Government guaranteed loans also do not, yet a default on these loans creates a fiscal obligation on the part of the federal government.

B.   Federal Budget Priorities: Federal budget shares reflect the spending priorities of the nation. For example, spending for national defense has dropped while spending for Social Security, welfare, and Medicare has grown very rapidly. Entitlement programs will grow, as medical costs are the fastest growing sector of the federal budget. Interest costs will increase unless Congress balances the federal budget.

VI.   THE DEBT BURDEN: The accumulated national debt is over $5.5 trillion or about $20,000 per capita. This debt is owed mostly to banks and financial institutions and individual investors. About 13 percent is owed to foreign banks or individuals. The floating of this huge debt depends on continued public confidence that the federal government can continue to pay interest on the debt, and pay off bonds when they become due.

    A.   Default and Hyperinflation: No one expects the U.S. government to default on its debt--refuse to pay interest when due. But in the past, other nations have done so. Some future administration may be tempted to monetarize the debt--that is, print more money to pay off bondholders. Such currency would flood the nation and soon become worthless, resulting in hyperinflation annual inflation between 100-1,000 percent. Both would appear to be unlikely in the near future.

    B.   Interest Burden for Future Generations: **FILL-IN.**

    C.   The Long-Sought Balanced Budget: In 1998, the U.S. government had a surplus for the first time in 30 years.

    D.   Politics, Deficits, and Surpluses: How should the surplus be spent? **FILL-IN.**

VII.   THE TAX BURDEN: The U.S. tax burden is modest compared to other countries. Federal revenue is derived from five sources:

    A.   Individual Income Tax: This is the government's largest source of revenue (See Figure 16-3). Individual income is now taxed at five marginal rates: 15, 28, 31, 36 and 39.6 percent. That is, up to a certain income level, one pays 15 percent, the next income level pays 28 percent, etc. Personal exemptions and refundable earned income tax credit relieve the poorest families from paying any income tax. Tax brackets, personal exemptions, and standard deductions are indexed to protect against inflation. Income tax is automatically deducted from the paychecks of employees. This withholding system is the backbone of the individual income tax. Naturally, the government pays no interest on the money it withholds. About half of personal income is not taxed due to exemptions, deductions, etc. These are called tax expenditures, which represent revenue lost to the government. Among the major tax expenditures are:

        1.   Personal exemptions.

2.   Home mortgage interest.
3.   Property taxes paid on first and second homes.
4.   Deferral of capital gains taxes on home sales.
5.   **FILL IN.**
6.   **FILL IN.**
7.   **FILL IN.**
8.   Exclusion of Social Security benefits.
9.   **FILL IN.**
10.   State and local income taxes paid.
11.   **FILL IN.**
12.   Accelerated depreciation for machinery, equipment and structures.
13.   Medical expenses over 7.5 percent of income.

Much of the political infighting in Washington involves the efforts of interest groups to obtain exemptions, deductions, special treatments, etc.

B.   Corporate Income Taxes: Corporate income tax provides only about 10 percent of the federal government's total revenue. The Tax Reform Act of 1986 lowered corporate tax from 46 to 34 percent and eliminated many of the provisions which had allowed many corporations to pay little or no tax up to this point. There remains a question of who really bears the burden of this tax-the corporations or the consumers to whom it is passed.

C.   Social Security Taxes: This is the second largest and fastest-growing source of federal revenue. It is also withheld from paychecks as an FICA tax and is currently 15.3 percent of income, one half paid by the employer and one-half by the employee. Since these taxes are largely earmarked for Social Security, those paying FICA feel they have a right to Social Security. After all, they have paid for it. Or have they? Less than 15 percent of benefits paid today to current Social Security recipients can be attributed to their prior contributions. Current taxpayers pay 85 percent of the benefits received by current retirees. Today 75 percent of taxpayers pay more in Social Security taxes than income taxes.

D.   Estate and Gift Taxes: Federal estate taxes begin on estates in excess of $650,000. Any amount over this is taxed at a range of 18 to 55 percent. To avoid the wealthy giving away their estate before death, any gift in excess of $10,000 is taxed.

E.   Excise Taxes and Custom Duties: Federal taxes on liquor, tobacco, gasoline, telephones, air travel and luxury times plus customs duties amount to about 30 percent of federal revenue.

VIII.   TAX POLITICS: Who bears the heaviest burden of taxes is at the heart of tax politics. <u>Progressive</u> <u>taxation</u> requires higher-income groups to pay a larger percentage of their income than lower-income groups. <u>Regressive</u> <u>taxation</u> takes a larger share from low-income groups. A <u>proportional</u> <u>or</u> <u>flat</u> <u>tax</u> requires all income groups to pay the same percent of their income.

A. The Argument for Progressivity: This type of taxation is based on the theory that those with the ability to pay more taxes should pay more taxes and the marginal utility theory as it applies to money. That is, each additional amount of income is less valuable to an individual. Thus, for someone earning $1 million a year, an additional $5,000 would hardly be noticed, but for someone earning $25,000 per year, an additional $5,000 would mean a great deal.

B. <u>The</u> <u>Argument</u> <u>for</u> <u>Proportionality</u>: **FILL-IN.**

C. Reagan's Reductions in Progressivity: The top marginal rate fell from 70 to 28 percent and the Tax Reform Act of 1986 reduced 14 tax brackets to only two-15 and 28 percent.

D. Read My Lips: At the Republican National Convention in 1988, George Bush promised not to raise taxes in his administration. Yet in a 1990 budget deal with the Democratic Congress he accepted a hike in the top marginal rate from 28 percent to 31 percent. Breaking the solemn pledge hurt Bush in the 1992 presidential campaign.

E. Soak the Rich: These proposals are always very popular. President Clinton pushed Congress to raise the top marginal rate to 36 percent for families earning $140,000 and 39.6 percent for those earning $250,000. These hikes did not bring in that much new revenue since so few families earn these amounts. Moreover, higher tax rates encouraged more people to find tax shelters and other means of tax avoidance.

F. Capital Gains Taxation: All income is not taxed equally. Interest income from municipal bonds is a tax expenditure for the federal government. Capital gains made on income producing property is taxed differently than personal income. The current top rate for capital gains is 20%, while for personal income it is 39.6%. This difference is testimony to the power of the real estate, investment firm, and stockbrokers lobby. A major goal of tax reform is to treat all income equally.

CHAPTER SIXTEEN SAMPLE QUESTIONS

TRUE-FALSE:

1. A free market economic system involves collective decisions, while a political system involves individual decisions.

2. A political liberal is more likely to favor Keynesian economic policies.

3. Currently, the federal deficit is at its highest point ever.

4. The Gross Domestic Product (GDP) is used as an indicator of economic performance.

5. The President's budget proposal is prepared by the Treasury Department.

6. The Federal Reserve regulates the supply of money in the market.

7. Since the Federal Reserve control the money supply which affects the economy, voters hold the Fed responsible for bad times.

8. Much of the growth in federal government spending can be attributed to "uncontrollable" budget items.

9. The capital gains tax is a tax on profits derived from the buying and selling of property.

10. The Social Security tax is the largest source of revenue in the federal government.

MULTIPLE-CHOICE:

11. Which of the following would be considered a reason for the increases in the size of the federal budget deficit?
    a. Increasing costs of in-kind benefits
    b. Interest on the national debt
    c. Backdoor spending
    d. All of the above

12. The major tax expenditures in the federal tax law include:
    a. Property tax on second homes
    b. Child care credit
    c. Charitable contributions
    d. All of the above
    e. None of the above

13. Whose ideas were codified in the Employment Act of 1946
    a. Adam Smith   b. John Smith
    c. John Maynard Keynes   d. Milton Freidman

14. Which of the following actions by a national government would not be acceptable according to Keynesian theory in a recession?
    a. Cut taxes   b. Increase government spending
    c. Raise taxes   d. Spend more than income

15. When the economy is moribund and prices are increasing, this phenomenon is called:
    a. Inflation   b. Stagflation
    c. Recession   d. Depression

16. Which one of the following is not a principal player in the executive branch in determining economic policy?
    a. OMB
    b. Council of Economic Advisors
    c. Treasury Department
    d. Commerce Department.

17. Federal reserve governors are appointed for_____year terms:
    a. 5   b. 10   c. 14   d. 4

18. Which of the following is not an uncontrolled budget item.
    a. Medicaid   b. Defense spending
    c. Social Security   d. Federal retirements

19. In the face of inflation, the Fed would take all but one of the following actions:
    a. Increase reserve requirement   b. Sell government securities
    c. Buy government securities   d. Raise the discount rate

20. Gross Domestic Product (GDP) includes all but one of the following:
    a. Annual production of goods and service
    b. Maid service
    c. Social security
    d. Bake goods

CHAPTER SIXTEEN SAMPLE QUESTION ANSWERS:

TRUE-FALSE:

1.   **FALSE.** It is just the opposite relationship. See page 591.

2.   **TRUE.** A political liberal is more likely to favor Keynesian economic policies. See page 594.

3.   **FALSE.** We have had higher deficits at various times in our history. See page 604.

4.   **TRUE.** See page 598.

5.   **FALSE.** It is done by OMB. See page 596.

6.   **TRUE.** See page 596.

7.   **FALSE.** They hold the president responsible. See page 597.

8.   **TRUE.** A large portion of federal expenditure over the years has been on "uncontrollables." See page 600.

9.   **TRUE.** See page 615.

10.   **FALSE.** Individual income taxes provide the most, but Social Security taxes are gaining rapidly. See page 611.

MULTIPLE-CHOICE:

11. **D.** Increasing costs of in-kind benefits, interest on the national debt, and backdoor spending all can be considered reasons for the increases in the size of the federal budget deficit. See page 602.

12. **D.** The major tax expenditures in the federal tax law include property tax on second homes, child care credit, and charitable contributions. See page 609.

13. **C.** Keyne's ideas were centered around full employment. See page 592.

14. **C.** Raising taxes would only be done in good times, not bad times. See page 592.

15. **B.** This condition is called stagflation. See page 593.

16. **D**. Only the Commerce Department is odd man out. See page 596.

17. **C**. Fourteen years is a long time, but this is what helps to ensure the Fed's independence. See page 596.

18. **B**. While many complain about defense spending, it has actually been coming down while entitlement spending has gone up. See page 602.

19. **C**. Selling government securities pulls money out of circulation, which helps to control inflation. Buying government securities puts money into circulation. See page 597.

20. **C**. Income transfers are not included, only final purchases. See page 598.

CHAPTER SEVENTEEN:
POLITICS AND SOCIAL WELFARE

I. **POWER AND SOCIAL WELFARE:** The federal government redistributes income from one group to another--from the working class to the poor, for example. This social welfare activity of the government is the largest and fastest growing portion of the federal budget and amounts to more than half of government outlays. Many people think of social welfare as a program for the poor, the estimated 35-40 million whose income is below the official poverty line. If the $1 trillion spent on social welfare were directly distributed to the nation's poor, each poor person would receive $25,000 per year. But most poor people are not the beneficiaries of social welfare which goes mostly in the form of Social Security and Medicare to the nonpoor. Thus, the middle class and not the poor class is the major beneficiary of the nation's social welfare.

II. **POVERTY IN THE UNITED STATES:** In 1998, the poverty line for a <u>family</u> <u>of</u> <u>four</u> was $17,000. This is the cash income considered necessary to maintain a decent standard of living. This definition of poverty has many critics:

    A. Liberal Criticism: Some critics believe poverty is underestimated for several reasons.

        1. The official definition includes cash income from social welfare and Social Security-without this income the number of poor would be much higher.

        2. It does not include the near poor, the 45-50 million Americans living below $20,000 of annual income for a family of four.

        3. It does not account for regional differences, costs of living, climate, and accepted styles of living.

        4. It does not consider what people think they need to live.

    B. Conservative Criticism:

        1. It does not consider the value of family assets. The elderly who own their own homes, furniture, and cars may have incomes below the poverty level, but not suffer hardship.

        2. **FILL-IN.**

        3. Many underreport their real income.

        4. In-kind benefits are not included: food stamps, free Medicare care, public housing, and free school lunches. If these were included, about 50 percent of the poor would move above the poverty line.

    C. Temporary Poverty: Poverty is not necessarily a lifetime experience. Only 6-8 percent of the nation's population has lived in poverty more than five years.

D. Persistent Poverty: About half of the poor on welfare rolls are persistently poor, or likely to remain on welfare more than five years. Welfare becomes a permanent part of their life. This prolonged poverty and welfare dependency it creates an underclass that suffers from many social ills-teen pregnancy, family instability, drugs, crime, etc. Government education, training, and job programs fail to benefit many of these people.

E. Family Structure: Poverty and welfare dependency are much more common in single-parent families headed by a female. Unwed parenthood has contributed to a rising number of children living in poverty. Traditionally, illegitimacy was held down by powerful religious and social structures but these have weakened over time, and the availability of welfare cash benefits has grown and removed much of the economic hardship once associated with unwed motherhood. Indeed, it is argued that well-meaning government welfare programs have perpetuated poverty and social dependency.

F. Teen Pregnancy: **FILL IN**.

G. The Truly Disadvantaged: The nation's largest cities have become the principal location of virtually most of the social problems facing our society. And the location of most of our poor class. Yet this is a recent event. As late as 1970, there were higher rates of poverty in rural areas than cities. The shift in the labor market from manufacturing jobs to professional, financial, and technical service have increasingly divided the market into high and low wage sectors. The shift in these better paying jobs to the suburbs has left inner-city dwellers with fewer and lower paying jobs, thus making a major contribution to poverty. This was compounded by the migration of middle class of the inner-city to the suburbs. The loss of these role models has made things worse.

III. SOCIAL WELFARE POLICY: Public welfare has been recognized as a government responsibility for many centuries. Today, more than one-third of the American population receives some form of government benefits. More than 50 percent of American families have at least one member who receives a government check. Thus, the welfare state covers a large part of our society. Major social welfare programs can be classified as either social insurance or public assistance. If the beneficiary made contributions for the government benefit, it is social insurance. If the program is financed out of general tax revenues and one has to prove poverty to receive the benefit, it is a public assistance program. These later programs are generally labeled welfare.

A. Entitlements: These are programs for which the government establishes an eligibility criteria--age, income, retirement, disability, unemployment, etc.

Everyone who meets the criteria is entitled to the benefits. Almost all of the entitlement programs were established either during the New Deal of Franklin Roosevelt-Social Security, AFDC, Unemployment Compensation, and Aid to Aged, Blind, and Disabled (now called Supplemental Security Income), or the Great Society of President Johnson, food stamps, Medicare, and Medicaid.

B.   Social Security: **FILL-IN. HOW MANY PEOPLE RECEIVE SOCIAL SECURITY? WHAT PERCENT OF THE WORK FORCE IS COVERED BY SOCIAL SECURITY?**

C.   Unemployment Compensation: Temporarily replaces some of the lost wages of those involuntarily out of a job and helps stabilize the economy during recessions. This program is overseen by the Department of Labor, but administered by the states and funded by federal and state unemployment taxes on employers.

D.   Supplemental Security Income: This is a means tested, federally funded program which provides a cash payment to the needy elderly (over 65), the blind and disabled (which has very loose definition covering alcoholism, drug abuse, and attention deficiency among children). This former factor has led to a rapid rise in SSI beneficiaries. Elderly immigrants were also able to collect SSI.

E.   Family Assistance: Formerly Aid to Families with Dependent Children (AFDC), this means tested, cash grant program for states is designed to assist needy children on a temporary basis. States administer the program and define eligibility (within federal guidelines).

F.   Medicare: **FILL-IN. WHAT DOES PART A COVER AND HOW IS IT FINANCED? WHAT DOES PART B COVER AND HOW IS IT FINANCED?**

G.   Medicaid: **FILL-IN. WHO RECEIVES MEDICAID?**

H.   Food Stamps: Provides low-income households with coupons to purchase food. Overseen by the federal government, but administered by the states.

I.   Earned Income Tax Credit: A "negative income tax" to assist the poor.

IV.   SENIOR POWER: Senior citizens are the most politically powerful group. While only 28 percent of the population, because they have high voter turnout, they equal more than 1/3 of voters. Compare the 65 or older turnout of 68 percent to the age 18-21 turnout of 36 percent for presidential elections and 61 percent compared to 19 percent for congressional elections. Seniors are also well represented in

Washington by the AARP.

A. The Aged in the Future: The baby boom following WWII until 1960 produced a large generation. During the boom, women averaged 3.5 births during their lifetime compared to our current 1.8 lifetime births. This boom generation will begin to retire in 2010 and by 2020 will equal 20 percent of our population. Better lifestyles (less smoking, more exercise and weight control) and advances in medicine may also extend life expectancy.

B. The Generational Compact: The framers of Social Security in 1935 created a trust fund. A reserve would be built from taxes paid by working persons. This reserve would earn interest and the combined reserve and interest would be used in later years to pay benefits. Now Social Security is financed on a pay-as-you-go basis. Income from Social Security taxes pays the benefits to those retired. This generation is paying for the last generation. This is viewed as a compact between one generation and the other.

C. The Rising Dependency Ratio: **FILL-IN. WHAT WAS THE DEPENDENCY RATIO AND WHY HAS IT INCREASED?**

D. Burdens on Generation X: Unless changes are made to the Social Security system, the current generation of young Americans may have to pay 40 percent of their income for Social Security taxes and would have to pay many times more than they would ever receive back in benefits.

E. Cost-of-Living (COLAs) Increases: **FILL-IN.**

F. Wealthy Retirees: There is no means test for Social Security. Large numbers of affluent Americans receive checks every month. Since the elderly experience less poverty than today's workers and possess more wealth, Social Security benefits for some are a negative redistribution of income-from the poorer to the more wealthy.

G. Saving Social Security: Questions continue on how to reform system.

H. The "Third Rail" of American Politics: While the most expensive program in the government, Social Security is also the most sacrosanct. For this reason, it is known as the third rail in politics--touch it and you die! Because more beneficiaries live longer and COLAs spending keeps increasing, Congress could change the law--raise the retirement age for full benefits (already scheduled to increase to age 67), limit or redefine COLAs, means test the benefit, etc.

V. POLITICS AND WELFARE REFORM: Americans face a dilemma in welfare policy. As a generous people, Americans feel government should aid those in need. On the other hand, many feel welfare fosters dependency, undermines the work ethic, contributes to illegitimate births and the breakup of families. While social insurance programs remain popular, public assistance programs are very controversial.

A.   Poverty and Public Policy: The effect of generous welfare benefits has been debated for quite some time. Surveys of welfare recipients show that they would prefer to work, but welfare benefits may have subtle effects on behavior which influence their ability to attain and keep secure jobs in the future.

B.   Reform Politics: Congress passed and President Clinton signed into law on August 22, 1996, legislation that ends 61 years of federal guarantees of cash assistance for poor children. Major elements of the welfare reform bill are:

1.   Federal cash assistance for poor children would end. Each state will receive a lump sum of federal money to run its welfare and work programs.

2.   Family heads must work within two years or the family will lose benefits.

3.   Lifetime welfare benefits are limited to five years. States may set stricter limits. Twenty percent of families can be exempt because of hardship.

4.   States may stop payments to unmarried teenage parents and may provide them only if a mother under 18 stays in school and lives with an adult.

5.   States can shift 30 percent of welfare block grants for child care, social services and child protection.

6.   States must retain their own spending on welfare at 75 percent of 1994 level or at 80 percent if they fail to put enough welfare recipients to work.

7.   States may pay benefits to cover additional children born to women on welfare.

8.   States must continue to provide Medicaid to those already covered under current law and for one year when recipients lose their benefits due to increased earnings.

9.   Future legal immigrants, not becoming citizens, would lose most benefits. SSI and food stamps for non-citizens will now end.

There was much consternation among liberals when President Clinton signed this legislation. The president indicated it was not perfect and that he would support some later changes or corrections. However, the legislation has removed people from welfare rolls.

VI.   HEALTH CARE IN AMERICA: The U.S. spends more of its resources on health care than any other nation, yet lags behind many other nations in measures of health, such as life expectancy and infant mortality. Most other democracies provide health care for all their citizens, while Americans have no guarantee of medical care. In short, the American medical care system is the most expensive and least universal in its coverage in the world.

A.   The Health of Americans: In historical terms, great advances have been made in sanitation, immunizations, clean water and air, sewage disposal, improved diets, and increased standards of living. Many of the causes of death today are linked to heredity, personal habits and lifestyles, and the physical environment. Better health is likely to be found in altered life styles and personal habits.

B.   Access to Care: **FILL-IN. WHAT PERCENTAGE OF THE AMERICAN POPULATION HAVE NO MEDICAL INSURANCE? WHAT RECOURSE DO THEY HAVE?**

C.   Coverage Gaps: Patients frequently have to pay deductibles or co-payments. Most plans do not provide prescription drugs, eyeglasses, hearing aids, or routine physical exams. Medicare does not pay for long-term care of catastrophic illness. Medicare covers only 100 days of nursing home care, if the patient is sent there from a hospital. Congress attempted to add catastrophic health care coverage to Medicare, but the surtax charge to Medicare users caused much opposition and the program was scuttled. As the elderly population grows, long-term care will be even more important. Medicaid pays for needy patient nursing-home care, but the middle class cannot qualify for Medicaid unless they spend down their savings. Thus, long term care threatens their assets and their children's inheritance. Private insurance to cover this benefit is too expensive. So senior citizens are trying to have long-term nursing care added to Medicare to be paid by all taxpayers. Also, Medicare does not pay for prescription drugs.

D.   Health Care Cost Inflation: **FILL-IN. WHAT FACTORS HAVE LED TO THE INFLATION IN HEALTH CARE?**

E.   Coping with Costs: <u>Managed care</u> is the buzzword. Private insurers have negotiated discounts from hospitals and physicians--preferred provider organizations (PPOs), health maintenance organizations (HMOs), and Medicare no longer pay hospitals what they charge, but pay fixed fees. But these reforms have generated more paperwork which medical professionals feel costs more than the savings.

VII.   POLITICS AND HEALTH CARE REFORM: Reform centers on two central problems: controlling costs and closing gaps in coverage. Both are interrelated.

A.   National Health Insurance Plans: A national health insurance plan would be paid for with tax revenue and government would be the single payer. A stipulated set of services would be an entitlement for everyone. Hospital budget costs would be negotiated. Physician fee schedules would be used. Some co-payments could be required. Most costs would be shifted from the private to the public sector.

B.   Employer-based Plans: Another option is to provide coverage through employer-based programs which would require employers to provide coverage and the government subsidies would be given to people living below the poverty line. Currently, most people attain medical coverage through employer-based programs, but the amount and type of coverage varies significantly.

C.   Clinton's Failed Comprehensive Health Care Plan: A 1992 committee headed by First Lady Hillary Clinton developed a comprehensive plan to restructure the health care system. It did not include national health insurance, but did shift reliance from the private area to the federal government. It included mandated employer-sponsored insurance, managed competition through government health purchasing alliances, and national spending caps. This proposal failed to gain congressional support. There are many reasons:

    1.   It was too comprehensive, rather than incremental. It would affect one-sixth of the national economy.

    2.   The health industry advertising campaign caused a great deal of public confusion. For the 85 percent of the population already covered by some type of health insurance, it raised more problems than it solved. Benefits went mostly to the 15 percent not insured.

    3.   Cost containment was ignored.

D.   Kennedy-Kassebaum Act: Modest reforms were attained in 1996 with this bill. It provided for the "portability" of health insurance.

E.   Prescription Drug Coverage Under Medicare: **FILL IN**.

F.   A Patients' Bill of Rights: **FILL-IN.**

G.   Interest Group Battles: **FILL IN. WHO ARE THE VARIOUS GROUPS THAT HAVE A STAKE IN THE HEALTH CARE DEBATE?**

CHAPTER SEVENTEEN SAMPLE QUESTIONS

TRUE-FALSE:

1. Poverty tends to be a long-term phenomena for most people.

2. The middle class, not the poor, are the major beneficiaries of the nation's social welfare system.

3. Wealthy retirees are not eligible for Social Security.

4. Black Americans experience poverty at roughly three times the rate of white Americans.

5. Today, nearly one-half of the U.S. population receives some form of government benefits.

6. Medicare helps low-income families obtain health care.

7. The dependency ratio is on the rise in part because people are living longer than they used to.

8. The United States spends more of its resources on health care than any other nation.

9. About 15 percent of the American population has no medical insurance.

10. Polls show that Americans are not willing to pay more taxes for comprehensive health care.

MULTIPLE-CHOICE:

11. Which of the following programs are NOT means tested?
    a. Supplemental Security Income (SSI)
    b. Family Assistance
    c. Unemployment Compensation
    d. None of the above

12. What is the poverty level for a family of four in 1999?
    a. $12,000   b. $14,000   c. $17,000   d. $19,000

13. Liberals criticize the official definition of poverty for all but one of the following reasons:
   a. The definition includes cash from welfare programs; without this income there would be more poor
   b. The definition does not include the near poor
   c. The definition does not consider what people think they need to live
   d. By using regional differences to calculate the poverty level, a lower poverty level is determined

14. A social welfare program in which no contributions are required in order to obtain benefits is a:
   a. Social insurance program
   b. Supplemental security program
   c. Entitlement program
   d. Public assistance program

15. Which one of the following groups has the largest number of poor?
   a. Blacks
   b. Families with female heads
   c. Hispanics
   d. Under age 18

16. Which of the following is the focus of our social problems?
   a. Rural areas
   b. Suburbs
   c. Indian reservations
   d. Nation's largest cities

17. All but one of the following have had a deleterious impact on the inner city:
   a. Changes in the labor market from industrial goods to professional, financial, and technical jobs
   b. Shift in manufacturing and commercial sales jobs to the suburbs
   c. Immigration of working-class to the inner city
   d. Poor schools

18. The 1996 Welfare Reform bill included all but one of the following provisions:
   a. The end of federal cash assistance for children
   b. Lifetime welfare benefits limited to two years
   c. States may stop payments to unmarried teenage mothers
   d. States must retain their own spending on welfare at either 75 percent or 80 percent of their 1994 level

19. Which of the following is not a social insurance program?
   a. Social Security
   b. Medicare
   c. Medicaid
   d. Unemployment Compensation

20. Which of the following interest groups do not have an interest in health care?
   a. Employees
   b. Senior citizen's lobby
   c. HMOs and PPOs
   d. Drug companies

CHAPTER SEVENTEEN SAMPLE QUESTION ANSWERS

TRUE-FALSE:

1.   **FALSE**. See page 621.

2.   **TRUE.** Although most think that social welfare is for the poor, this is not the case. See page 620.

3.   **FALSE**. Social Security is provided for all retirees, regardless of personal wealth or need. See page 626.

4.   **TRUE.** Compared to whites, black Americans experience far more poverty. See page 622.

5.   **FALSE.** Only one-third of Americans receive benefits, but this is still a large number. See page 624.

6.   **FALSE.** Medicaid provides health care assistance for low-income families. See page 627.

7.   **TRUE.** See page 629.

8.   **TRUE.** See page 637.

9.   **TRUE.** An estimated 35-40 million Americans cannot afford health insurance and are not covered by any employer-provided insurance. See page 638.

10.   **FALSE.** While polls show Americans would support paying more taxes, they would prefer these be sin taxes, which would not raise sufficient revenue. See page 641.

MULTIPLE-CHOICE:

11. **C**. Unemployment compensation is not a means tested program. See page 627.

12. **C.** In 1995, the poverty level was $16,000 but rose to $16,500 in 1998. See page 620.

13. **D.** Regional differences are not used, and this is what irritates liberals since some regions may be more expensive than others, re: cost-of-living, climate, etc. See page 620.

14. **D.** A social welfare program in which no contributions are required in order to obtain

benefits is a public assistance program. See page 624.

15. **B.** Families headed by single females experience the most poverty. See page 622.

16. **D.** Our nation's largest cities, especially the inner-city has become the concentration point of our social ills. See page 623.

17. **C.** The out-migration of the working and middle class (those who could afford to move) has depleted the inner city of a stable, role model class. See page 623.

18. **B.** Lifetime benefits are limited to five years; consecutive years on welfare can be limited to two years. See page 635.

19. **C.** Medicaid is a public assistance program. See page 627.

20. **A.** Employees generally do not have a special interest group speaking for them on health care unless it is a union. Employers on the other hand are represented by professional and technical interest groups and are extremely interested in reforms of health care that may cost them more money. See pages 642-643.

CHAPTER EIGHTEEN:
POLITICS AND NATIONAL SECURITY

I. POWER AMONG NATIONS: International politics is a global struggle for power. This struggle has led to many attempts to bring order to the international system.

   A. The Balance of Power System: Practiced in the eighteenth and nineteenth centuries by European powers, it was a system of alliances designed to balance one group against the other, thereby discouraging war. For almost a century, from the Napoleonic Wars to World War I, it appeared to be effective. But, one defect in the system is that a small conflict between two nations that are members of separate alliances could draw all members into the conflict and quickly turn a small conflict into a major war. This is what essentially happened in WWI, when a minor conflict in the Balkans turned into WWI. This disaster led to calls for a new system-collective security.

   B. Collective Security: This is a system where all nations join together to guarantee each other's security against external aggression. This was the central idea of the League of Nations established in 1919. Even though it was the brainchild of our President Woodrow Wilson, the Senate refused to confirm the treaty because of opposition to international involvement. Further, the League failed to deal with acts of aggression by the Axis powers: Germany, Italy and, Japan. The result was an even more devastating World War II.

   C. Formation of the United Nations: Another attempt at collective security, the victorious allies established the UN in 1945. Its essential components are:

      1. Security Council: Consists of 11 members, five of which are permanent--the U.S., China, Britain, France and the Soviet Union (Russia). Permanent members have an absolute veto--they can stop and defeat any matter before the Council. Has primary responsibility for maintaining international peace and security.

      2. General Assembly: This is the main body of the UN, composed of all the member states. Each nation has a single vote.

      3. Secretariat: **FILL-IN.**

      4. Specialized Organizations: Examples include: the Economic and Social Council, Trusteeship Council, and International Court of Justice at The Hague.

D. The United Nations in the Cold War: The UN was largely ineffective in the Cold War. While the UN grew from 51 to 185 members, many of these new countries were headed by authoritarian regimes of one sort or another. Western democracies were outgunned in the General Assembly, and the Soviet Union used its veto in the Security Council to prevent any action. Anti-U.S. and anti-democratic speeches became the order of the day in the General Assembly. In reality, the UN was overshadowed by the world's two superpowers: the U.S. and Soviet Union.

E. Regional Security: **FILL-IN. WHY DID THESE COME INTO EXISTENCE? WHAT WAS THE SOVIET REACTION TO THE FORMATION OF NATO? WHAT HAPPENED TO THE WARSAW PACT?**

F. The UN Today: The end of the Cold War has injected new life into the UN. Russia inherited the seat on the security council that once belonged to the Soviet Union. There is now greater cooperation on the Security Council to support a new world order. But the help of the U.S., as the remaining superpower, is still necessary to help the UN enforce its resolutions. The U.S. Congress has refused to pay the U.S. dues to the UN until it makes reforms in its bureaucracy and reduces its costs.

II. THE LEGACY OF THE COLD WAR: For more than 40 years, the U.S. and USSR confronted each other in a protracted military, political, economic, and ideological struggle which became known as the Cold War.

A. Origins: During WWII, the U.S. and the Soviets were allies. Upon conclusion of the war, the U.S. demobilized its armed forces, while the Soviet Union used theirs to install Communist governments in the countries of Eastern Europe. Germany and Berlin were divided into occupation zones of the Allied powers. The divided city of Berlin lay 200 miles inside the Eastern German border. In 1948, the East German government with the connivance of the Soviet Union blockaded the rail lines and roads into the Western part of Berlin. The U.S. provided supplies by air for over four months. In 1946, former Prime Minster Churchill of England warned of an iron curtain falling across Europe. The formal start of the Cold War is marked by the establishment of the Truman Doctrine in 1947 under which military and economic aid was provided to Greece and Turkey fighting against Soviet-backed guerillas. The doctrine promised aid to support free peoples fighting armed minorities or outside forces.

B. Containment: Russian expert George F. Kennan in a seminal article in *Foreign Affairs* called for a policy of containment. That is, the U.S. should try to contain communism within its present boundaries. One of the first concrete efforts in this regard was the Marshall Plan to economically build a weakened Europe which, if not aided, might fall to communism.

C.   The Korean War: This was the first military test of containment. North Korea with the concurrence of the Soviet Union launched a surprise attack on South Korea. The U.S. brought the matter to the UN Security Council, which the Russians were boycotting because of its refusal to seat the new Communist government of China. The Security Council passed a resolution calling on member nations to send troops or other support to repel the invasion. The U.S. had drastically reduced its armed forces and only had about 30,000 troops in Korea. U.S. and Korean forces were pushed down the peninsula of Korea until their backs were at the sea in the port of Pusan. As U.S. reinforcements moved to hold the line, General Douglas MacArthur launched a surprise amphibious attack at Inchon on the western side of Korea cutting off the North Korean army. As the trapped North Korean army raced north, the U.N. forces were in hot pursuit. In spite of warnings by the Chinese government about approaching their border with North Korea, the UN forces kept pressing north. In December, 1950, one million Chinese troops poured across the border and entered the conflict. The sheer mass of this assault forces the UN forces to retreat south. General MacArthur wanted to retaliate against the Chinese mainland, but President Truman did not want to expand the war. MacArthur took his plans and complaints public and Truman showing great courage, fired the hero of WWII. The Korean War became a stalemate in which the UN forces suffered many casualties. Eisenhower was elected president in 1952 and promised to end the conflict using nuclear weapons if necessary. Eventually, an armistice was signed which reestablished the boundary between South and North Korea along the 38th parallel. While Communist expansion was contained, the cost was high-38,000 U.S. military personnel were killed.

D. The Cuban Missile Crisis: During the Cold War, the Soviets sought to expand their influence in the Third World. Many new countries were former colonies that had become independent. Fidel Castro fought a guerilla war in Cuba against the repressive regime of Batista. In 1959, Castro was successful and soon thereafter allied his government with Moscow. The U.S. sought his ouster, and in 1961, the CIA planned a covert operation involving a brigade of Cuban exiles. The plan, developed when Eisenhower was president, called for the U.S. to provide air cover, but the new president, Kennedy, refused to provide the air cover. Without it, the invasion failed. Kennedy was also tested in the same year by the erection of the Berlin Wall. Despite heated words, the U.S. did nothing concrete and the wall became a symbol of Soviet repression. Taking advantage of the perceived weakness of the young American president, in 1962, the Soviets sought to secretly install nuclear weapons in Cuba which would threaten U.S. cities. U.S. intelligence photos showed the installation of the missiles, which led to a direct confrontation with the Soviets. Rejecting military advice to bomb the installations, Kennedy instead opted for a blockade of Cuba, threatening to halt Soviet missile-carrying ships by force, if necessary. This confrontation was the most serious threat of nuclear holocaust during the entire Cold War--U.S. nuclear forces were on alert. If the U.S. had to use force against Soviet ships, we were not sure what would be the reaction of the Soviets. Secret diplomacy was used--the U.S. agreed in writing never to invade Cuba and to remove missiles from Turkey, which threatened the Soviet Union. The Soviets agreed to remove their missiles from Cuba. Since most Americans did not know of the deal, Kennedy was hailed as a hero. Khrushchev was soon removed from power because of adventurism.

E.	The Vietnam War: Vietnam was another test of Asian containment. The domino theory was prevalent at this time and arguments were made that if the U.S. did not stop the war in Vietnam, it would spread to Laos and Cambodia. Vietnam was part of what was known as French Indochina. President Eisenhower declined to intervene in the former French colony when the forces of Ho Chi Minh defeated the French army at Dien Bien Phu in 1954. The Geneva Accords of 1956 divided Vietnam into two parts-North and South. Shortly thereafter, the Viet Cong, southern-based Communist guerillas, began operations in South Vietnam. With the South Vietnamese government threatened, President Kennedy sent a force of 12,000 advisors and counter-insurgency forces to assist the South Vietnamese. By 1964, elements of the regular North Vietnamese army were assisting the Viet Cong. An alleged attack by North Korean gunboats in the Tonkin Gulf led Congress to pass the Tonkin Gulf Resolution, which basically opened the door to U.S. involvement in the war. President Johnson ordered U.S. combat troops to Vietnam and authorized limited air strikes against North Vietnam. This precipitous action was not undertaken with specific congressional approval, nor was any attempt made to mobilize American public opinion. Eventually over 500,000 troops were sent to Vietnam in what became a war of attrition. Instead of a decisive victory, the war dragged on and popular support started to slip away. Viet Cong and North Vietnamese forces launched a surprise attach during the Tet holiday. They struck on January 31, 1968, and a Viet Cong unit actually captured the U.S. Embassy in Saigon for six hours. All attacks were eventually repulsed and Communist losses were severe. The communists were hoping for popular uprisings and support which never materialized. However, the Communist defeat on the battlefield became a victory in the field of American public opinion. The American media turned vicious and portrayed the action a defeat for the U.S. and South Vietnam and began a campaign to force U.S. withdrawal. In early 1968, President Johnson halted the bombing on North Vietnam and announced he would not seek another term in office. Formal peace talks opened in Paris on May 13th. In late 1968, Richard Nixon was elected as president. Nixon and Henry Kissinger, his national security advisor, wanted to end the war, but honorably. They also wanted a peace settlement that would give South Vietnam a fighting chance for survival. The North Vietnamese stonewalled the peace negotiations. In January 1973, the Vietnamese returned to the negotiating table and quickly agreed to peace terms. This agreement called for the return of POWs and allowed the Thieu government to remain in South Vietnam. The agreement also called for the U.S. government to provide economic assistance to North Vietnam. The U.S. did not fulfill any promise either to North or South that it made in the agreement. Congress refused to appropriate any further funds. This and the forced resignation of Nixon in August 1974 convinced the North Vietnamese that the U.S. would not interfere any further in South Vietnam. In early 1975, the North Vietnamese army launched an attack. The U.S. did not intervene,,, and the U.S. ambassador had to flee from the roof of the embassy by helicopter. By April 1975 Vietnam was unified. For the U.S., it was a period of national humiliation.

F.   The Vietnam Syndrome: A new period of isolationism permeated U.S. foreign policy. No more Vietnams became the rally cry. The Soviet Union took advantage of our isolationist mentality by expanding its military and political influence in Asia, Africa, the Middle East, the Caribbean,, and Central and South America. The U.S. did little to halt this expansion. The Soviet invasion of Afghanistan finally galvanized the U.S. to have the CIA back, in a covert way, the Afghan guerillas, which forced the Soviet Union's armed forces into a stalemate which some dubbed Russia's Vietnam.

G.   Rebuilding America's Defenses: **FILL-IN.**

H.   Gorbachev, Perestroika, and Glasnost: Gorbachev was committed to a policy of perestroika (restructuring of the Soviet command economy by decentralization of state planning) and also called for glasnost (openness) in Soviet life and politics. Gorbachev also began a reduction of the Soviet armed forces, and indicated that these armed forces would no longer be used to keep Communist governments in power in Eastern Europe. This announcement encouraged democratic forces in all of Eastern Europe and one after the other, Communist governments fell from power, culminating in the destruction of the Berlin Wall.

I.   The Collapse of Communism: **FILL-IN.**

J.   The Disintegration of the Soviet Union: Strong independence movements began life as the power of the Soviet Communist Party waned. The Baltic countries of Lithuania, Estonia, and Latvia led the charge. Soon all 15 republics of the Soviet Union had declared their independence, and the USSR ceased to exist at the end of 1991.

K. Russia After Communism: Difficult political, social, and economic problems followed. Putin became president in 2000.

III. NUCLEAR THREATS; While nuclear weapons raised the threshold of a nuclear holocaust, they also acted to restrain the superpowers. While there were scores of clashes in the Cold War, there were never any directed between the forces of the Soviet Union and the U.S.

A. Deterrence: This doctrine is predicaated on the notion that one nation could absorb a first nuclear strike and still have enough residual nuclear forces to retaliate against the attacking country in a devastating counter-attack. Rationally, this assured counter-attack should prevent the first attack. This logic is based on second-strike capability.

B. MAD Balance of Terror: By the 1970s, each side had enough missiles and delivery systems to destroy the other side. This mutual balance of terror, in essence, meant each country's populations was held hostage against a nuclear attack.

C. Limiting Nuclear Arms: SALT: The development of space-based satellite intelligence enabled both sides to see what the other was doing in regards to strategic weapons. Verification was always one of the principal hangups with arms reduction talks. Now with space intelligence, verification of arms reductions was easier. First talks about nuclear arms reductions were initiated during the Nixon administration. In 1972, the Strategic Arms Limitation Treaty (SALT) I was concluded which froze existing nuclear weapons at their current levels and included an anti-ballistic Missile (ABM) agreement. The ABM treaty essentially ratified the idea that each country's citizens were nuclear hostages as it severely limited the construction of defensive anti-ballistic missile batteries. The U.S. never did construct an ABM site. While each side could upgrade and develop new nuclear weapons, they would have to dismantle older weapons to stay within the ceiling limits. Both sides also agreed not to interfere with the space intelligence-gathering activities of the other. In 1979, after seven years of hard negotiations, the SALT II Treaty was concluded. It set an overall limit on strategic nuclear launch vehicles to 2,250 for each side. When the Soviet Union invaded Afghanistan, President Carter withdrew the treaty from further Senate consideration, and to this date the treaty has never been ratified by the U.S. Senate, although the U.S. has continued to abide by its provisions.

D. Reducing Nuclear Arms: START: The Reagan administration wanted to achieve three things in further negotiations: reductions of nuclear inventories, equality between the U.S. and USSR, and on-site verification. The START I

Treaty was signed by Presidents Bush and Gorbachev in 1991 and was the first treaty to actually call for the reduction of weapons. The START I Treaty called for a ceiling of 1,600 delivery systems from 2,250. In 1993, the START II Treaty was signed. All MIRV warheads are to be eliminated by the year 2003, all Russian SS-18 missiles will be eliminated, the U.S. will eliminate all MX missiles, and convert all MIRV Minuteman missiles into single warheads. The overall level of nuclear warheads is to be reduced to 3,500.

E.   Nuclear Testing and Nonproliferation: **FILL-IN.**

F.   Continued Minimal Deterrence: With the changes in Russia, the U.S. assessment of Russian intentions has changed. While we assume that responsible leaders will maintain control over these weapons, the U.S. must continue to maintain some level of nuclear forces to deter attack or intimidation from any leader that may come into control of these awesome weapons. The U.S. will retain some 500 single, shot Minuteman missiles and its Trident SLBM force.

G.   Nuclear Terrorism: The possibility of an attack by a terrorist nation or group is a real threat as nuclear proliferation and theft of fissionable materials may enable some group to use a nuclear weapon as a form of terrorism. To guard against this or some accidental launch, some feel a ballistic missile defense (BMD) system should be developed and deployed. Some research has been done, but there are no current plans to proceed any further.

IV. POST-COLD WAR THREATS: The end of the Cold War does not mean that the world is at peace. It simply means that the bi-polar conflict between the U.S. and Russia has ended.

A.   Guarding against Reversal of Democratic Trends: If former Communist countries made a full transition to democracy and a market economy, the world should be more peaceful. But dangers lurk on the horizon:

1.   Continuing economic deterioration in Russia may undermine the weak conditions of democracy.
2.   **FILL-IN.**
3.   Continued differences among the former Soviet republics may rekindle ancient hatreds among ethnic groups and result in armed conflict.
4.   **FILL-IN.**

B.   Western Europe and the Future of NATO: Today, the Russian threat to Western Europe is relatively small. The Russian armed forces have been reduced and morale is low and their equipment is in a poor state. This raises the question of why we still maintain troops in Europe. The complete withdrawal of troops would most likely wreck NATO. Which raises a further question: What is the future role of NATO?

C.   NATO Expansion: Yet another question facing NATO at the end of the Cold war was whether or not to expand membership to include the former Communist nations. Expansion, it was argued, would encourage democracy. Russia opposed expansion as a threat to its security. Poland, Hungary, and the Czech Republic were eventually admitted to NATO, but only after Russia had been reassured of the peaceful intentions of the alliance.

D.   European Ethnic Conflicts: These are as old as the continent. The questions for the U.S. and NATO are: Do such conflicts, such as in Bosnia, threaten the security of Western Europe? And if so, what should be done about them?

E.   Regional Threats: These appear to be the most likely threats in the future, especially in both the <u>Middle East</u> and <u>Asia</u>.

   1.   Iraq: Saddam Hussein's military forces were considerably reduced in the Gulf War, but he remains a threat in the area.

   2.   Iran: **FILL-IN.**

   3.   Syria: It still has a powerful military force, but since the former Soviet Union was its main supplier, it now has to look for other support. It still is technically at war with Israel and its troops still occupy large parts of Lebanon.

   4.   Libya: Libya's threat lies in its role as a major base for worldwide terrorism.

   5.   North Korea: It remains the world's most authoritarian and militarist regime. It spends a great deal on its military forces and has a well-developed nuclear weapons program. It still poses a threat to South Korea, and U.S. support of South Korea would be necessary in the event of hostilities.

   6.   China: Currently, China has the world's largest armed forces and has nuclear weapons. The role of Taiwan as a province or independent state remains a contentious issue. While China has made some market reforms, it still maintains tight political control.

   7.   Terrorism: This threat creates two military requirements: Punish any

aggressor and deter other nations from supporting terrorism.

F. Unanticipated Threats: The record of forecasting future threats is very poor. Which simply means, the U.S. must always be ready to respond to unanticipated threats on a global scale.

V. THE USE OF MILITARY FORCE: One of the most agonizing decisions faced by a president--the end must justify the means.

A. To Protect Vital Interests: The U.S. learned some very important lessons from Vietnam about the use of force.

1. Use force only to protect vital national interests.
2. Forces must have clearly defined military objectives.
3. Sufficient forces should be provided to ensure overwhelming and decisive victory.
4. Support of the American people is needed.
5. Use force as a last resort.

These guidelines were followed in the Desert Storm operation and are strongly supported by military leaders. Contrary to some stereotypes, military leaders are reluctant to go to war if these criteria are not met.

B. In Support of Important Political Objectives: Political leaders and diplomats view war differently than do military leaders; they see it as a continuation of politics. In addition to carrying out conventional war, U.S. military forces must be prepared for a variety of missions, including:

1. Demonstrating U.S. resolve in a crisis situation.
2. Demonstrating U.S. support for democratic governments.
3. **FILL-IN**.
4. **FILL-IN**.
5. Peacekeeping among warring factions or nations.
6. Peacekeeping missions to support a peace agreement.
7. Provision of humanitarian aid under hostile conditions.
8. Assist in an international war against drug trafficking.

In pursuit of these objectives, U.S. forces have been sent to Lebanon, Grenada, Panama, Somalia, Haiti, and Bosnia. Opponents of some of these actions claim we are acting as the world's policeman. Proponents argue that each case is evaluated on a cost-benefit basis.

VI. MILITARY FORCE LEVELS: In theory, the overall level of military forces of any nation should be determined by the size and nature of a perceived threat to its national security. Political influences often distort this determination--the buying of certain weapons systems is often dictated by powerful political leaders as is the construction of military bases. For over 40 years the Soviet threat drove our defense policy--force planning, training, strategy and tactics, weapons research and procurement, force deployments, and budgets. With the new world order, a complete reexamination was in order.

A. Reductions in Forces: Post-Cold War reductions began in 1990 under the Bush administration and called for a reduction of U.S. military forces from 2.1 to 1.6 million. While still maintaining a presence in Europe, U.S. force levels in Europe were cut by more than half. Later, the Clinton administration argued that the end of the Cold War called for a complete "bottom-up" review of threats facing the nation.

B. Iraqi-Equivalent Regional Threats: Current force planning envisions having sufficient forces to fight and win two nearly simultaneous major regional conflicts. Nearly simultaneous is very ambiguous and recognizes the U.S. may not have sufficient airlift and sealift to move the necessary forces. Under these restrictions, it is planned that we will fight to win one regional conflict while holding the aggressor at bay in the other. Once victory is obtained in the first, forces can be repositioned to defeat the second aggressor.

C. Future Force Levels: The revised threat assesment calls for major reductions in the size and budget of the military. The Army will have 10 divisions (15,000-18,000 personnel), the Air Force 13 fighter wings (72 combat aircraft), the Navy will have 11 carrier battle groups (one in a training status), the Marine Corps will retain its three expeditionary forces.

D. Criticism: **FILL-IN. WHAT ARE THE MAIN POINTS OF CRITICISM?**

E. Historical Trends in Defense Spending: In 1955, defense spending consumed 58 percent of the federal budget and equaled 10.5 percent of GDP. Ten years later, it was 40.1 percent of the federal budget and 7.5 percent of GDP. By 1978, the defense sector cost 23 percent of federal spending and 4.5 percent of GDP. This was the low point, and it began to creep up during the last budget of President Carter. During the Reagan era, defense spending rose to 29 percent of budget and 6.5 percent of GDP.

F. Post-Cold War Defense Spending: Current projections are down, and defense spending is projected to equal less than 15 percent of the federal budget and less than 3 percent of GDP--or roughly defense spending levels before the attack on Pearl Harbor in 1941.

CHAPTER EIGHTEEN SAMPLE QUESTIONS

TRUE-FALSE:

1. International politics is a struggle for power.

2. Because of its size and contribution to the UN budget, the U.S. has three votes in the General Assembly.

3. Disappointment with the concept of collective security led to the concept of regional security.

4. The Korean War was the first military test of the containment policy.

5. The UN was a highly effective tool for preventing conflict during the Cold War.

6. American isolationism was one of the legacies of Vietnam.

7. War, or the use of force can only be used to accomplish precise military objectives.

8. Nuclear weapons caused the superpowers to be more cautious with each other.

9. One effect of the MAD policy was to hold hostage the civilian populations of the USSR and U.S.

10. U.S. military force levels are designed to confront and win two, nearly simultaneous regional conflicts.

MULTIPLE-CHOICE:

11. In the eighteenth and nineteenth centuries, European countries employed _____ to stabilize international relations.
    a. Containment
    b. Balance of Power
    c. Collective Security
    d. Balance of Terror

12. All but one of the following are examples of collective security:
    a. NATO
    b. UN
    c. League of Nations
    d. U.S.-Korean Mutual Defense Treaty

13. The UN Security Council has how many permanent members?
    a. 5   b. 11   c. 13   d. 15

14. The nuclear policy which is based on the idea that an attack can be prevented by having the capability to return fire after being attacked is called:
    a. Mutual assured destruction
    b. Detente
    c. Containment
    d. Deterrence

15. Which of the following is NOT considered a regional threat in the world today?
    a. China
    b. Turkey
    c. Iran
    d. Syria

16. What marked the beginnings of the cold war
    a. The Yalta conference
    b. Churchill's "iron curtain" speech in Fulton, Missouri
    c. The initiation of the "Truman Doctrine"
    d. U.S. development of the atomic bomb
    e. The East German blockade of Berlin

17. "Nondeterrable" nuclear threats include:
    a. Accidental missile launches
    b. Unauthorized missile launches by elements in the former Soviet Union
    c. Missile launches by terrorist nations
    d. All of the above
    e. None of the above

18. The lessons learned from Vietnam include all of the following EXCEPT:
    a. Support of the U.S., public is needed prior to committing troops
    b. Military forces should have clearly defined missions
    c. Involvement in a civil war is fruitless without strong public support from within the nation in question.
    d. Forces must be of sufficient strength to ensure victory.

19. Which of the following Soviet words means restructuring?
    a. Gorbachev
    b. Perestroika
    c. Glasnost
    d. Apparatchniks

20. Which arms control treaty banned MIRV warheads from missiles after 2003?
    a. SALT I
    b. SALT II
    c. START I
    d. START II

CHAPTER EIGHTEEN SAMPLE QUESTION ANSWERS

TRUE-FALSE:

1. **TRUE.** All types of politics involves a struggle for power. See page 647.

2. **FALSE.** And this is a major bone of contention on the part of the U.S. See page 648.

3. **TRUE.** This was the major reason for the creation of NATO. See page 649.

4. **TRUE.** But it was not to be the last! See page 650.

5. **FALSE.** See page 649.

6. **TRUE.** See page 654.

7. **FALSE.** War can be used for political objectives as well. See page 670.

8. **TRUE.** This was somewhat paradoxical considering their destructive power. See page 657.

9. **TRUE.** As bizarre as this may seem. See page 657.

10. **TRUE.** See page 674.

MULTIPLE-CHOICE:

11. **B.** It lasted from the Congress of Vienna in 1815 until the outbreak of WWI. See page 647.

12. **D.** A bi-lateral defense treaty cannot be an example of collective security, which involves many nations, not just two. See page 649.

13. **A.** While the Council has 11 members, only five are permanent. See page 649.

14. **D.** The nuclear policy which is based on the idea that an attack can be prevented by having the capability to return fire after being attacked is called deterrence. See page 657.

15. **B.** Turkey is NOT considered a regional threat in the world today. See pages 665-667.

16. **C.** The initiation of the Truman Doctrine marked the formal beginning of the Cold War. See page 650.

17. **D**. "Nondeterrable" nuclear threats include accidental missile launches, unauthorized missile launches by elements in the former Soviet Union, and missile launches by terrorist nations. See page 663.

18. **C.** See page 667.

19. **B.** Perestroika was supposed to restructure and strengthen the Communist nation. See page 653.

20. **D**. The last major treaty was the START II, and this was a major accomplishment of this treaty. See page 659.

CHAPTER NINETEEN
THE SOCIAL AND ECONOMIC MILIEU OF TEXAS POLITICS

I.   DECADES OF CHANGE AND CHALLENGE: The problems faced by Texas as it adjusts to the changing economy, society and political landscape directly influence Texas politics.

    A.   Challenges of the 2000s: The 1990s have seen the economic recovery in Texas, but this has not alleviated the problems faced by the state. Continued population growth along with the increased demand for state services which accompany it-crime, poverty, an inequitable public education system, and the loss of energy revenues-remain problematic for state leaders. Potential policy solutions to these problems are influenced by the significant changes which have occurred in the social, economic, and political structures of the state. Texas is now the second most populous state with a highly urban population and a diverse ethnic and racial makeup.

II.   TEXAS MYTHS: Texans share political myths concerning the state's history and culture. The Alamo and being an independent republic distinguishes Texas from any other state in terms of its autonomy. The individualism evident in the image of the Texas ranger and the cowboy are seen in the political culture of self-reliance. This is translated into politics by the lack of state services and the belief in a minimal role of government.

III.   THE POLITICAL CULTURE OF TEXAS: Political culture is a widely shared set of views, attitudes, beliefs, and customs of a people about how their government should be organized and run. Three political subcultures can be identified across the United States.

    A.   The Individualistic Subculture: This culture entails the view that government should interfere as little as possible in the private activities of its citizens, while assuring that adequate public facilities and a favorable business climate are available to permit individuals to pursue their self-interest.

    B.   The Moralistic Subculture: **FILL IN.**

    C.   The Traditionalistic Subculture: This is the view that political power should be concentrated in the hands of a few elite citizens who belong to established families or influential social groups. Public policy basically serves the interests of this small group.

    D.   Historical Origins of Political Subcultures: The historical beginnings of the different subcultures can be explained by the settlement patterns of the early U.S. and the cultural differences of the people who settled each area of the nation. The New England colonists were influenced by the Puritans and developed a moralistic culture, while the settlers of the mid-Atlantic states were motivated by entrepreneurial interests and developed an individualistic culture. The South was settled by elites with a traditionalistic culture. Texas was primarily settled by those from individualistic and traditionalistic cultures, thus providing the unique blend of the two found in Texas.

IV. THE PEOPLE OF TEXAS: The politics and government of Texas can be understood, in part, from the perspective of the people living in the state.

    A. Native Americans: Native Americans make up less than one-half of one percent of the state"s population. The Alabama-Coushatta, Tigua, and Kickapoo peoples live on reservations in Texas and comprise the largest groups of Native Americans in the state.

    B. Hispanics: As of 1990, Hispanics represented 25 percent of the state's population, with estimates reaching 31 percent by the year 2000 and 41 percent by 2020. Traditionally Hispanics were concentrated in the South and Border regions of Texas, but now have migrated throughout the state. The number and distribution of Hispanics has produced significant political power and influence. As of 1994 more Hispanics held elected office in Texas than in any other state.

    C. African Americans: Today African Americans constitute approximately 12 percent of the state's population, even though that figure was significantly higher in the period following the Civil War. East Texas and the urban areas of Dallas, Fort Worth, Houston, and Austin have the largest concentrations of African Americans. They have achieved political power in selected areas, but not on a statewide level. In 1998, there were 474 African Americans elected to statewide office.

    D. Anglos: Anglos migrated to the state from the upper South in the early nineteenth century and settled primarily in Northeast Texas. A second wave of migration occurred when slavery was legalized and Anglos from the lower South settled initially in the southeastern part of the state. Two subcultures are evident among Anglos. Those living in the northern section of the state were influenced by an individualistic culture, while those in the south are more traditionalistic. Anglos make up about 60 percent of the state's population, and this is expected to drop off to about 55 percent by the year 2000.

    E. The Asian American Population: There has been a rapid increase in the number of Asian Americans in Texas, and the number is expected to reach 4.2 percent of the population by the year 2020. The largest concentration of Asian Americans can be found in Houston, where they have started to gain significant political power.

V.   POLITICS, RACE, AND ETHNICITY: Despite the changes in the law and other efforts to rectify racial and ethnic discrimination, there is still some evidence of employment and housing discrimination in Texas. These considerations remain implicit in political and policy issues today, even though the emphasis has shifted from questions of race to those of class and economic standing.

VI.   THE POLITICAL IMPLICATIONS OF DEMOGRAPHICS:

A.   Population Increase: The population of Texas has increased at a much faster pace than the rest of the nation in the last fifty years, making it the second most populous state. This growth is only partially explained by birth rate. A great percentage of the Texas population increase is due to migration from other states, as the nation experienced a shift in population from the Northeast and Midwest to the South and West. This influx of new citizens has changed the traditional one-party nature of the political system, making Texas a two-party state.

B.   The Aging Population: The over sixty-five population is estimated to reach 17 percent by the year 2030. This aging population places serious demands on the public and private sectors for goods and services, including expanded health care and long-term care.

C.   Urbanization: Today approximately 80 percent of the state's population lives in urban areas. Texas cities have experienced phenomenal growth since the 1960s. Like urban areas throughout the country, Texas's largest cities are increasingly populated by minorities. This is due not only to higher birth rates in minority populations, but also "white flight."

D.   Population Density: **DEFINE.** There are significant differences in the population density of Texas counties. These differences have led to conflict between the urban and rural areas of the state, which have been magnified by the dominance of rural lawmakers in the state legislature and the constitutional restrictions developed when the state was primarily rural.

E.   Wealth and Income Distribution: There is a wide disparity in income distribution in Texas. Despite the tremendous wealth of some, the state's average family and household incomes are below the national average. On all measures of income, Hispanics and African Americans fall significantly below Anglos, and many Texans live in severe poverty. Seven of the twenty poorest counties in the nation are in Texas, and these have large Hispanic populations. Over all, over 16.7 percent of the state's population falls below the poverty level. Financial resources can be translated into political power and influence. Therefore it is clear that some Texans have enormous resources in relation to others. By 1997, the average household income in Texas was $35,075, compared to $37,005 in the rest of the U.S.

F. Education and Literacy: Litigation has forced the state to deal with the problem of educational equity and financing, and the issue promises to remain on the forefront of policy debate. The 1990 census indicated that approximately 72 percent of the over twenty-five population had a high school degree and 20 percent had completed college. By 1996, 76.4 percent of those twenty-five and older had completed high school. These attainments are not evenly distributed across ethnic and racial groups. Asian Americans and Anglos had a significantly higher high school and college completion rate than did Hispanics, African Americans, and Native Americans. As education directly affects employment, income, and political participation, the level of educational attainment of the state influences political power.

VII. THE ECONOMY OF TEXAS: Politics and the state of the economy are closely linked. A strong economy provides flexibility and policy options which are impossible in tough economic times. In the 1980s, Texas experienced a period of phenomenal growth which permitted an expansion of state services. By the early 1990s however, the state was forced to cut back due to severe recessions.

The state's economy has traditionally been linked to oil and natural gas. This connection has accounted for the periods of boom and bust in the Texas economy. Sensitivity to the strength of the Mexican peso and the electronics industry compounded the economic problems faced by the state in the late 1980s. During that period, the state's banks and savings and loan industry experienced more bank failures than any other time since the Great Depression.

State and local governments were forced in the periods of economic hardship and declining tax revenues to find creative budgetary methods. Some of these have included regressive taxes such as the sales tax. **DEFINE REGRESSIVE TAX.**

The changes in the Texas economy in the last decade provide hope that the state will be less susceptible to economic fluctuations. Economic diversification has led to a growth in the service sector and high-tech industries. **DEFINE ECONOMIC DIVERSIFICATION.** There has also been a trend toward the globalization of the state's economy. In 1999, Texas had a gross state product of $596 billion. If Texas were a nation, its economy would rank eleventh in the world.

VIII. ECONOMIC REGIONS OF TEXAS: There are ten distinct economic regions in Texas.

A. The High Plains Region: Agriculture is the dominant industry in this area, which includes Amarillo and Lubbock. Oil and gas production is also important, but the percentage of employment in this area has declined, as has the overall population.

B. The Northwest Texas Region: This region experienced virtually no population growth in the last decade and is expected to lose population in the next. Agriculture and oil and gas are dominant industries, even though many energy related jobs were lost in the last recession. Although there is some manufacturing, the service sector is expected to provide the major source of employment in the future.

C. The Metroplex Region. **FILL IN.**

D. The Upper East Texas Region: This region includes cities such as Texarkana, Marshall, Tyler, and Longview. The area's economy has traditionally been based on oil and gas, lumber, cotton, and cattle, but has now diversified to include more manufacturing.

E. The Southeast Texas Region: This region includes the cities of Beaumont, Port Arthur, and Orange. Population growth in the area has been slow in the last decade and is expected to continue as such. Oil and gas as well as lumber have been the primary industries. Future growth is expected to be in construction, health services, and poultry processing.

F. The Gulf Coast Region: This region has a highly diversified economy with an emphasis on petroleum and chemical production, water transportation, and trade. Cities in the region include Houston, Galveston, and Angleton. The region is more cosmopolitan than other parts of the state and is in a good position to take advantage of the globalization of the state's economy.

G. The Central Texas Region: **FILL IN**.

H. The South Texas Region. This region is geographically diverse and encompasses the cities of San Antonio, Corpus Christi, McAllen, and Laredo. This area has experienced significant population growth in the last decade and it is expected to continue. Construction and the North American Free Trade Agreement have given a boost to the economy of this region, but it still has some of the poorest counties in the country. Government employment and services, oil and gas as well as chemical production, agriculture, livestock, and food processing are all significant components in the regional economy.

I. The West Texas Region: **FILL IN.**

J. The Upper Rio Grande Region: This region, which includes El Paso and the Big Bend National Park, grew significantly in the 1980s and is expected to continue to do so at a faster rate than the overall state. Manufacturing accounts for a major proportion of the employment. Industrialization along the border and North American Free Trade Agreement is expected to benefit the region significantly.

IX. TRANSNATIONAL REGIONALISM. **DEFINE.**
The interests of Texas and Mexico have long been bound by geopolitical factors, economics, and demographics.

A. Maquiladoras: The maquiladora program was created by the Mexican government in 1964 to promote economic growth along the border. Manufacturing and industry were to be promoted along the Mexican-U.S.border with special tax incentives on imports and changes in Mexican law concerning foreign ownership of industry. The program was not overwhelmingly successful, although some Texas counties did benefit.

B. The North American Free Trade Agreement (NAFTA): **DEFINE.**
Most estimates project that NAFTA will increase trade among the partners and thus strengthen economic ties. Opponents fear that cheap labor available in Mexico will mean the loss of American jobs, the opening of highways to Mexican trucks will cause safety problems, increased commerce will compound environmental problems, and that the dominance of U.S. corporations will reduce Mexican control over their own economy. NAFTA critics also noted the political corruption and human rights violations of the ruling political party in Mexico (PRI).

C. Trade Patterns between Texas and Mexico: Mexico is now the U.S.'s third largest trading partner and is responsible for thousands of jobs in Texas and the U.S. Approximately 5 percent of Texas jobs are related to trade with Mexico. The movement of goods and people between Texas and Mexico is significant and challenges both governments to provide the infrastructure and services needed. Texas exports to Mexico increased from 8.8 billion dollars in 1987 to 41 billion dollars in 1999.

D. Common Borders, Common Problems: The interdependence of Texas and Mexico has led to common problems. Problems such as health care do not stop at the border. The number of people living in slums (which create major health problems) on both sides of the border is serious. The tendency for Mexican mothers to cross the border to the U.S. in order to give birth has created "binational families." Environmental problems created by the growth in population and industrial development are not easily rectified when each nation has varying standards. Aspects of NAFTA are intended to address these problems, but the concerns remain.

E. Illegal Immigration: The attraction of economic opportunities in the U.S. has long induced illegal immigration from Mexico and other Latin American countries. There are an estimated 3.5-4 million people living in the U.S. illegally. Large segments of the Texas economy have come to depend on the cheap labor these immigrants provide. Despite the attempt to stem the tide of illegal immigrants with the 1986 Immigration Reform and Control Act, the migration continues. The cost of health care for illegal immigrants and the education of their children has placed a notable burden on taxpayers. The controversy on how to resolve this situation continues.

CHAPTER NINETEEN SAMPLE QUESTIONS

TRUE-FALSE:

1.	The political myth of individualism in Texas has led to the expectation of minimal government assistance.

2.	Family and social relationships form the basis for maintaining the elite structure of the traditionalistic political culture.

3.	The growth of the Hispanic population has not produced significant political power and influence.

4.	An aging population in Texas will place unprecedented demands for resources on both the public and private sectors.

5.	Thirty percent of America's ten largest cities are located in Texas.

6.	The population density of the state is unequally distributed around the state.

7.	Wealth and income are fairly evenly distributed across the state.

8.	The largest growth sector in the Texas economy is the service industry.

9.	The primary purpose of the North American Free Trade Agreement (NAFTA) was to reduce tariffs and increase trade among Mexico, the U.S. and Canada.

10.	It has always been illegal for American companies to hire illegal immigrants.

MULTIPLE CHOICE:

1.	The political subculture which views political power as being best concentrated in the hands of a few elite citizens is:
	a. Traditionalistic
	c. Moralistic
	b. Individualistic
	d. None of the above

2.	The first wave of Anglo migration into Texas occurred in the early nineteenth century and was comprised of people from the _____ region of the U.S.
	a. Lower South
	c. Upper South
	b. Mid West
	d. Far West

3. Compared to the rest of the nation in the last 50 years, the Texas population growth has:
    a. Grown at approximately the same rate
    b. Grown at a faster rate
    c. Grown at a slower rate
    d. Been negative

4. In 1995, the average household income in Texas was:
    a. Below the national average
    b. Slightly above the national average
    c. Well above the national average
    d. About the same as the national average

5. This economic region in Texas (which includes Bryan College Station, Waco, and Temple) is already a high-tech center and is expected to show strong growth in manufacturing, high-tech industries, and health services employment in the future. Which is it?
    a. Southeast   b. Gulf Coast
    c. South Texas   d. Central Texas

6. Which of the following agencies was NOT created by NAFTA to address problems arising from the treaty/
    a. Border Environmental Cooperation Commission
    b. Commission for Labor Cooperation
    c. Agency for International Development
    d. Working Group on Emergency Action

7. Which of the following was NOT a result of the 1986 Immigration Reform and Control Act?
    a. It imposed fines on employers who hired illegal immigrants
    b. It required employees to show proof of right to work status
    c. It gave amnesty to illegals who moved to the U.S. before 1982
    d. It denied benefits to the citizen children of illegal immigrants

8. Which of the following was NOT a goal of the maquiladora program?
    a. Increased foreign currency exchange
    b. Increased technology transfer to Mexico
    c. Increased industrial development
    d. Increased employment
    e. All of the above ARE goals of the maquiladora program

9. The economic conditions of the 1980s and 1990s have _____ the state's reliance on oil and gas as the major industry.
      a. Increased   b. Decreased
      c. Not altered   d. None of the above

10. The term "transnational regionalism" refers to:
      a. The interdependence of south Texas and Mexico
      b. The interdependence of the economic regions of Texas
      c. The interdependence of Texas and it surrounding states
      d. none of the above

CHAPTER NINETEEN SAMPLE QUESTION ANSWERS

TRUE-FALSE

1. **TRUE.** Individualism is the belief that citizens can take care of themselves with minimal government assistance. See page 685.

2. **TRUE.** The traditionalistic political culture is based on family and not political participation by the masses. See page 687.

3. **FALSE.** Hispanics have attained political power and influence as is evident in the number of Hispanic candidates elected to office. See page 689.

4. **TRUE.** By 2030, 17 percent of the Texas population will be older than the age of 65. See page 693.

5. **TRUE**. Houston, San Antonio, and Dallas are all among the nation's top ten largest cities. See page 694.

6. **TRUE.** The population density of the state is unequally distributed around the state. See page 695.

7. **FALSE.** There is great disparity in the distribution of wealth and income. See page 695.

8. **TRUE.** This industry include both low and high wage jobs. See page 702.

9. **TRUE.** The primary purpose of the North American Free Trade Agreement (NAFTA) was to reduce tariffs and increase trade among Mexico, the U.S. and Canada. See page 706.

10. **FALSE**. The hiring of illegal aliens was not a crime until the passage of the Immigration and Reform Control Act in 1986. See page 710.

MULTIPLE CHOICE:

1. **A.** The political subculture which views political power as being best concentrated in the hands of a few elite citizens is traditionalistic. See page 687.

2. **C.** The first wave of Anglo migration into Texas occurred in the early nineteenth century and was comprised of people from the upper South region of the U.S. See page 691.

3. **B.** Texas's population has grown at a much faster pace that the rest of the U.S. See page 692.

4. **A.** In 1995, the national average household income was $34,076. In Texas it was only $32,039 See page 694.

5. **D.** The Central Texas region has a well-balanced economy consisting of agriculture, trade government, health services, universities, and military bases. It also includes Killeen and Austin. See page 704.

6. **C.** NAFTA did not create the Agency for International Development. This is a State Department-related agency. See pages 706-707.

7. **D.** The 1986 Immigration Reform and Control Act does not directly affect children of illegal immigrants born in this country as they are citizens of the U.S. See page 710.

8. **E.** Maquiladoras are aimed at improving the general Mexican economy—they are aimed at improving all of the conditions listed here. See page 705.

9. **B.** The economic conditions of the 1980s and 1990s have decreased the state's reliance on oil and gas as the major industry. See page 700.

10. **A.** The term "transnational regionalism" refers to the interdependence of south Texas and Mexico. See page 705.

CHAPTER TWENTY:
THE TEXAS CONSTITUTION

I.   THE CONSTITUTIONAL LEGACY. The current Texas Constitution has been amended many times and is generally considered outdated and in need of revision. A total rewrite has been elusive as many special interests prefer to have the document unchanged. Texas has had seven constitutions and each was written in a distinct historical setting.

      A.   The Texas Constitution in a Comparative Perspective: Scholars believe that constitutions should be brief and include general principles while leaving specifics for statutory law. They should also not be overly restrictive and thus require modification as society changes. The U.S. Constitution is an excellent example of such a document. It is brief and flexible, being amended only twenty-seven times since its creation. The Texas Constitution, by contrast, is long and detailed with many amendments.

      B.   The Constitution of Coahuila y Texas, 1827: The first constitution of Texas was written as part of the Mexican political system. It had unicameral legislature, a governor, and vice governor. Catholicism was made the state religion, although this was not enforced on the Anglo settlers of Texas. Increased Anglo immigration and the perceived threat of U.S. expansionary policies led Mexico to attempt to exert more control over Texans, and eventually to the Revolution of 1836.

      C.   The Constitution of the Republic of Texas, 1836: In 1835, the Mexican constitution was replaced with a document which provided for a unitary system of power. **DEFINE UNITARY**.

           In response, Texas declared its independence. The new constitution created a bicameral legislature, an elected President, and no official state religion. The nine-year period of independence significantly influenced the state's political culture and myths.

      D.   The Constitution of 1845: **FILL-IN**.

      E.   The Civil War Constitution, 1861: When Texas seceded from the Union, the state constitution was revised once again. Significant changes in the state's constitution were made in line with membership in the Confederacy, although many elements of the previous version were left in tact. One party dominance and an emphasis on states rights were the lasting effects of the Civil War and Texas's participation in the Confederacy.

      F.   The Constitution of 1866: After the Civil War, the Constitution of 1845 was revived and the federally required alterations of abolition of slavery, repudiation of the Secession Ordinance of 1861, and repudiation of all debts and obligations incurred under the Confederacy were included. The new constitution was soon invalidated by the Radical Reconstructionist in Congress, and Texas was placed under military government once again.

G. The Reconstruction Constitution 1869: This constitution did not reflect the views of the majority of Texans at the time, but rather the wishes of the Republican delegates to the state constitutional convention. The new document centralized power, gave the governor a four-year term and appointive powers, provided for annual legislative sessions, gave African Americans the right to vote, and created a statewide system of public schools. Under this constitution, Governor Davis promoted some of the most repressive and unpopular policies in the history of the state.

H. The Constitution of 1876: Retrenchment and Reform: In response to gubernatorial excess, the people of Texas elected a Democratic governor and legislature which took steps to write a new constitution. Many of the delegates to the constitutional convention represented agricultural interests, and about half of the delegates were members of the Grange. **DEFINE GRANGE**.

The economic problems and governmental corruption which permeated the state and federal administrations propelled the framers to write a constitution with an antigovernment nature. Control was placed in the hands of local government, strict limits were placed on taxation, and the powers of the legislature, governor and courts were restricted.

II. GENERAL PRINCIPLES OF THE TEXAS CONSTITUTION: The Texas Constitution embodies three important principles: popular sovereignty, limited government, and separation of powers. Popular sovereignty is the constitutional principle of self-government and is found in the Preamble and first two sections of the Bill of Rights. Limited government is the principle restricting governmental authority and is found throughout the constitution. The Texas Constitution specifically calls for the separation of powers. This is the division of authority among the legislative, executive, and judicial branches.

III. WEAKNESSES AND CRITICISMS OF THE CONSTITUTION OF 1876:

A. Executive Branch: Critics argue that the constitution fragments authority and responsibility excessively in the executive branch. The Texas governor has little control over the other elected state executives and the numerous boards and commissions. Such fragmented government is also seen at the county level, with numerous county officials sharing power.

B.   Legislative Branch: The constitution set up a low-paid, part-time legislature and in doing so, created a legislature which is easily influenced by special interests. Strict limitations on the frequency and subject of legislative operations hinder the ability to meet the complex needs of a changing Texas society.

C.   Judicial Branch: The constitution created numerous locally elected judicial offices, in which judges have a great deal of autonomy.

D.   Education: The centralized public school system set forth in the Constitution of 1869 was abolished in the 1876 version and local governments were given authority and responsibility for education. Disparities in the ability of local governments to finance schools has led to an inequitable education system.

E.   Individual Rights: **FILL IN**.

F.   Consequences of Details: The Texas Constitution is burdened with specifics of policy implementation and other details better dealt with in statutory law. This excessive detail has caused parts of the document to become obsolete. Numerous amendments have been added to enable the constitution to adapt to changing social and political conditions. Several attempts have been made to delete the obsolete sections of the document, but the problem remains and more amendments can be expected.

IV.   CONSTITUTIONAL CHANGE AND ADAPTATION:

A.   Amendment: The amendment process in Texas is fairly easy. Proposed constitutional amendments can only be submitted by the legislature. Approval of two-thirds of the House and Senate will place the amendment on the ballot, where it must be approved by a majority vote. The constitution has been amended 340 times as of 1999. Amendments have been added to address statewide issues, correct obsolete sections of the document, and to meet the needs of small groups.

Texans cannot force a constitutional amendment to be placed on the ballot. Texas does not have initiative or referendum. **DEFINE INITIATIVE AND REFERENDUM**.

B.   Constitutional Convention: The constitution can also be revised by the use of a constitutional convention called by the legislature with the approval of the voters. Delegates to the convention are elected by the public to revise the constitution, which is then put to the voters for approval.

C.   Constitutional Reform Efforts of 1971-1975: A major reform effort was undertaken beginning in 1971. After a Constitutional Revision Commission held public hearings around the state and made recommendations, the convention convened in January of 1974. Special interests dominated and the convention finally adjourned without attaining the two-thirds majority needed to send the proposed changes to the voters. The failure of the convention can be partially explained by the fight over whether to include the state's right-to-work provision (prohibiting union membership as a condition of employment) in the constitution. The failure of Governor Briscoe to support the new state charter, the makeup of the delegates, and involvement of numerous special interests also served to undermine the convention.

D.   Further Piecemeal Reforms: After the failure of the constitutional convention, 143 amendments were added to the constitution between 1975-1999. These amendments dealt with issues such as a lottery, personal income tax, and the role of the comptroller.

E.   Constitutional Provisions, Interest Groups, and Elites: A very small number of people may be responsible for deciding on changes to the constitution. Turnout in elections where constitutional amendments are the only issues on the ballot is alarmingly low--often less than 20 percent. Even when other material is on the ballot, turnout in state elections is low. Interest groups have made great efforts to protect their interests by including them or maintaining their position in the state constitution. Placing favorable amendments on the ballot in years which promise low turnout is just one way to accomplish such goals. Campaigning to stop proposed amendments has also been a successful strategy of interest groups.

Many of the most recent constitutional changes have had an economic development, pro-business orientation. This has included tax breaks and bond proposals for numerous industries. This constitutional emphasis has led critics to argue that the document serves only the elites. In order to overcome this bias, non-elites are forced to turn to the courts.

F.   Change through Court Interpretation: While it may not have been the case in the past, the Texas courts now appear ready to take a more active role in interpreting the constitution. Rulings such as the one in *Edgewood v. Kirby* demonstrate the controversy involved with the courts' more active role.

V.   CONSTITUTIONAL RESTRAINTS AND THE ABILITY TO GOVERN:

A.   Prospects for Future Change: The prospects for significant change to the Texas Constitution in the future seem slim. There is not a sense in the general public that the document needs revision, and therefore the required public approval is hard to attain. The number of special interests with a stake in maintaining the current situation and opposing change is also notable. Finally, most Texans are unfamiliar with the constitution so there is little call for reform or interest therein.

CHAPTER TWENTY SAMPLE QUESTIONS

TRUE-FALSE:

1.   The terms of Texas' admission into the Union provided that Texas could divide itself into as many as five states.

2.   Elements of the Mexican legal system are still found in Texas land and property law, water and water rights law, and community property laws.

3.   The state of Texas has two courts of last resort.

4.   Women and minorities were initially given full citizenship under the 1876 Texas Constitution.

5.   Texas State Treasurer was a rarity in politics—an officeholder who campaigned to abolish her own job.

6.   Voter turnout in elections where constitutional amendments are the only items on the ballot is high.

7.   The prospects are good for major revisions of the current Texas Constitution in the future.

8.   The Constitution of Coahuila y Texas in 1827 set up a unicameral legislature.

9.   The Radical Reconstructionist invalidated the Constitution of 1866 and forced the revisions entailed in the 1869 version.

10.   Any change to the Texas Constitution requires popular approval.

MULTIPLE CHOICE:

1.   When the first constitution was adopted in 1827, Texas was still:
        a. Dominated by Native Americans
        b. Petitioning for statehood
        c. Part of Mexico
        d. Considered a territory of Louisiana

2. Which of the following was <u>not</u> an aspect of the first Texas constitution?
    a. A governor and vice-governor
    b. A unicameral legislature
    c. Catholicism as the official state religion
    d. All of the above were components of the first Texas constitution

3. _____ is a constitutional arrangement in which power is formally divided between the national and subnational governments.
    a. Federalism   b. Unitary
    c. Unicameral   d. Bicameral

4. Reflecting the distrust of government that was widespread when it was written, the Texas Constitution is less a set of basic governmental principles than a(n)
    a. Assemblage of succinct guidelines
    b. Assortment of flexible responsibilities
    c. Listing of elected state officials
    d. Compilation of detailed statutory language

5. Which of the following is NOT one of the general principles found in the Texas Constitution?
    a. Separation of powers
    b. Popular sovereignty
    c. Centralization of power
    d. Limited government

6. The southern states, Texas included, are the only states whose constitutions formally acknowledge the supremacy of the U.S. Constitution, a statement required by the Radical Reconstructionist for:
    a. Application for war loan repayments
    b. Readmission of the former Confederate states to the Union
    c. Adoption of any new state constitutions
    d. Reduction of state representation in the U.S. House

7. The most recent constitutional amendments have tended to favor:
    a. Local government
    b. Public interests
    c. Business
    d. None of the above

8. To ensure the election of citizen-lawmakers, the Texas Constitution created a:
    a. Full-time, well-paid legislature
    b. Low-paid, part-time legislature
    c. Full-time, low-paid legislature
    d. Part-time, well-paid legislature

9. Although the drafters filled the Texas Constitution with a multitude of restrictive provisions, they also:
   a. Created a progressive document
   b. Developed a sense of individualism
   c. Provided an extremely difficult method of amending it
   d. Provided a relatively easy method of amending it

10. The restraints in the Texas Constitution limit the policy options of state government and have generally protected:
    a. The landowners
    b. The poor
    c. Legislators
    d. Elites

CHAPTER TWENTY SAMPLE QUESTIONS ANSWERS

TRUE-FALSE:

1.   **TRUE.** This clause was forgotten until 1991, when a representative proposed doing just this. The proposal was not taken seriously. See page 720.

2.   **TRUE**. These elements are holdovers from the rule under Mexican law. See page 718.

3.   **TRUE**. The Court of Criminal Appeals is the court of last resort for criminal cases. The Texas Supreme Court is the court of last resort for civil cases. See page 726.

4.   **FALSE.**   Women were not guaranteed the right to vote until 1920 under amendment to the U.S. Constitution.   African American voters did not receive suffrage until the 1960s. See page 725.

5.   **TRUE**. In 1994, Whitehead defeated her Republican challenger for the JOB by promising to abolish the office. She won, and the office was abolished. See page 736.

6.   **FALSE**. Voter turnout in elections where constitutional amendments are the only items on the ballot is traditionally very low. See page 735.

7.   **FALSE**. The prospects are not good for major revisions of the current Texas constitution in the future. See page 738.

8.   **TRUE**. The Constitution of Coahuila y Texas in 1827 set up a unicameral legislature. See page 718.

9.   **TRUE**. The Radical Reconstructionist invalidated the constitution of 1866 and forced the revisions entailed in the 1869 version. See page 722.

10.   **TRUE**. Any change to the Texas constitution requires popular approval. See page 729.

MULTIPLE CHOICE:

1. **C**. Texas was originally a territory of Mexico. The Constitution of Coahuila y Texas was written in 1827. See page 718.

2. **D.** The first Texas Constitution, the Coahuila y Texas Constitution, had a governor and vice governor, a unicameral legislature, and Catholicism was the official state religion. See page 718.

3. **A.** Federalism is a constitutional arrangement in which power is formally divided between the national and subnational governments. See page 719.

4. **D.** At 80,000 words, the Texas Constitution is extremely detailed. The U.S. Constitution is much smaller and broader. See page 717.

5. **C.** The separation of powers, popular sovereignty, and limited government are the general principles found in the Texas Constitution. Centralization of power is not. See page 725.

6. **B.** The U.S. Congress, elected in 1866, demanded tougher requirements for reconstruction than Presidents Abraham Lincoln, Andrew, and Johnson This was one such requirement for reentry into the Union. See page 722.

7. **C.** The most recent constitutional amendments have tended to favor business. See page 737.

8. **B.** This was intended to prevent a class of professional politicians isolated from the people they served. See page 727.

9. **D.** This easy amendment process has contributed to the length and detail of the Texas Constitution. See page 728.

10. **D.** The restraints in the Texas constitution limit the policy options of state government and have generally protected elites See page 737.

CHAPTER TWENTY-ONE
INTEREST GROUPS, POLITICAL PARTIES, AND ELECTIONS IN TEXAS

I.   THE POWER OF INTEREST GROUPS: Interest groups tend to be very strong in states with weak political party systems. Thus the one-party dominance of the Democratic Party in Texas facilitated the development of strong interest groups. Interest groups spend millions of dollars each year in attempts to influence campaign outcomes and lobbying efforts.

II.   PLURALISM OR ELITISM: **DEFINE PLURALISM. DEFINE ELITISM.**

III.   DOMINANT INTEREST GROUPS IN TEXAS: Large corporations, banks, oil companies, and agricultural interests have long dominated state government, but the redistricting of the 1970s enabled other interests to have access as well. **DEFINE SINGLE-MEMBER DISTRICT.**

    A.   Business Groups: Business groups have organized in three basic ways in Texas. Associations which represent broad based business interests, trade associations, and individual corporate lobbying are mechanisms used by business to influence state government.

    B.   Professional Groups: Groups such as the Texas Medical Association (TMA) and Lawyers Involved for Texas (LIFT) have been tremendously active and influential. The war over tort law has been a recurrent issue. Candidate contributions made through political action committees (PACs) have enabled these groups to finance political campaigns and become key players in state politics.

    C.   Education Groups: Education groups, particularly higher education interests, have been very active in Austin. Although it is technically illegal for state employees to attempt to influence legislation, chancellors and other university officials have found ways of promoting their interests in the legislature. The numerous groups representing elementary and secondary educations have been very active since 1990. Nevertheless, the number of groups and their varying perspectives have sometimes sent conflicting signals to the legislature, and thus reduced potential effectiveness.

    D.   Public Interest Groups: Most public interest groups active in Austin promote protection of consumers, the elderly, the poor, the young, the disabled, or promote higher ethical standards for public officials. The use of paid lobbyists, as well as grass roots activists by these groups is common.

    E.   Minority Interest Groups: The last twenty years have seen the legislature become more responsive to minority interest groups. Hispanic organizations have been particularly influential in election and educational reform. The National Association for the Advancement of Colored People (NAACP), while also concerned with educational and electoral issues, has focused a great deal on employment opportunities.

F. Organized Labor Groups: While generally weak across the state, organized labor enjoys selected areas of strength. One such area is the southeastern part of the state, where oil workers are highly unionized. Unions can provide strong grass roots organizations for political candidates, but labor candidates have not fared well in recent elections. Texas has about 230,000 members of unions affiliated with the Texas AFL-CIO.

G. Government Lobbyists: Counties, cities, and other local governments faced with ever tightening budgets have started to be active in Austin. Umbrella organizations which represent numerous government entities have also employed full-time lobbyists to aid in their attempts to gain support from the state.

H. Agriculture Groups: Given the historical importance of agriculture in the state, the influence of agricultural groups is not surprising. Groups such as the Texas Farm Bureau continue to be a major influence, despite the urbanization of the state.

I. Religious Groups: Religious groups have influenced policy in Texas, and conservative groups have become particularly powerful within the Republican party. In their attempts to improve social conditions, many groups have started community based organizations which are becoming important policy players. Note the importance of the Religious Right.

IV. DEVELOPMENT OF THE TWO-PARTY SYSTEM IN TEXAS:

A. One-Party Politics: For more than a century, Texas was a one-party Democratic state. Social and economic development of the last 30 years have increased the viability of the Republican Party and two-party competition. The success of the Democratic Party in Texas since the Civil War is in part due to the anti-Republican sentiment remaining after the rule of the Radical Republicans. The Democratic Party also ensured their dominance through efforts to forestall the political and economic coalitions of small farmers, African Americans, and the urban laborers. The political power of Democratic elites was solidified with constitutional restrictions and segregation legislation.

B. Factionalism in the Democratic Party: The Depression and FDR's New Deal politics dramatically altered the political landscape of Texas. The New Deal policies which entailed federal economic intervention, as well as social programs such as Social Security, were tremendously popular and yet at odds with portions of the Texas Democratic Party. Texans supported Roosevelt in each of his elections, but the split between liberal and conservative Democrats became problematic. The conservative wing of the party, nevertheless, controlled state politics with only rare interruptions. The bifactionalism of the Democratic Party was tested by factors such as the national party's commitment to civil rights, efforts by the oil interests to regain control of the tidelands, and the election of Republican John Tower to the U.S. Senate.

C.   Two-Party Politics in Texas: The realignment of Texas did not occur as part of a critical election, but rather occurred gradually due to several catalysts. The civil rights movement and economic factors led to greater participation of minorities and the development of Democratic affiliation of these groups. The migration of northern Republicans to the state in the 1970s and 1980s also facilitated the evolution of two-party politics. Elections throughout the state in the 1990s demonstrate, the viability of both parties.

D.   Toward Republican Dominance? Governor Bush won reelection to office in 1998 and Republicans swept all statewide offices. Republicans also made significant gains at the county level.

E.   Third Parties: Although none have enjoyed statewide electoral success, Texas has a long tradition of third party activity. Political organizations on the local level which are not affiliated with either the Democratic or Republican Parties have, however, gained significant influence.

V.   CHANGING PATTERNS OF PARTY SUPPORT AND IDENTIFICATION: Party identification in Texas has changed greatly in the last 30 years. While,, in 1964,, less than 10 percent of the population classified themselves as Republicans, today about 34 percent call themselves Republicans, 26 percent Democrats. There are, however important differences in the social and economic characteristics of party identifiers. Republicans tend to be Anglos, college educated, have high incomes, be younger than 45, and live in large metropolitan areas. Democrats, on the other hand, tend to be minorities, less educated, have lower incomes,, and be older. In 1998, Governor Bush attracted about 40 percent of the Hispanic vote.

VI.   THE PARTY ORGANIZATION: Political parties in Texas have established both permanent and temporary organizations to promote their candidates and agendas. The Democratic and Republican Parties have no membership requirements, and the declaration of party affiliation upon registration is not required in Texas.

Therefore, the right to participate in the party's electoral and nominating activities is based on voting in the party's primary. That act identifies a voter as a Republican or Democrat.

A. The Permanent Organization: The first level of the party organization is the precinct. County commissioners in each county establish precincts for which precinct chairs are elected in each party. The precinct chair is responsible for organizing the precinct convention and serves on the county executive committee. There were an estimated 8,350 precintsin Texas in 2000.

The second level of the party organization is the county executive committee. The committee is comprised of the precinct chairs and a county chair elected by countywide primary voters. The county executive committee is responsible for management of the primary election within the county, even though funding for this is provided by the state organization.

The state executive committee is the third level of the party organization. This committee is the statewide governing board for the political party. It has representatives from each of the state's senatorial districts, as well as the state party chair and vice chair. The committee is responsible for organizing the state convention, fundraising, and development of party policy.

B. Temporary Organization: The series of conventions held every two years are the temporary organizations of the political parties. The convention system helps to organize the permanent structure, as well as provide an opportunity for party activists to gather. These conventions are particularly important in presidential election years, for the delegates to the national convention are chosen here.

C. Precinct Conventions: Any party member who voted in the party primary is entitled to participate in the precinct convention. The main purpose of the convention is to select delegates to the district convention and the development of policy statements for possible inclusion in the state and national party platform. Participation in precinct conventions is very low in nonpresidential election years.

D. County or Senatorial District Conventions: Delegates from multiple precincts come together at district conventions in order to select delegates for the state convention and consider platform recommendations.

E. State Conventions: State conventions are held in June of even-numbered years. The party platform is adopted, the state party chair and vice chair elected, and the nominees to statewide office are certified at this convention. In presidential selection years the delegates to the national convention are also chosen, members of the national committee elected, and presidential electors are chosen.

VII.   PARTIES AND GOVERNMENT: Critics of political parties in Texas point out that they do not fit the responsible party model. **DEFINE RESPONSIBLE PARTY MODEL.**

The decentralization of parties and the inability to discipline party members, the sheer number of elected officials in the state, the coalitions of groups and individuals with differing views created to pass policy, and the long standing anti-party tradition in American politics explain the difficulties political parties in Texas have in conforming to the responsible party model.

VIII.   MINORITIES AND POLITICAL PARTICIPATION: Despite the very low turnout, Texas today has some of the most progressive voter registration laws in the country. Texas has a history, however, of excluding African Americans, Hispanics, and low-income whites. Techniques such as the poll tax, the all-white primary, and restrictive registration systems were all used to deny voting opportunities to various groups.

IX.   POLITICAL GAINS BY MINORITIES AND WOMEN: The elimination of restrictive voting laws, a progressive registration system, registration drives of groups such as the NAACP, and the federal Voting Rights Act have helped minorities make considerable electoral progress.

    A.   Hispanics: Although Hispanics make up approximately 30.7 percent of the state's population, voter turnout would not indicate that degree of prominence. In recent elections, Hispanics accounted for only 12-15 percent of those voting. Of those Hispanics who do vote, there is a strong affiliation with the Democratic Party.

    B.   African Americans: African Americans make up approximately 11.5 percent of the state's population and about 9 to 10 percent of the voters. Like the Hispanics, there is a very strong affiliation with the Democratic Party, and if African Americans were to vote as a cohesive group their political power would be impressive.

    C.   Women: Although Texas politics has long been dominated by men, women are gaining political ground. In the last two decades the state has elected numerous women to high office including governor, U.S. Senate, U.S. House of Representatives, state Senate, Texas House and mayor of the three largest cities in the state.

X.   ELECTIONS IN TEXAS: The low voter turnout in Texas may in part be due to the numerous elections and the corresponding voter fatigue. Turnout and interest in the general election of presidential years is the highest, but can be very low in local elections.

A. Primary Elections: **DEFINE DIRECT PRIMARY. DEFINE OPEN PRIMARY.** Only 4.8 percent of the voting age population voted in the 2000 Democratic presidential primary, compared to 7.1 percent in the 2000 GOP presidential primary.

B. General Elections: The general election for state and federal offices is held the first Tuesday after the first Monday in November in even-numbered years. Candidates from both the major parties, as well as those from third parties who have met the petition requirements, are listed on the ballot. Voter turnout in Texas has long been weak, and only about a third of the voters voted in the 1994 election and 27 percent in 1998.

C. City, School Board, and Single-Purpose District Elections: Most local elections are held in April of odd-numbered years and are nonpartisan. While the competitiveness of these elections varies, the turnout is rarely as high as in the general elections. From 1990-1994, thirteen PACs made contributions in excess of $200,000 to candidates.

D. Special Elections: Special elections can be held to consider constitutional amendments, local bond issues, local initiatives and referenda, to recall public officials, and to fill certain statewide offices. Turnout in these elections is normally very poor.

E. Extended Absentee Balloting: In an effort to aid turnout, Texas extended the absentee balloting period in 1988. There has been a striking increase in the number of ballots cast early, and now candidates are having to adjust campaign strategies accordingly.

XI. CAMPAIGN FINANCES:

A. Campaign Costs: The cost of campaigning in Texas is considered high, but exact data are not available due to the differing reporting requirements across offices. Modern campaign techniques, the rising cost of television advertising, and true two-party competition have raised the cost of campaigning significantly.

B. Fund Raising: Texas places no limit on the amount of money an individual or PAC can contribute to a candidate for state election, other than judicial candidates. This has led to the criticism that the system is little more than legalized bribery.

C. Political Action Committees: PACs represent individual companies or special interest groups and accumulate money from their members to contribute to candidates. The lack of campaign contribution limits has made PACs exceptionally influential in Texas politics. From 1990-1994, thirteen PACs made contributions in excess of $200,000 to candidates.

D. Attempts at Reform: Campaign reform remains a continual struggle. After the Sharpstown scandal, a list of reforms was enacted which, while they did not limit contributions, required reporting of contributions and sources for the first time.

CHAPTER TWENTY-ONE SAMPLE QUESTIONS

TRUE-FALSE:

1. Many lobbyists are former legislators.

2. Public interest groups are those which represent the interests of public employees.

3. Most university regents, chancellors, and presidents are politically well-connected.

4. Urbanization has reduced the importance of agricultural interest groups.

5. Texas now has a viable Republican Party and competitive two-party politics.

6. People must declare their party affiliation when they register to vote in Texas.

7. Minority interest groups have often found that the courthouse is a shorter route to success than the statehouse.

8. Turnout in local elections is approximately the same as in presidential elections.

9. Texas offers an extended period for absentee balloting.

10. Like the federal government, Texas places limits on campaign contributions given to all candidates for state offices.

MULTIPLE CHOICE:

1. Which of the following is NOT one of the ways business interests organize in Texas?
   a. Trade associations
   b. Mobilizing public opinion
   c. Individual corporate lobbying
   d. Business associations

2. Powerful pressure groups usually evolve in states with:
   a. Strong economic bases
   b. Strong political parties
   c. Weak political parties
   d. Weak educational systems

3. The "Religious Right" combined Christianity with which of the following political positions?
   a. Anti-civil rights
   b. Anticommunism
   c. Anti-New Deal
   d. All of the above

4. The influence of trial lawyers has been expanded for all the following reasons EXCEPT:
   a. Litigation over medical malpractice
   b. Product liability
   c. Workers' compensation
   d. False advertising

5. Which of the following is not a characteristic of Texas Republicans?
   a. Anglo
   b. Over 45
   c. Live in large metropolitan areas
   d. All of the above are characteristics of Texas Republicans

6. Under Roosevelt, the regulatory function of the federal government was expanded to exercise control and authority over:
   a. The expansion of communism
   b. The growth of big business and labor
   c. The development of integration programs
   d. Much of the nation's economy

7. The state party convention:
   a. Is held in June of even numbered years
   b. Has delegates elect the party's state leadership
   c. Adopts a party platform
   d. All of the above

8. Although none has had statewide electoral success in Texas, there has been a tradition of:
   a. Special interests
   b. Labor unions
   c. Republican Party activity
   d. Third parties

9. Which of the following has been used in Texas to discourage certain groups from voting?
   a. The poll tax
   b. The white primary
   c. Restrictive registration requirements
   d. All of the above

10. Selection of candidates for government office through direct election by the voters of a political party is the:
    a. White primary
    b. Direct primary
    c. Open primary
    d. Blanket primary

CHAPTER TWENTY-ONE SAMPLE QUESTIONS ANSWERS

TRUE-FALSE:

1.   **TRUE.** Former governmental officials have specialized knowledge about how policies are mad–that's why many become lobbyists after their public careers are over. See page 745.

2.   **FALSE.** Public interest groups are those which represent the interests of the general public as opposed to a particular company or industry. See page 748.

3.   **TRUE.** Universities often use nontaxed funds and donations to pay lobbyists. See page 748.

4.   **FALSE.** Urbanization has not reduced the importance of agricultural interest groups. See page 750.

5.   **TRUE.** Although once a one-party Democratic state, the 1980s saw the resurgence of the Republican Party in Texas. See pages 754-756.

6.   **FALSE.** People do not have to declare their party affiliation when they register to vote in Texas. See page 761.

7.   **TRUE.** This is true because sometimes the legislature cannot or will not address the problems. See page 749.

8.   **FALSE.** Turnout in local elections is much lower than in presidential elections. See page 770.

9.   **TRUE.** In 1988, Texas passed a law enabling citizens to vote in an election up to twenty days before election day. See page 771.

10. **FALSE.** Unlike the federal government, Texas does not place limits on campaign contributions given to all candidates for state offices. See page 777.

MULTIPLE CHOICE:

1. **B.** Business interests in Texas organize by using trade associations, individual corporate lobbying, and business associations. See page 746.

2. **C.** For most of Texas's history, political parties have not been competitive, allowing interest groups to have an entry into the system. See page 744.

3. **D.** The "Religious Right" combined Christianity with the political positions of anti-civil rights, anticommunism, and anti-New Deal. See page 750.

4. **D.** Lawyers have managed to influence Texas politics in significant ways, like influencing the election of Texas Supreme Court justices. See page 747.

5. **B.** Texas Republicans tend to be Anglo and live in large metropolitan areas. They do not tend to be over 45. See pages 760-761.

6. **D.** Roosevelt introduced many programs to help improve the U.S. depressed economy. See page 753.

7. **D.** The state party convention is held in June of even-numbered years, has delegates elect the party's state leadership, and adopts a party platform. See page 763.

8. **D.** The most successful third party in Texas in recent years has been the Libertarian Party See page 757.

9. **D.** Texas has used the poll tax, the white primary, and restrictive registration requirements to discourage certain groups from voting. See page 765.

10. **B.** This direct primary is used in most states to choose candidates for political office. See page 769.

CHAPTER TWENTY-TWO:
THE TEXAS LEGISLATURE

I. THE INSTITUTIONALIZATION OF THE TEXAS LEGISLATURE: The Texas legislature operates under numerous constitutional restrictions. One of the most difficult is the requirement that they meet for only 140 consecutive days, once every two years. Also, the conditions in which the legislature functions have changed greatly over the last 30 years and altered the legislature itself. **DEFINE INSTITUTIONALIZATION.**

II. THE ORGANIZATION AND COMPOSITION OF THE TEXAS LEGISLATURE: Based on the fear of a strong central government, the framers of the Texas Constitution created a part-time, bicameral legislature with 31 Senators and 150 members of the House of Representatives.

   A. Legislative Sessions: Regular sessions of the legislature are limited to 140 days, once every two years and begin on the second Tuesday in January of odd-numbered years. The governor is given the ability to call the legislature into a special session, but these are limited to 30 days and the subject matter is specified by the governor. There is, however, no limit on the number of special sessions a governor may call. Special sessions have been used frequently in the recent past, and some critics argue that they are evidence for the need of a full-time legislature.

   B. Terms of Office and Qualifications: Members of the Senate serve four-year staggered terms, while House members serve two-year terms. A candidate for the Senate must be a qualified voter, at least twenty-six years old, a resident of Texas for five years, and a resident of the district for one year prior to election. A candidate for the House must also be a qualified voter, at least twenty-one years old, and a resident of Texas for two years and of the district one year prior to election. There is no limit on the number of terms a member of the House or Senate may serve.

   C. Pay and Compensation: The pay of legislature is set by the state constitution and can only be raised with voter approval. The pay is very low, and critics have argued it should be raised in an effort to professionalize the legislature. The base pay is $7,200 per year.

   D. Physical Facilities: Recent renovation added significant office space and meeting rooms to an overcrowded capital building. The Senate chamber is in the east wing of the capitol and the House is in the west. Seating on the floor of the chambers is arranged by seniority as opposed to party affiliation, as is the case in the U.S. Congress.

E. Membership and Careers: Changing political attitudes, court-ordered single-member districts, and redrawn political boundaries have significantly changed the composition of the legislature in the last 25 years. The legislature is much more inclusive and representative of the ethnic and gender makeup of the state than it once was. Legislators tend to come from the ranks of business and the law, and many have little or no previous political or government experience prior to taking office.

F. Legislative Turnover: Turnover in the Texas legislature is high. The average tenure in the House is 7 years, and 11 years in the Senate. The high turnover is in part due to the low pay, high personal costs of holding office, and redistricting.

III. REPRESENTATION AND REDISTRICTING: **DEFINE PROPORTIONAL REPRESENTATION. DEFINE SINGLE-MEMBER DISTRICT.**

Despite constitutional requirements that the legislature redraw district lines every ten years in light of the U.S. census and the creation of the Legislative Redistricting Board to force the legislature to comply with redistricting requirements, the legislature has traditionally underrepresented urban areas. Court cases such as *Baker v. Carr* and *Reynolds v. Sims* forced the legislature into an apportionment system which impartially represents all sectors of the state. At-large districts were also eliminated in the 1970s, giving greater access to minorities.

IV. LEGISLATIVE LEADERSHIP: The dominance of the Democratic Party and the personal leadership it created precluded the need for a highly organized institutional leadership until recently.

A. House Leadership: The presiding officer of the House is elected by the House members and is called the Speaker. Although it is illegal for Speaker candidates to make clear promises in return for support, the control the Speaker has over the committee assignment process precludes the need for such promises. Membership on House committees is partially determined by seniority, but the Speaker controls the designation of committee chairs and vice chairs, as well as appointing all members of the procedural committees. Prior to the 1950s, it was unusual for a Speaker to serve more than two terms. This tradition has since been eliminated. The Speaker appoints the Speaker pro tempore to be part of the Speaker's team and aid in the passage of legislation. This person is usually a close personal ally of the Speaker. (James E. "Pete" Laney in 2000.)

B. Senate Leadership: The presiding officer of the Texas Senate is the lieutenant governor, who is elected by the voters of the state for a four-year term. The lieutenant governor is elected separately from the governor and can be tremendously powerful due to his/her legislative influence and state wide electoral base. The lieutenant governor has a great deal of control in the Senate. He/she determines when (and if) a bill will be considered by the full chamber, as well as appoints the members to the standing committees.

The president pro tempore of the Senate is chosen by the members of the Senate and is usually rotated among the most senior members of the chamber. The president pro tempore takes over leadership of the chamber in the absence of the lieutenant governor and is third in line of succession to the governorship. In 2000, the Lieutenant Governor was Rick Perry.

V. INFLUENCE AND CONTROL OVER THE LEGISLATIVE PROCESS: Both the lieutenant governor and the Speaker of the House have the ability to assign any piece of legislation to committee and thus influence the fate of that legislation. While both chambers have mechanisms to overrule such assignments, challenges to leadership are rare. The presiding officers exert control through the application of the rules of the chamber, the state constitution, and through their informal relations with other members. They customarily adopt the pretense of being neutral on any given piece of legislation. The Speaker can vote on any piece of legislation and the lieutenant governor can break ties, but both avoid any position, taking unless necessary.

VI. LEADERSHIP TEAMS: The committee chairs make up the Speaker's and lieutenant governor's teams and act as the presiding officer's unofficial floor leaders. The absence of a formalized leadership structure based on party and the use of teams is an artifact of the long-time Democratic control of the legislature.

VII. THE COMMITTEE SYSTEM: Committees are responsible for consideration of proposed legislation, holding hearings, correction of drafting errors, compromise, consolidation of similar legislation, and the screening of unworthy legislation. Only a small percentage of the legislation proposed is eventually passed, most is dispensed with in committee. Therefore, the chairs of committees can be tremendously influential as they control the fate of legislation in their committee.

A. Standing Committee: There are 37 standing committees in the House and 15 in the Senate. These committees are created to consider legislation or perform a procedural role in the legislative process. Membership composition of the committee will vary with the chamber and substantive responsibilities.

The importance of a committee is determined by its policy jurisdiction. In the Texas House the Calendars committee is particularly influential, despite recent reforms, in that it schedules the order of legislative debate on the floor. Other important committees in the House include the Appropriations and Ways and Means and in the Senate Finance and State Affairs are powerful.

B. Standing Subcommittees: The formal standing subcommittee system has just started to develop in Texas. In the past, subcommittees had been created simply as the need arose.

C. Conference Committees: Conference committees are designed to resolve the differences in versions of legislation passed by the House and Senate. Conference committee members are assigned by the presiding officers and legislation must be approved by a majority of the House conference committee members as well as the Senate members prior to being sent back to the chambers for approval.

D. Special Committees: The governor, lieutenant governor, and the Speaker occasionally appoint members to select committees which are temporary committees used to examine major policy issues and make legislative recommendations.

VIII. RULES AND PROCEDURES:

A. How a Bill Becomes a Law: The first reading of a bill is the first step in the legislative process and entails introduction of the legislation and its referral to committee. After committee consideration, if the bill gains committee approval, it is given a second reading by the full chamber. At this point it can be debated and amended. The amendment process may help or hinder the legislation. If the bill is approved on the second reading, it will be sent to the other chamber for consideration. This is the third reading. If the bill is approved on the third reading, then it is presented to the governor. However, if the second chamber makes any changes to the legislation, these changes must be presented to the original chamber for approval.

The governor may sign, veto, or ignore the legislation. If the governor of Texas fails to sign a piece of legislation by a certain deadline, it will become law. A gubernatorial veto can be overridden by a two-thirds vote of each chamber. The Texas governor has the line-item veto only on appropriations bills. **DEFINE LINE-ITEM VETO.**

B. Procedural Obstacles to Legislation: Numerous obstructions can be found throughout the legislative process. Like the Calendars committee in the House, the two-thirds rule in the Senate can bar floor debate on a given piece of legislation. **DEFINE THE TWO-THIRDS RULE. DEFINE A TAG. DEFINE A FILIBUSTER.**

C. Shortcuts, Obfuscation, and Confusion: There are numerous ways legislators can circumvent the obstacles placed in front of their bills. These include attaching a bill which is being otherwise detained to another piece of legislation as an amendment and the use of the local and consent calendars.

Compromises on important bills are often made off the floor of the chamber and behind the scenes. This, the use of division votes, and the aversion to record votes often leaves the public in the dark concerning the decision,making process of their legislature. Other practices such as taking the voting lead from the sponsors of a bill, and the casting of votes for members not present are also used to get legislation passed. The time limits placed on the legislature and the last minute rush that ensues causes such measures to be used.

IX.   THE EMERGING PARTY SYSTEM: The realignment of the populace has caused the emergence of partisan conflict in the legislature. Legislative organization in Texas has not been arranged by party, and even the evolution of the Republican Party in the last twenty years has not altered this. Republicans and conservative Democrats have formed coalitions which have been effective in promoting their policy objectives, without a formal party structure.

   A.   The Growth of Partisanship: The rise of the Republican Party has seen an increase in partisan conflicts. In the past it was very common for presiding officers to appoint Republicans to important committees, assured of their cooperation. This type of appointment generosity is not likely to continue. Nevertheless, currently there is still a fair amount of cooperation between the two parties. Still, the case of James Byrd, Jr. shows that partisanship is a permanent part of the legislature.

   B.   Republican Contenders: The increase in the number of Republicans in both chambers of the Texas legislature and the establishment of the first Republican caucus indicate the political viability of the party. The changes generated by a Republican majority could be significant. Republicans sought a House majority in 2000.

X.   OTHER LEGISLATIVE CAUCUSES: The cohesive voting blocs of the Hispanic and African-American caucus have enabled these groups of legislators to have a large impact on Speakers' elections and important statewide issues. Recognizing the value of such caucuses, legislators from some urban areas such as Harris County have started to form their own caucuses.

XI.   LEGISLATORS AND THEIR CONSTITUENTS: Legislators have great leeway in representing their constituents for they represent a tremendous number of interests, lack of public attention to state legislative action is high, and media coverage is meager and uneven. These factors make legislators more responsive to interest groups or those sections of their constituency which are attentive.

XII.   LEGISLATIVE DECISION MAKING: The legislature has both formal and informal rules of conduct. The rules and norms are designed to give conflict an air of civility and courtesy. Debate is focused on issues and personal attacks are avoided.

The sheer number of issues and pieces of legislation presented each session makes it very difficult for any member to be informed on all of them. Legislators use informational shortcuts and the norms of the legislature to help them make decisions. The clues given by bill sponsors, political parties, legislative staffs, interest groups, the wishes of constituents, information and insight provided by other legislators, gubernatorial pressures, and media coverage all play a part in legislative decision making. The importance of any of these on an individual legislator will vary by legislator and issue.

XIII. THE DEVELOPMENT OF LEGISLATIVE STAFF: The quality and quantity of legislative staff have increased in the last twenty years with the increased professionalization of the legislature. Legislative staff include the permanent employees of the Budget Board, Legislative Council, and Reference Library, as well as the secretarial staff who manage offices, lawyers who aid in writing legislation, and personal staff which handle constituent concerns. Funding for individual legislative staff is limited, and on these funds offices in the district, as well as those in Austin, must be maintained.

XIV. LEGISLATIVE ETHICS AND REFORMS: The millions of dollars spent by interest groups to influence the legislature and the faults of a few members have undermined the confidence most Texans have in their legislature. Most legislators are hard-working, honest people and there are stiff penalties for ethical failings. Accordingly, most attempts to codify legislative ethics stem from scandal. Reforms to the campaign finance laws have been slow in coming, and although, have been more common in the recent past, still have a long way to go to eliminate corruption.

CHAPTER TWENTY-TWO SAMPLE QUESTIONS

TRUE-FALSE:

1.   The Texas legislature can be classified as highly professional.

2.   Texas legislators have the ability to set their own pay, without the approval of the voters.

3.   The governor has the authority to call special sessions when necessary.

4.   The number of terms an individual can serve in the legislature is limited to three for House members and two in the Senate.

5.   The committee system in Texas is the backbone of the legislative process.

6.   In 1997, law and business careers were no longer the dominant occupation of the Texas legislators.

7.   The various techniques used to circumvent procedural obstacles make it very easy to pass legislation with which a majority of legislators are not familiar.

8.   Despite the growth of the Republican Party, the lack of open partisan conflict in the Texas legislature is likely to continue.

9.   Legislative staff often play an important role in influencing the decisions made by Texas legislators.

10.   Unlike the president of the U.S., the governor of Texas may visit the House or Senate to demonstrate support for a piece of legislation.

MULTIPLE CHOICE:

1.   The Texas legislators meet in regular session for:
     a. Six months annually
     b. Six months every three years
     c. 140 days annually
     d. 140 days every two years

2. The Texas legislature has become more professional due to:
   a. Structuralization
   b. Institutionalization
   c. Internalization
   d. Functionalizing

3. In 1964, the U.S. Supreme Court, in *Reynolds v. Sims*, held that state legislative districts had to be apportioned on the:
   a. Proportional representation principle
   b. Single-member district principle
   c. "One person, one vote" principle
   d. "Separate but equal" principle

4. The Speaker of the House in the Texas legislature has all of the following powers EXCEPT:
   a. Schedule debate on a bill
   b. Assign legislation to committees
   c. Assign members to committees
   d. All of the above are powers of the Speaker

5. A _____ is a committee created to consider legislation or perform a procedural role in the lawmaking process.
   a. Subcommittee
   b. Calendars committee
   c. Standing committee
   d. Rules committee

6. The voters in a statewide election choose the presiding officer of the Texas Senate, the:
   a. Speaker of the Senate
   b. Vice governor
   c. Lieutenant governor
   d. Majority leader of the Senate

7. Which of the following was not a provision in the 1973 ethics reforms laws?
   a. Requirements that lobbyists register with the secretary of state
   b. Report of lobbyists' expenditures
   c. Submit journal of legislative proposals to legislative leaders
   d. File public reports identifying their sources of income

8. A group of legislators who come together based on common political goals, partisan ties, or ethnic or geographic similarities is called a:
   a. Caucus
   b. Congregation
   c. Assembly
   d. Conference

9. Which of the following are influences on the decision making of Texas legislators?
   a. The governor
   b. The legislative staff
   c. The Legislative Budget Board
   d. All of the above

10. Legislative staff are used for all of the following EXCEPT:
    a. Research
    b. Writing legislation
    c. Handling the personal business of the legislator
    d. Responding to constituent needs

CHAPTER TWENTY-TWO SAMPLE QUESTION ANSWERS

TRUE-FALSE:

1. **FALSE.** The Texas legislature cannot be classified as highly professional. See page 778.

2. **FALSE** Texas legislators do not have the ability to set their own pay without the approval of the voters. See pages 779-780.

3. **TRUE.** Special sessions are limited to specific topics and cannot be used to introduce new issues. See page 778.

4. **FALSE.** There are no term limits in Texas. See page 779.

5. **TRUE.** Most of the work done in the Texas legislature is done in committee. See page 790.

6. **FALSE.** In 1997, 11 of 31 senators and 47 of 150 House members were lawyers. See page 781.

7. **TRUE.** The various techniques used to circumvent procedural obstacles make it very easy to pass legislation with which a majority of legislators are not familiar. See page 796.

8. **FALSE.** Despite the growth of the Republican Party, the lack of open partisan conflict in the Texas legislature is not likely to continue. See page 798.

9. **TRUE.** Legislative staff often inform members as to the political implications or the substantive merits of legislation. See page 804.

10. **TRUE.** Unlike the president of the U.S., the Governor of Texas may visit the House or Senate to demonstrate support for a piece of legislation. See page 804.

MULTIPLE-CHOICE:

1. **D.** Texas legislators are only part-time to prevent them from being isolated from their constituents See page 779.

2. **B.** The Texas legislature is still not as professional as some state legislatures. See page 778.

3. **C**. This change was made because urban districts were underrepresented. See page 783.

4. **A**. The Speaker of the House in the Texas legislature cannot schedule debate on a bill. He can assign legislation to committees and assign members to committees. See page 785.

5. **C**. A standing committee is a committee created to consider legislation or perform a procedural role in the lawmaking process. See page 791.

6. **C**. This is important because, unlike the U.S. vice president, the lieutenant governor has extensive legislative responsibilities. See page 787.

7. **C**. This law was passed as a response to the 1972 Sharpstown scandal. See page 808.

8. **A**. A group of legislators who come together based on common political goals, partisan ties, or ethnic or geographic similarities is called a caucus. See page 799.

9. **D**. The governor, the legislative staff, and the Legislative Budget Board are all influences on the decision making of Texas legislators. See pages 803-805.

10. **C**. Legislative staff are used for research, writing legislation, and responding to constituent needs. They do not handle the personal business of the legislators. See pages 805-806.

CHAPTER TWENTY-THREE
THE TEXAS EXECUTIVE AND BUREAUCRACY

I.   A FRAGMENTED GOVERNMENT: Constitutional restrictions make the Texas governor one of the weakest in the nation. The governor has no appointed cabinet and the heads of some of the most important state agencies are independently elected. Reforms have increased gubernatorial control but the main powers remain the ability to veto legislation, call the legislature into special session and set its agenda, and make limited appointments.

II.   THE STRUCTURE OF THE PLURAL EXECUTIVE: The Texas Constitution sets up a plural executive system, in which the executive officeholders are elected independently of the governor and fragments authority. The members of the executive system which are elected separately from the governor who, include the lieutenant governor, comptroller of public accounts, treasurer, commissioner of the general land office, attorney general, agriculture commissioner, railroad commissioners, and the members of the board of education.

The agencies which are headed by the independently elected executives are only subject to minimal gubernatorial control. Although there has been minimal conflict in the past, the ability of agency heads to claim their own electoral mandate may cause friction between the governor and agency heads as Texas becomes more of a two-party state. Such discord makes the coordination of policy difficult and severely limits gubernatorial power.

III. THE GOVERNOR:

    A.   Backgrounds and Requirements for Governorship: To be governor in the state of Texas, an individual must be thirty years old, a U.S. citizen, and a resident of Texas for five years. The practical requirements for the position are somewhat more numerous. Most governors have been white, well-educated, middle-aged, wealthy males with some form of previous statewide government experience.

    B.   Impeachment and Incapacitation: Texas is one of the few states which allow for the removal of the governor through impeachment. **DEFINE IMPEACHMENT.**

The Lieutenant governor takes over the position of governor in the case that the Governor dies, is incapacitated, is impeached, or leaves the state.

    C.   Salary and Perks of the Office: Staff, travel expenses, access to state cars and planes, a governor's mansion, and a salary of $115,345 are provided for the governor.

D. Legislative Powers of the Governor: The annual State of the State address gives the governor the opportunity to set forth a policy agenda, which can be supplemented by gubernatorial communications to the full legislature or individual members. The two primary legislative powers given the governor are the ability to call the legislature into special session and the veto.

The governor may call as many special sessions as he/she feels the need for and designate the issue to be dealt with during that time. The aversion many legislators feel toward special sessions often makes the mere gubernatorial threat of a session a tool to sway legislative action. Governors are not likely to call special sessions casually because they entail the expenditure of gubernatorial capital and influence. If the legislature fails to adopt the policy agenda of the governor, he/she may end up looking foolish. The power of the Speaker and the Lieutenant governor in the process also requires gubernatorial prudence in calling a session.

The Texas governor has one of the strongest veto powers in the nation. He/she has ten days after passage to sign, veto or allow legislation to become law without his/her signature. The governor also has a line-item veto on budget bills. The threat of veto is often an influential tool. George Bush vetoed 37 bills in 1997 and 31 in 1999.

E. Budgetary Powers of the Governor: The governor of Texas has weaker budgetary power than most. The legislature's use of the Legislative Budget Board reduces the governor's ability to influence the creation of the budget. Recently the legislature has also used creative appropriation techniques to limit the governor's use of the line-item veto.

F. Appointive and Removal Powers of the Governor: The Texas governor has the ability to appoint numerous members of the more than 200 boards and commissions, but these officials serve six-year staggered terms, making it difficult for governors to gain control of the bureaucracy. The governor cannot remove appointees from previous administrations and needs a two-thirds majority of the Senate to removed his/her own appointees. **DEFINE SENATORIAL COURTESY.**

Gubernatorial appointments to the various boards and commissions require a two-thirds majority approval vote of the Texas Senate. The Governor also fills midterm vacancies in the U.S. Senate or other statewide offices (except for lieutenant governor).

G. Judicial Powers of the Governor: The judicial powers of the governor include the appointment of the members of the Board of Pardons and Paroles, the ability to grant executive clemency, and to carry out prisoner extraditions.

H.   Military Powers of the Governor: The Governor appoints the adjunct general and is the commander-in-chief of the state's military. These gubernatorial powers and troops are to be used to protect lives and property, and to keep the peace during times of domestic violence or natural disaster.

I.   Informal Resources of the Governor: To overcome the constitutional limitations of the office, Governors are often forced to rely on other resources. These informal resources may include their own personality, leadership styles, work habits, and administrative methods.

J.   The Governor's Staff: The size of the Governor's staff has grown significantly as the complexity of the office has increased. Staffers are usually chosen for their political beliefs and loyalty, and may be responsible for gathering support for gubernatorial proposals, scheduling the governor's time and appointments, and representing the governor at meetings.

K.   The Governor and the Mass Media: The critical role of the media in modern politics forces governors to be accessible to reporters, give press conferences, and adapt their campaigns to media requirements.

L.   The Governor and the Political Party: The dominance of the Democratic Party and the factionalism within it has, in the past, provided the governor little advantage as head of the party. The rise of the two-party competition may, however, make the Governor's role in the party more of a resource. For example, Bush strengthened his anti-abortion credentials with conservatives in 1999.

M.   The Governor and Interest Groups: Governors often solicit the support of interest groups, which in return seek gubernatorial responsiveness to their policy interests.

IV. OTHER OFFICES OF THE EXECUTIVE BRANCH:

A. Lieutenant governor: Not only does the lieutenant governor take over the Governorship if the governor were to die or be impeached, he/she is the presiding officer of the Senate and exerts a tremendous amount of influence over the legislative process. In fact, the second highest office in the state is primarily a legislative position.

B. Attorney General: The attorney general is the state's chief legal officer and is responsible for defending the state's laws and agency orders. He/she has little responsibility for criminal enforcement, but rather is responsible for civil procedures.

C. Comptroller of Public Accounts: Texas law requires that the state operate on a pay-as-you-go principle which necessitates that there be accurate estimates of the revenues available to spend. This is the responsibility of the comptroller. So important is this function that state law mandates that no budget can become law without comptroller certification. He/she also has the ability to conduct audits of state agencies.

D. Commissioner of the General Land Office: The land commissioner is responsible for managing the approximately 22 million acres of public land owned by the state of Texas. This includes the collection of revenue from the mineral rights and other land use fees which have been designated as funding for programs such as education.

E. Commissioner of Agriculture: The agriculture commissioner, as head of the state Department of Agriculture, regulates and promotes the agriculture industry, provides support for agricultural research, and administers various consumer protection laws.

F. Secretary of State: The secretary of state's primary responsibility is the administration of the state's election laws. This includes the development of the state's voter registration policy, monitoring of election procedures, and receiving and tabulating election results. The secretary of state is the only constitutional office which the governor can appoint.

G. State Treasurer: This office was eliminated in 1993, but had been designated as the guardian of the states funds.

V. ELECTED BOARDS AND COMMISSIONS: The Texas Railroad Commission and the State Board of Education are the only two, of the over two hundred boards and commissions, which are elected.

A. Texas Railroad Commission: While this commission's purpose of regulating intrastate railroad operations has largely been taken over by the federal government, it remains powerful today due to its responsibility for the regulation of oil and natural gas production. The three commissioners are elected for six-year staggered terms, and the position of chair rotates among the three. The commission has been widely criticized for being co-opted by the oil and gas industry. Governor Bush appointed the first African American to the commission in 1999.

B. State Board of Education: After significant revision, the current board has fifteen elected members who represent districts across the state. The board nominates (and the governor appoints) the commissioner of education who is responsible for managing the Texas Education Agency. The legislature has reduced its powers in recent years.

VI. THE TEXAS BUREAUCRACY: A bureaucracy is responsible for conducting the day-to-day activities of governing. The Texas bureaucracy has been criticized for being highly fragmented. It is, however, particularly influential in Texas because it not only carries out the functions of government but it also lacks a full-time legislature to oversee it.

VII. THE GROWTH OF GOVERNMENT IN TEXAS: The Texas government has grown significantly in the last thirty years, both in terms of the number of employees and state expenditures. Approximately 80 percent of state employees work in the areas of higher education, public safety and corrections, and social services. Efforts to limit the growth of government have not been successful due to the continued call for services, federal government mandates, and interest group activity.

VIII. BUREAUCRATS AND PUBLIC POLICY: The discretion given to agencies to interpret the laws passed by the legislature provides the bureaucracy a significant amount of influence. While the legislature maintains oversight and budgetary authority which can be used to keep agencies in line, the bureaucracy has its own sources of legislative and executive influence to protect its interests.

A. Policy Implementation: The duty of implementing legislative actions is not always exclusively the responsibility of a single agency. Not only is there often a question of departmental overlap in responsibility and jurisdiction, the courts may influence the way bureaucrats carry out their duties. The actual implementation process is, in reality, the composite of numerous actions by a tremendous number of bureaucrats.

B. Obstacles to Policy Implementation: The ability of the bureaucracy to carry out legislative initiatives may be hampered by unclear or misguided mandates, inadequate funding, and interest group or industry interference.

DEFINE IRON TRIANGLE.

The active involvement of regulated industries in their regulation has been common in Texas and has stimulated much criticism of the bureaucracy. The sunset review process and gubernatorial efforts have reduced some of the influence of regulated industries, but it remains problematic.

IX. STRATEGIES FOR CONTROLLING THE BUREAUCRACY: There are numerous ways for elected leaders to manage the actions of the bureaucracy. These include transferring authority for a program, reducing programmatic discretion, manipulation of an agency's budget, abolition of an agency, protection of whistleblowers, and revolving door restrictions.

A. The Revolving Door: The experience and regulatory knowledge provided by employment in the bureaucracy has led to the tendency for employees to stay in the agency only long enough to gain experience and make connections. They then leave the agency for more lucrative employment in the regulated industry. This revolving door of the bureaucracy has generated serious ethical questions and recent reforms designed to restrict the revolving door.

B. Legislative Budgetary Control: In practice, there is very little legislative budgetary control. Legislators meet every two years to adopt a state budget, but are not present for substantive oversight of agency expenditures. This shortage of legislative oversight has been exacerbated by the growing tendency to lump agency funds in the budget to avoid gubernatorial use of the line-item veto. The failure to specify appropriations simply gives additional discretion to agency officials.

C. Sunset Legislation: Texas is one of the few states which has sunset legislation, requiring the periodic review of all state agencies to ensure their continued need and service. While few agencies have been abolished and the size of the state government has not been reduced, major bureaucratic restructuring and revisions have resulted from the review process.

The Sunset Advisory Commission, made up of members of the House and Senate as well as two members of the public, review state agencies on a twelve-year cycle. The report of the commission on any agency is considered by the full legislature, where a failure to approve the bill or fund the agency will lead to the termination of the agency. Universities, the courts, and the agencies created in the state constitution are exempt from sunset review.

D. Performance Reviews: Budgetary shortfalls precipitated the use of performance reviews by the state comptroller to identify inefficiency and mismanagement. Over $6 million in spending cuts and agency changes were eventually made upon the reviews, and the Council of Competitive Government was created. This organization is designed to provide state services more efficiently by giving Texas businesses more opportunity to bid on state contracts.

E.   Merit Systems and Professional Management. **DEFINE MERIT SYSTEM. DEFINE PATRONAGE.**

The Texas employment and personnel system is a highly fragmented arrangement, lacking a central agency to develop and coordinate hiring and personnel policies. The legislature is responsible for setting vacation, holiday, and retirement policies. All employment opportunities are listed with the Texas Employment Commission, but the fragmentation permits many jobs to be filled based on friendship and personal connections.

CHAPTER TWENTY-THREE SAMPLE QUESTIONS

TRUE-FALSE:

1.   The Texas governor is one of the weakest in the nation.

2.   Only the Texas secretary of state is appointed by the governor, while the other officeholders are elected statewide.

3.   Texas is one of the few states that allows for the governor to be removed through impeachment.

4.   Until the election of Republican Bill Clements in 1978, every Texas governor since 1874 has been a Democrat.

5.   The Texas governor has line-item veto authority over the state budget.

6.   The governor gains significant power and influence from being the head of his/her political party.

7.   The executive powers of the lieutenant governor are limited.

8.   The Texas attorney general is primarily a criminal lawyer.

9.   The tendency of bureaucratic agency employees working for interest groups, while still employed by the agency, is called the revolving door phenomena.

10.   The Railroad Commission and the State Board of Education are the only two of the 200-plus boards and commissions that head most state agencies that are elected.

MULTIPLE-CHOICE:

1.   Texas governors have tended to be all of the following EXCEPT:
       a. Wealthy
       b. Highly educated
       c. Catholic
       d. Anglos

2.   The legislative powers of the governor include all of the following EXCEPT:
       a. The line-item veto
       b. Calling special sessions of the legislature
       c. Giving the State of the State address
       d. All of the above are part of the governor's legislative powers

3. A fragmented system of authority under which most statewide, executive officeholders are elected independently is known as a:
   a. Bifurcated executive
   b. Multiple executive
   c. Plural executive
   d. Collective executive

4. Otherwise qualified prospects are dissuaded from running for governor and other offices because of the difficult burden of:
   a. Fund raising.
   b. Media bashing.
   c. Lack of privacy.
   d. Public recognition.

5. Because of the key legislative role and statewide constituency, many experts consider the office of _____ one of the most powerful offices in state government.
   a. Governor
   b. Lieutenant governor.
   c. Attorney general
   d. Comptroller of public accounts

6. The elective officer, abolished by voters in 1995 and whose duties were transferred to the comptroller's office, was the:
   a. Treasurer
   b. Land commissioner
   c. Agriculture commissioner
   d. Secretary of state

7. An elected panel that oversees the administration of public education in Texas is the:
   a. Texas Education Agency
   b. Coordinating Board
   c. Texas State Teachers Commission
   d. State Board of Education

8. The Texas Railroad Commission:
   a. Lost much of its power to regulate trucking and railroads to the federal government
   b. Regulates oil and natural gas production
   c. Has elected commissioners
   d. All of the above
   e. None of the above

9. An iron triangle is the relationship among a:
    a. bureaucratic agency, legislative committee and the media
    b. bureaucratic agency, legislative committee and the courts
    c. bureaucratic agency, legislative committee and an interest group
    d. bureaucratic agency, interest group and the courts

10. Which of the following are obstacles to bureaucratic policy implementation?
    a. Bureaucratic apathy
    b. Interest group influence
    c. Bureaucratic incompetence
    d. All of the above

CHAPTER TWENTY-THREE SAMPLE QUESTIONS ANSWERS

TRUE-FALSE:

1.   **TRUE.** The Texas Governor is one of the weakest in the nation. See page 815.

2.   **TRUE.** Most of these offices were mandated by the 1876 Texas Constitution. See page 816.

3.   **TRUE.** Texas is one of the few states that allows for the governor to be removed through impeachment. See page 819.

4.   **TRUE.** This, and Governor George Bush's election, are evidence OF an emerging two-party system in Texas. See page 819.

5.   **TRUE.** The Governor of Texas has line-item veto authority on no other kinds of legislation. See page 822.

6.   **FALSE.** The Governor does not gain much power or influence from being the head of his/her political party. See pages 828-830.

7.   **TRUE.** The executive powers of the lieutenant governor are very limited. See page 831.

8.   **FALSE.** The Texas attorney general is primarily a civil lawyer. See page 832.

9.   **FALSE.** The revolving door phenomena refers to the tendency for agency employees to leave the agency and go to work for an interest group. See page 842.

10.   **FALSE.** The majority of commissioners and heads of state boards are appointed. See page 836.

MULTIPLE-CHOICE:

1. **C.** Texas governors have tended to be wealthy, highly educated, Anglo, Protestants. See page 818.

2. **D.** The legislative powers of the governor include the line-item veto, calling special sessions of the legislature, and giving the State of the State address. See pages 821-822.

3. **B.** This way, no single elected official is responsible for the executive. See page 816.

4. **A.** Clayton Williams, for instance, spent millions of his own dollars and lost in 1990.

4. **A.** Clayton Williams, for instance, spent millions of his own dollars and lost in 1990. See page 818.

5. **B.** The lt. governor's executive powers are limited—the position is primarily legislative. See page 832.

6. **A.** Martha Whitehead, who ran for the office with the platform that she would oversee the dismantling of the office, won this post in 1995. See page 836.

7. **D.** The State Board of Education was an appointive board until 1986, when the voters changed it to an elected board. See page 837.

8. **D.** The Texas Railroad Commission lost much of its power to regulate trucking and railroads to the federal government, regulates oil and natural gas production and has elected commissioners. See page 836.

9. **C.** An iron triangle is the relationship among a bureaucratic agency, legislative committee, and an interest group. See page 840.

10. **B.** Interest group influence is an obstacle to bureaucratic policy implementation. See page 840.

CHAPTER TWENTY-FOUR
THE TEXAS JUDICIARY

I. THE POWER OF THE COURTS IN TEXAS: State courts in Texas are responsible for both civil and criminal legal matters, as well as limited public policy making.

   A. The State Courts in the Federal System: The rulings and interpretations of the federal courts have had a significant impact on state policies and state court activities. The federal courts have set the tone for state action in the areas of civil rights, elections, the treatment of prisoners and the mentally ill, and the procedures used by police officers. Despite the growth of such federal action, more than 95 percent of all court cases still occur at the state level.

   B. The Legal Framework of the Judicial System: The basic legal framework for the state of Texas is set forth in the state Constitution. Beyond that, the legislature created criminal and civil laws and codes for court procedures. The details of illegal activities and their penalties are set forth in the penal code. **DEFINE FELONY. DEFINE MISDEMEANOR**.

   Civil cases involve disputes between individuals, whereas criminal cases entail the state charging an individual of some wrongful action. **DEFINE PLAINTIFF.**

II. THE STRUCTURE OF THE TEXAS COURT SYSTEM: There are five levels in the Texas court system, although there is some overlap in authority and jurisdiction. **DEFINE ORIGINAL JURISDICTION. DEFINE APPELLATE JURISDICTION**.

   The highest level of the Texas courts is a bifurcated system, meaning that there are two courts of last resort. There is a separate court for criminal cases (the Court of Criminal Appeals) and for civil cases (the Texas Supreme Court).

   Judges in Texas, except for municipal judges, are elected in partisan elections. Midterm vacancies in the district and appellate courts are filled by gubernatorial appointment, while the justice of the peace and county court positions are filled by county commissioner appointment.

   A. Courts of Limited Jurisdiction: The municipal and justice of the peace courts make up the lowest level of court system in Texas. The municipal courts have original jurisdiction over city ordinances and are not courts of record. **DEFINE DE NOVO.**

   Justice of the peace (JOP) courts have original jurisdiction over civil cases where the amount in question is less than $5,000, and in criminal cases punishable with fines alone. Each county of the state is required to have at least one JOP court, but large counties may have up to sixteen. Justices are elected, and justices are not required to have legal training to hold office. JOP courts, like municipal courts, are not courts of record.

B.   County Courts: Each county has a constitutional county court which shares original jurisdiction with the JOP and municipal courts. This court also has jurisdiction over criminal misdemeanors punishable with fines of $500 or more and jail sentences of less than a year.

The county judge of a constitutional county court is elected on a countywide basis and presides over the county commissioners court. Judges are not required to be lawyers but must be "well informed in the law" and take courses in evidence and legal procedures.

The legislature has also created the statutory county courts which were designed to deal with specific local problems, so the jurisdiction of these courts vary. The judges in the statutory county courts must be attorneys and are elected.

C.   Courts of General Jurisdiction: The principal trial courts in the state of Texas are the district courts. District courts have original jurisdiction over civil cases of $200 or more, divorces, contested elections, suits over land titles, slander or defamation, and all felony criminal cases. Judges are elected, must be twenty-five years old, and have served as a judge in another court or have practiced law for four years.

The legislature has the authority to specify judicial districts, and there has been a significant increase in the number of district courts in the recent past. The population growth and the corresponding increase in the number of cases in some areas of the state have lead to the uneven development of district courts. Some urban counties have many district courts, while other rural areas may have only one to serve several counties. The Judicial Districts Board was created in 1985 to deal with this inequity, but political pressures forced the continuation of the status quo as late as 1994. **DEFINE PLEA BARGAIN.**

D.   Intermediate Courts of Appeals: Appeals from criminal and civil cases in the district courts are sent to one of the fourteen courts of appeals. Each court of appeal represents one of thirteen regions of the state and is responsible for the cases from that area. The Houston area is allotted two appellate courts because of the number of cases in that area. Each court has at least a chief justice and two additional justices. The legislature has the authority to provide, and has provided additional justices to each court in order to aid with the workload.

Appellate judges are elected to six-year terms, must be thirty-five years old, and have ten years of experience as an attorney or as a judge of a court of record. The case load of the appellate courts varies greatly, and the Texas Supreme Court has the authority to transfer cases between courts to even the load.

E.   Highest Appellate Courts: In an attempt to fragment government power and ensure the prompt consideration of criminal appeals, the framers of the constitution created two separate final courts. The Texas Supreme Court, which handles civil cases, is also responsible for a limited coordination of the state judicial system, in that it develops the administrative procedures for the state courts, appoints the Board of Law Examiners, has oversight of the State Bar, and has disciplinary authority over state judges. The Texas Court of Criminal Appeals has jurisdiction over criminal cases.

Both the Texas Supreme Court and the Court of Criminal Appeals have presiding justices and eight other judges. These judges serve six-year staggered terms, must be thirty-five years old, and have been a practicing attorney, judge of a court of record, or both, for the preceding ten years.

F.   Texas Judges: Approximately two-thirds of the judges on the intermediate and highest appellate courts come to the office from private practice, not from the lower courts. Most of the district judges also were in private law practices before obtaining a seat on the bench, but career patterns for lower court justices are more varied. The number of Republican justices is on the increase as the two-party system strengthens throughout the state. Although the number of women and minority justices is growing, there remains a white male bias.

G.   Other Participants in the State Judiciary: Besides the judges, other elected officials of the judicial system include the district and county clerks, who maintain the court records, and the county and district attorneys, who are responsible for prosecuting criminal cases. The bailiff and other law enforcement officers, although not elected, are also important participants in the legal system.

H.   Efforts to Reform the Judicial System: The overlapping jurisdictions and other problems of the Texas judicial system has prompted calls for reform since the 1970s. Despite this, reorganization has been slow in coming, due to the opposition of many of the participants in the legal system.

III.   THE JURY SYSTEM:

A.   The Grand Jury: **DEFINE AND EXPLAIN GRAND JURY, VENIREMAN.**

B.   The Petit Jury: **DEFINE AND EXPLAIN PETIT JURY.**

IV.   JUDICIAL PROCEDURES AND DECISION MAKING: The basic trial procedure includes the presentation of opening arguments by both sides, the examination and cross-examination of witnesses, the presentation of evidence, rebuttal, and summation. The procedures are slightly different in criminal and civil cases, and most litigants can waive their right to trial and have their case heard exclusively by a judge.

At the appellate level there is no jury or re-presentation of evidence. Judges simply examine the record of the lower court proceedings and legal briefs filed with the appeal, and consider the conformance to constitutional and statutory requirements. Except for death penalty cases, civil and criminal appeals are sent initially to one of the courts of appeals. From there they may be appealed to the Texas Supreme Court or the Court of Criminal Appeals.

Most of the cases reaching the Texas Supreme Court do so based on writs of error, which claim that the lower court has ruled inappropriately on a rule of law. Appeals based on writs of error are distributed among the nine justices for examination and preparation of a memorandum to be shared with the other justices. The justices then meet to consider the memorandum prepared, and four of the nine justices must agree to hear the appeal for it to be considered by the Court. Once the Court has agreed to hear a case, the attorneys in the case will present oral arguments and answer questions from the justices in open court. The justices will then consider and debate the arguments and legal points in the case privately and issue their opinions at a later date, which often takes months.
EXPLAIN WRIT OF MANDAMUS AND WRITS OF ERROR

The Texas Court of Criminal Appeals has jurisdiction on cases appealed from the intermediate appellate courts, as well as the capital punishment cases which may be appealed directly to the highest level. Four justices must agree to hear a petition for a case to be given discretionary review. The procedure for hearing arguments and writing opinions in the Court of Criminal Appeals is similar to that in the Texas Supreme Court.

V.   JUDICIAL CONCERNS AND CONTROVERSIES: The 1980s and 1990s brought a period of controversy for the Texas legal system. The influence of money in judicial elections and the absence of minority judges undermined the public perception of the court system.

A.   Judicial/Activism/Impropriety: The traditional dominance of conservative, pro-business interests extended to the Texas courts and justices, who historically considered their role to be a limited, constructionist position. The 1970s saw a shift in the orientation of the Texas courts towards a more activist position as groups such as the Texas Trial Lawyers Association started to participate in judicial elections and sought legislative changes to encourage judicial activism. Allegations against Justices for improper contact with attorneys and the Pennzoil case led some to call for changes in judicial selection.

B.   Campaign Contributions and Republican Gains: The potential influence campaign contributions may have on judicial decisions has stimulated significant discussion about judicial ethics and the need for reform. The problems of the Texas Supreme Court in the 1980s and the subsequent midterm resignations opened the door for Republicans on the high court. By the late 1980s there was a significant Republican contingent on the court. Recent rulings indicate the philosophical orientation of the court has gradually shifted away from the judicial activist position to a more conservative, pro-business stance. **EXPLAIN MERIT SELECTION.**

C.   Legislative Reaction to Judicial Activism: The business community responded to the increase in judicial activism and their opposition to the trial lawyers by taking their case to the legislature. Tort reform was a direct attempt to limit judicial activism. **DEFINE TORT REFORM.**

D.   Winners and Losers: In a 1999 study by Texas Watch, a consumer group, it was stated that doctors, hospitals, etc. had been winners before the Texas Supreme Court. Consumers have recently fared better under Bush.

E.   Minorities and the Judicial System: The high cost of judicial elections, the splintering of voters along ethnic lines, poor voter turnout among minorities and the shortage of minority lawyers has caused the lack of minority representation on the high courts. African American and Hispanic groups sought to change this through actions in the federal courts. At the time of the case *League of United Latin American Citizens et al. v. Mattox et al.,* only 42 of the state's 375 district judges and 3 of 80 intermediate court of appeals judges were African American or Hispanic. While the case did little to change the judicial selection system, it highlights the political stakes involved.

Minority groups argued that the county wide election of district judges diluted minority voting strength and thus was a violation of Section 2 of the Voting Rights Act. The U.S. Fifth Circuit Court eventually ruled that evidence for this dilution was minimal and that partisanship was much more a factor in judicial elections. Five years of legal wrangling thus left the question of judicial selection in the hands of the legislature, which had refused to deal with the problem for years. By 1995 little had changed in the distribution of minority judges in the Texas court system.

The first Hispanic, Raul A. Gonzalez, was appointed to the Texas Supreme Court in 1984 to a fill a midterm vacancy and subsequently won re-election in 1986. Fortunato P. Benavides was the first Hispanic appointed to the Texas Court of Criminal Appeals. Appointed in 1991 to fill a midterm vacancy, Benavides lost a 1992 re-election bid. In 1990 the first African American was appointed and elected to the Texas Court of Criminal Appeals.

G. Women in the Judiciary: In 1982, Governor Clements appointed Ruby Sondock who, although she did not seek re-election, became the first woman elected to the Texas Supreme Court. It was not until 1992 that a woman was elected to the state Supreme Court and 1994 when a woman was elected to the state Court of Criminal Appeals. Women did, however, attain judgeships lower in the state system as early as 1935. By 1998, more than 140 women were judges at the county court level or higher.

H. The Search for Solutions: Reforms such as campaign contribution limits, nonpartisan elections, and the merit selection system, while often promoted as solutions to the judicial problems faced by the state, are not without ramifications of their own. Contribution limits may hinder the ability of minority candidates to attain office more than the nonminority candidates, and alternative selection methods do little to reduce undue influence on the judiciary.

VI. CRIME AND PUNISHMENT: The U.S. and Texas Constitutions provide certain rights to individuals which must be afforded even those accused of the most abhorrent crimes. The rights owed the accused have gradually been applied to the states, through the application of the due process and equal protection clauses of the U.S. Constitution. **EXPLAIN MIRANDA RULE. EXPLAIN NOLO CONTENDERE.**

In criminal cases the defendant is entitled to a trial by jury, but may waive this right, except in capital murder cases. If the defendant chooses to have his/her case decided by a judge, then the judge also determines punishment upon a guilty verdict. If a jury trial is selected, the defendant may also decide if the jury or judge should determine punishment. Juries are required to unanimously agree "beyond a reasonable doubt" upon the guilt of a defendant, otherwise a mistrial is declared. The Texas Court of Criminal Appeals recently took steps to refine the meaning of "beyond a reasonable doubt," stating that the evidence must be so convincing that jurors would be willing to rely on it "without hesitation." In capital murder cases the jurors must also consider whether the defendant would be a continued threat to the community and any mitigating circumstances before assigning the death penalty.

The use of the death penalty has undergone several changes over the last generation. The actual method used to carry it out, the restrictions placed on its use, and even its existence have been influenced by federal rulings.

Felonies, or the most serious crimes in society, are classified according to the seriousness of the act and have potential punishments which reflect this. First-degree felonies include actions such as aggravated assault and noncapital murder and are punishable by up to 99 years' imprisonment. Second-degree felonies encompass actions such as burglary or bribery and can be punished by up to twenty years in prison. Third-degree felonies carry a maximum punishment of ten years' imprisonment for actions such as the intentional bodily injury of a child. Nonviolent felonies are punishable by up to two years in prison and represent a new category of felonies for actions such as property crimes and drug offenses.

The least serious crimes are called misdemeanors and are categorized as Class A, B, or C. Class A misdemeanors are the most serious and entail the largest fines (up to $4,000) and longest jail terms (up to one year). **DEFINE PROBATION.**

VII.   THE POLITICS OF CRIMINAL JUSTICE: The Texas Court of Criminal Appeals has been accused of being overly concerned with the right of criminals. It is important to note that the court is caught between competing interests. Prosecutors and judges, who face re-election, do not like to see convictions overturned, while defense attorneys and civil libertarians seek the protection of individual rights. As the composition of the court has shifted over the last 30 years, so has the leanings of the court on the question of individual rights.

VIII.   INCREASED POLICY ROLE OF THE STATE COURTS: The Texas Supreme Court has taken on an increasing role in policy making. This is evident in landmark cases which dealt with the financing of the state's education system, the ability of parents to educate their children at home rather than in accredited schools, and abortion/free speech cases.

A.   The Courts and Education: Since the *Edgewood v. Kirby* case of 1989 required that the state change the method it used to finance public schools, the courts have taken a leading role in educational reform. Though financing the schools more equitably has been the chief concern of the courts in regard to education, other issues have arisen, such as home schooling and minimum skills tests.

B. The Courts and Abortion Rights: In 1993, the Texas Supreme Court had to walk a fine line between abortion rights and free speech. The Court struck down a rule that abortion protesters had to stay 100 feet from clinics. The U.S. Supreme Court later passed a law that allowed judges to limit demonstrations, but prevented them from limiting demonstrators.

C. The Courts and Gay Rights: The Texas Supreme Court ruled against a gay GOP group that had been denied a booth at the Republican state convention in San Antonio.

CHAPTER TWENTY-FOUR SAMPLE QUESTIONS

TRUE-FALSE:

1.   It is estimated that more than 95 percent of all litigation is based on state laws or local ordinances.

2.   The Texas Supreme Court is the single highest court in the state.

3.   No detailed transcript of trial proceedings is kept in most of the municipal courts.

4.   Justices of the peace are required by the constitution to be licensed attorneys.

5.   Reform efforts have been very successful in streamlining the Texas court system.

6.   The appellate courts provide the opportunity for an individual to have his/heer case heard at a higher level with a new jury.

7.   It is legal for attorneys to make campaign contributions to judicial candidates in front of whom they practice.

8.   Although it decides only civil appeals, the Texas Supreme Court is probably viewed by most Texans as the titular head of the state judiciary.

9.   Grand jury meetings and deliberations are conducted openly.

10.   Unanimous jury verdicts are required to convict a defendant in a criminal case.

MULTIPLE CHOICE:

1.   A serious crime, which is punishable by long term imprisonment and/or fines, is a
     a. Misdemeanor
     b. Penal code
     c. Felony
     d. All of the above

2.   The jurisdiction over violations of federal laws, including criminal offenses that occur across state lines, and over banking, securities, and other activities regulated by the federal government is held by the:
     a. National government
     b. Local judiciary
     c. State judiciary
     d. Federal judiciary

3. A judicial system which has two courts at the highest level to handle appeals from two separate areas of law is called a:
   a. Dual judiciary
   b. Paired judiciary
   c. Bifurcated judiciary
   d. None of the above

4. If a state judiciary vacancy occurs before the term expires, the vacancy is filled:
   a. Through a special election called by the governor
   b. By gubernatorial appointment
   c. From lower level judges
   d. In the next general election

5. The court which has the responsibility for developing administrative procedures for the state courts and appoints the Board of Law Examiners is the:
   a. Texas Supreme Court
   b. Court of Criminal Appeals
   c. Texas Appeals Court
   d. All of the above share responsibility

6. A nine member court with final appellate jurisdiction over criminal cases is the Texas:
   a. Constitutional Court.
   b. Supreme Court.
   c. Court of Criminal Appeals.
   d. Court of Last Resort.

7. A _____ alleges that constitutional or procedural mistakes were made by a lower court and therefore the case should be reviewed.
   a. Writ of mandamus
   d. Writ of habeas corpus
   c. Writ of error
   d. None of the above

8. In appellate court procedures, judges review the decisions and the procedures of the lower courts for conformance to constitutional and statutory requirements, but there is NO:
   a. Decision handed down
   b. Jury to rehear evidence
   c. Further appeal allowed
   d. Argument reviewed

9. Which of the following has been suggested as a solution to the problems faced by the Texas judiciary?
   a. Limits on campaign contributions to judicial candidates
   b. Use of the merit selection system
   c. Nonpartisan judicial elections
   d. All of the above

10. The Texas school finance case in 1989 that unanimously ordered major, basic changes in the financing of public education to provide more equity between rich and poor school districts is the
    a. *Miranda v. Arizona* case
    b. *Brown v. Board of Education* decision
    c. *Plessy v. Ferguson* doctrine
    d. *Edgewood v. Kirby* case

CHAPTER TWENTY-FOUR SAMPLE QUESTIONS ANSWERS

TRUE-FALSE:

1. **TRUE.** Federal courts are limited to trying only a few cases. See page 852.

2. **FALSE.** The Texas Supreme Court and the Court of Criminal Appeals share the status of the highest courts in the state. See page 858.

3. **TRUE.** No detailed transcript of trial proceedings is kept in most of the municipal courts. See page 855.

4. **FALSE.** There are no requirements except to be elected to the post. See page 855.

5. **FALSE.** Reform efforts have not been very successful in streamlining the Texas court system. See page 860.

6. **FALSE.** There is no jury to rehear evidence in the appellate courts. Appellate judges simply review the transcripts of the lower court proceedings. See page 863.

7. **TRUE.** It is legal for attorneys to make campaign contributions to judicial candidates in front of whom they practice. See page 866.

8. **TRUE.** Though the courts are bifurcated between civil and criminal cases, most people believe that the Supreme Court has the final legal say. See page 855.

9. **FALSE.** To protect the jury, grand juries are held in secret. See page 861.

10. **TRUE.** This is to ensure that juries are convinced that defendants are guilty beyond a reasonable doubt. See page 862.

MULTIPLE-CHOICE:

1. **C.** A serious crime which is punishable by long-term imprisonment and/or fines is a felony. See page 852.

2. **D.** State and local laws cover most other contingencies. See page 852.

3. **C.** A judicial system which has two courts at the highest level to handle appeals from two separate areas of law is called a bifurcated system. See page 852.

4. **B.** Justice of the peace and county court vacancies are filled by county commissioners courts. See page 855.

5. **A.** The court which has the responsibility for developing administrative procedures for the state courts and appoints the Board of Law Examiners is the Texas Supreme Court. See page 858.

6. **C.** The court with final appellate jurisdiction is the Texas Supreme Court. See page 858.

7. **C.** A writ of error alleges that constitutional or procedural mistakes were made by a lower court and therefore the case should be reviewed. See page 863.

8. **B.** Appellate courts determine if the courts have carried careful and legal procedures. See page 863.

9. **D.** Limits on campaign contributions to judicial candidates, the use of the merit selection system, and nonpartisan judicial elections have all been suggested as solutions to the problems faced by the Texas judiciary. See pages 866-867.

10. **D.** *Edgewood* caused a flurry of cases and rulings about public education finance. See page 881.

CHAPTER TWENTY-FIVE
LOCAL GOVERNMENT IN TEXAS:
CITIES, TOWNS, COUNTIES, AND SPECIAL DISTRICTS

I.   THE POWER OF LOCAL GOVERNMENT: Americans have long held the belief of local sovereignty and the power of the states. Despite this, the relationship between local and state governments is a unitary system. **DEFINE UNITARY SYSTEM**.

The idea that local governments are simply the creations of the state is referred to as Dillon's r
Rule.

II. LOCAL GOVERNMENTS IN THE TEXAS POLITICAL SYSTEM: All forms of local government, including counties, cities, and special districts are created by the state and constrained by state constitutional limitations. This can be difficult as the needs of a growing and changing state force local government action. Local governments not only carry out many of the responsibilities of the state, but are also faced with the demands of local concerns. The state of Texas provides a great deal of autonomy to its cities, but very little to its counties.

III. MUNICIPAL GOVERNMENT IN TEXAS: Today, Texas is a highly urban state with the basic forms of city government defined by statutory and constitutional law. Despite this legal setup, there is significant variation in the forms of local government across the state.

A.   General Law and Home Rule Cities: The state constitution sets forth two forms of cities. The general law cities are permitted to exercise only those powers specifically granted to them by the legislature and have fewer than 5000 residents. Home rule cities, on the other hand, have larger populations and a great deal more autonomy.

IV. FORMS OF CITY GOVERNMENT IN TEXAS: There are basically three forms of city government found in Texas.

A.   Mayor-Council: The mayor-council is the most common form of city government in Texas. This form is based on the idea of the separation of power, giving the legislative authority to the city council and the executive powers to the mayor. In most Texas cities, the mayor is weak, but this form of government may be either a strong mayor or weak mayor system as set forth in the city charter.

In a weak mayor system, the mayor has little influence over policy implementation and his/her powers are limited by numerous constraints by the restriction of traditional executive responsibilities. The strong mayor system provides for some of the traditional executive powers, such as appointive and removal authority and some control over the budget process. Although the strong mayor system is found in many of the larger cities across the nation, it has never been popular in Texas.

B. City Commission: The efforts to reform city government, make it more efficient and avoid partisan conflict, led to the development of the city commission form of government. Critics, however, suggest that the sharing of power among the members of the commission leaves no one individual in charge and a vacuum of leadership, and minimal budget oversight and review. The pure form of commission government calls for three commissioners (one mayor and two commissioners), with each having primary responsibility for a specific area of city functions. Few cities use this pure form of commission.

C. Council-Manager: **DEFINE AND EXPLAIN THE COUNCIL-MANAGER FORM OF GOVERNMENT**.

V. MUNICIPAL ELECTION SYSTEMS: The strong feelings against the influence of political parties in local government of the 1920-1950s, led city reformers to call for nonpartisan elections. This is the form used in most cities in the state of Texas.

A. At-Large Elections: Texas cities also widely make use of at-large elections or the place system. **DEFINE AND EXPLAIN AT-LARGE ELECTIONS AND THE PLACE SYSTEM**.

B. Single-Member Districts: The single-member district or ward elections are the opposite of at-large elections. In single-member district elections, the city is divided into sections and an individual is elected from a single district of the city.

C. Legal Attacks on At-Large Elections: Minority groups have successfully opposed the use of at-large elections, claiming that this electoral system makes it particularly difficult for a minority person to get elected.

VI. CITY REVENUES AND EXPENDITURES: Cities overwhelmingly rely on property and fee for service taxes, which are highly regressive. The state limitations on the taxing ability of local government and the ability of the citizens to have a rollback election have created significant hardships for city government. General obligation and revenue bonds are often used to finance city projects, given the requirement that cities have a balanced budget.

VII.   URBAN PROBLEMS IN TEXAS:

A.   The Graying of Texas Cities: The state's population is aging, and this causes additional calls for city services. This severely strains city budgets, as many cities have granted homestead exemptions to people over sixty-five, and the ability to levy additional local property taxes may be exhausted. **DEFINE HOMESTEAD EXEMPTION**.

B.   "White Flight": "White Flight" is the propensity of nonminorities to move out of urban areas. This concentrates minorities, who traditionally have been among the poorest Texans, in cities, thus undermining the tax base and increasing the calls for services.

C.   Declining Infrastructures: The maintenance of the streets, bridges, water and sewer systems, and other facilities can be costly. Paying for these projects is often done through the issuance of bonds based on the ability to tax and property values. The decline in property values in the 1980s made the financing of infrastructure improvements difficult. By the end of the 1990s, property values were increasing across most areas of the state.

D.   Crime and Urban Violence: Most types of crime actually declined in the mid-1990s, although public opinion did not reflect this. Therefore, tough-on-crime stances and the promise for additional crime-related expenditures has become a key issue for candidates. The budgets of many local governments are unable to handle the promised crime-related expenditures.

E.   State-and-Federal-Mandated Programs: The federal and state governments have increasingly relied on laws and regulations forcing local governments to carry out a specific action. These mandates have been used in everything from education to transportation. Many of these mandates are handed down without supplemental funding, placing a tremendous burden on local government.

VIII.   COUNTY GOVERNMENT IN TEXAS: Counties are the administrative subunits of the state, created to carry out the tasks assigned to them by the state, without the legislative power to make ordinances. The structure and operations of all counties are determined by constitutional design.

A.   Structure of County Government: The commissioners court is the governing body of a county, although it has no judicial functions. Other elected officials share responsibility for governing the county with the commissioners, severely fragmenting government.

B. The Commissioners Court and County Judge: The commissioners court is made up of a county judge and four county commissioners. The commissioners are elected by precinct and the county judge is elected county wide. The county judge presides over actions of the court and fills midterm commissioner vacancies. The commissioners court has authority over the county budget and in this way exerts influence over other county officials.

C. County Clerk: The county clerk is elected to act as the clerk for the commissioners court, the county courts and, in some cases, the district courts. He/she is also responsible for maintaining the vital statistics of the county, issuing licenses, and administering elections.

D. District Clerk: The district clerk is elected to aid the county clerk in his/her court functions.

E. County and District Attorneys: **FILL IN**.

F. Tax Assessor-Collector: The tax assessor-collector is elected to ascertain who owns what property and the amount of tax each owes. Property tax is the primary source of revenue for counties, therefore this office is an important one. In the 1970s the legislature required that each county have an appraisal district to determine the value of property and took that responsibility away from the assessor-collector to reduce potential abuses.

G. County Law Enforcement: **FILL IN**.

H. County Auditor: The county auditor is appointed by the district judges to examine every bill and expenditure of the county. This is done to ensure the legality of the expenditure and, in effect, places budgetary restrictions on the commissioners court.

I. County Treasurer: The treasurer's job has been, to a great extent, taken over by the auditor, and the position has been abolished in numerous counties. The treasurer is responsible for receiving and distributing county funds.

IX. CRITICISMS OF COUNTY GOVERNMENT: The county government system in Texas has been criticized for the limited supervision by the state, the differences in the way counties across the state interpret and carry out their functions, the fragmentation caused by numerous elected officials, and the reliance on property taxes.

X. SPECIAL DISTRICTS IN TEXAS: Special districts are units of local government created to carry out specific functions not met by existing cities or counties.

    A. Functions and Structures: The functions of special districts vary greatly, based on the need at the time of creation. Special districts are governed by a board of elected or appointed officials and many districts have the power to tax and borrow. Districts are often created in order to finance a particular governmental service, have been promoted for personal gain, and to serve a specific geographical area.

    B. Consequences of Single-Purpose Districts: Special districts often serve to compound the already fragmented governmental system in the state. Some special districts are unprofessional in their operations and management, have expanded beyond the function for which they were created, and are not highly visible, thus hiding mistakes and abuses from exposure.

XI. INDEPENDENT SCHOOL DISTRICTS: The Constitution of 1876 permitted cities and towns to create independent school districts and impose taxes to support them.

    A. Inequities in the Public Education System: The inequities in Texas have been evident for quite some time. Reformers note the problems with the adequacy and equity in funding, quality curricula, and teacher preparation.

    B. Local School Governance: The State Board of Education and the Texas Education Agency (TEA) are responsible for the regulation and coordination of the state's education system, but most of the administration of education is done by the local school districts. These districts vary tremendously in size and budget.

    Each school district is governed by a school board with three to nine elected officials, who serve from two to six-year terms. Elections are nonpartisan and may be single-member or at-large districts. Voter turnout in school board elections is low, and it is often difficult to find qualified candidates.

    The school superintendent is chosen by the school board and is responsible for the day-to-day management of the district's operations.

XII. COUNCILS OF GOVERNMENT: Councils of Government (COGs) are regional planning organizations created in response to federal requirements. There are twenty-four COGS in Texas, with voluntary membership and a governing body made up primarily of elected officials from the member counties and cities. COG funding comes predominately from the state and national government, even though member governments pay dues.

XIII.	SOLUTIONS TO THE PROBLEMS OF LOCAL GOVERNMENT:

A.	Privatization of Functions: Some local governments have turned to privatization as a means of providing services, in the belief that this will increase efficiency. **DEFINE PRIVATIZATION**.

B.	Annexation and Extraterritorial Jurisdiction: Annexation powers and extraterritorial jurisdictions vary according to the size and charter of the city in question. Nevertheless, the ability to appropriate surrounding territory and control the development of nearby unincorporated areas is significant. These powers have facilitated several large cities to grow and control future expansion of surrounding areas.

C.	Modernization of County Government: The overlapping, fragmented status of Texas local government has lead to the call for modernization of county government. Suggestions for modernization include county home rule, giving counties some legislative authority, creating the office of county administrator to run the departments now under the county commissioner, and the extension of the civil service.

D.	Economic Development:	**FILL-IN**.

E.	Interlocal Contracting: Small governments often contract with larger ones to provide services due to limited tax bases and/or staff. While not a consolidation of local governments, this may improve efficiency through the reduction of overlap.

F.	Metro Government and Consolidation: In the large urban areas of Texas there are numerous governments with overlapping jurisdictions and functions. One suggestion to reduce this fragmentation is the consolidation of the various city and county governments into a metro government. While there has been discussion of this in the San Antonio area, there has been little interest in this proposal state wide.

G.	Public Improvement Districts: **FILL-IN**.

CHAPTER TWENTY-FIVE SAMPLE QUESTIONS

TRUE-FALSE:

1.   Texas gives a great deal of discretionary authority to its cities, and very little to its counties.

2.   In many areas of the young country, local governments existed before there was a viable state or federal government.

3.   Texas relies on the federal government to carry out many of its responsibilities.

4.   In the city commission form of government, the commissioners act both as part of the policy, making body and individually as the heads of city agencies.

5.   Professionalism is one of the key attributes of the council-manager form of government.

6.   Despite budgetary difficulties, many Texas cities give additional homestead exemptions for people over sixty-five.

7.   As more and more people become old enough to claim exemptions, younger taxpayers will be called upon to shoulder the burden through higher tax rates.

8.   Special districts are not given the ability to tax and/or borrow money in Texas.

9.   Turnout in school board elections is good because people are concerned about the quality of their children's education.

10.   Incorporated cities are able to control the development of surrounding unincorporated areas.

MULTIPLE CHOICE:

1.   The principle that holds that local government are simply the creations of the state and should have only those powers given to them by the state is:
        a. Unitary Rule
        b. Dillon's Rule
        c. State's Rule
        d. None Of The Above

2. Cities which are given the ability to write their own charter and adopt any form of local government they choose are called:
    a. Home rule cities
    b. General law cities
    c. Charter cities
    d. all of the above

3. Cities that have fewer than 5,000 residents and have more restrictions in organizing their governments, setting taxes, and annexing territory are referred to as
    a. Common law cities
    b. Home rule cities
    c. General law cities
    d. Charter law cities

4. A form of city government in which policy is set by an elected city council, which hires a professional city manager to head the daily administration of city government is referred to as:
    a. Weak mayor
    b. Strong mayor
    c. City commission
    d. Council-manager

5. Elections in which officeholders are elected from specific geographic areas are called:
    a. At-large elections
    b. Place elections
    c. Single-member district elections
    d. General elections

6. A method for a city to borrow money to pay for new construction projects is:
    a. Regressive taxes
    b. General obligation bonds
    c. Revenue bonds
    d. Infrastructur

7. Which of the following is not a function of the county's tax assessor-collector's office?
    a. Prosecutes serious tax offenders
    b. Ascertains who owns what property
    c. Determines how much tax is owed on property
    d. Collects the tax

8.   A local government in which city and county governments consolidate to avoid duplication of public services is called:
a. Privatization
b. Extraterritorial jurisdiction
c. Metro government
d. Public improvement district

9.   The consequences of single-purpose districts include all of the following EXCEPT:
a. Geographic over-taxation
b. The governing boards are often dominated by a small group of people
c. Increased fragmentation in government
d. Poor funding leads to unprofessional and poorly paid staff

10.   Which of the following have been suggested by reformers as problems for the Texas educational system?
a. School financing
b. Curricula
c. Teacher preparation
d. All of the above

CHAPTER TWENTY-FIVE SAMPLE QUESTION ANSWERS

TRUE-FALSE:

1. **TRUE.** Texas gives a great deal of discretionary authority to its cities, and very little to its counties. See pages 887-888.

2. **TRUE.** There has always been a strong commitment to local government in the U.S. See page 887.

3. **FALSE.** Much of the burden is on the local governments to carry out the wishes of the state. See pages 887-888.

4. **TRUE.** In the city commission form of government, the commissioners act both as part of the policy-making body and individually as the heads of city agencies. See page 894.

5. **TRUE.** This form of government was developed to reduce partisan politics in city government. See page 895.

6. **TRUE.** Despite budgetary difficulties, many Texas cities give additional homestead exemptions for people over sixty-five. See page 901.

7. **TRUE.** This is just one of the problems facing an aging population in Texas. See page 901.

8. **FALSE.** Many special districts are given the ability to tax and/or borrow money in Texas. See pages 909-910.

9. **TRUE.** Self-evident. See page 903.

10. **TRUE.** Incorporated cities are able to control the development of surrounding unincorporated areas. This power is referred to as extraterritorial jurisdiction. See page 915.

MULTPLE CHOICE:

1. **B.** The principle that holds that local government are simply the creations of the state and should have only those powers give to them by the state is Dillon's rule. See page 888.

2. **A.** Cities which are given the ability to write their own charter and adopt any form of local government they choose are called home rule cities. See page 880.

3. **C.** Most Texas cities are general law cities. See page 890.

4. **D.** The principle characteristics of the council manager form of local government are professional city management, a clear distinction between policy making and administration, and nonpartisan city elections. See page 892.

5. **C.** Elections in which officeholders are elected from specific geographic areas are called single-member district elections. See page 900.

6. **B.** General obligation bonds require voter approval and are repaid with tax revenues. See page 901.

7. **B.** This does not fall under the jurisdiction of the tax-collector. See page 907.

8. **C.** About a dozen cities outside Texas use this kind of government. See page 919.

9. **A.** The consequences of single-purpose districts include the governing boards are often dominated by a small group of people, increased fragmentation in government, and poor funding leads to unprofessional and poorly paid staff. See pages 909-910.

10. **D.** School financing, curricula, and teacher preparation have been suggested by reformers as problems of the Texas educational system. See page 912.